Calvin, The Man and The Legacy

Calvin, The Man and The Legacy

Edited by
Murray Rae, Peter Matheson
and Brett Knowles

ATF Theology
Adelaide

2014

Text copyright © 2014 remains with the individual authors for all papers in this collection.

All rights reserved. Except for any fair dealing permitted under the Copyright Act, no part of this book may be reproduced by any means without prior permission. Inquiries should be made to the publisher.

Cover design by Astrid Sengkey
Layout/Artwork by Anna Dimasi

Text Minion Pro Size 11

Published by:

An imprint of the ATF Ltd.
PO Box 504
Hindmarsh, SA 5007
ABN 90 116 359 963
www.atfpress.com

CONTENTS

Preface
   Peter Matheson   vii

Part 1: The Man and His Thought

1. Graham Redding
Medicine for Poor Sick Souls?:
Calvin's Communion Service in Profile   3

2. Jason A Goroncy
John Calvin: Servant of the Word   13

3. Randall Zachman
The Grateful Humility of the Children of God:
Knowledge of Ourselves in Calvin's Theology   41

4. Elsie McKee
A Week in the Life of John Calvin   61

5. Murray Rae
Calvin on the Authority of Scripture   79

6. Randall Zachman
Calvin's Interpretation of Scripture   97

Part II: The Legacy and the Caricature

7. John Roxborogh
Thomas Chalmers and Scottish Calvinism
in the Nineteenth Century   123

8. John Stenhouse
Calvin's Own Country? Calvinists,
Anti-Calvinists and the Making
of New Zealand Culture   143

9. Peter Matheson
The Reception of Calvin and Calvinism in New Zealand:
Preliminary Trawl   171

10. Alison Clarke
Popular Piety, the Sacraments and Calvinism
in Colonial New Zealand   189

11. Kirstine Moffat
'Mr Calvin and Mr Knox':
The Calvinist Legacy in the Fiction and Poetry
of New Zealand Scots   213

12. Ian Breward
Calvin in Australia and New Zealand   235

Contributors   257

Index   261

Preface

Peter Matheson

The history of Otago and Southland, set on the South-east coast of the South Island of New Zealand, is unthinkable without the influence of Calvinism. Indeed the whole of New Zealand was marked by it, not least through the influence of the Presbyterian Church, which in 1900, for example, was arguably the best-attended and most articulate church in the land. The University of Otago, the first in New Zealand, and church life and thought itself owed much to their Calvinist heritage. Community life and values in Dunedin, Invercargill, Gore and the surrounding countryside continue to manifest its influence in countless ways. It was natural, therefore, that when the 500th anniversary of Calvin's birth in 1509 came round that thought should be given to an appropriate way to mark his impact in New Zealand, as had already been done in 1909, and in 1936. This volume is one of the happy outcomes of these celebrations.

An organizing committee began to meet in 2008, and was encouraged by the preliminary soundings it made with the Mayor of Dunedin, Peter Chin, with the Synod of Otago and Southland, and with the University of Otago, as well as with other interested parties. From the beginning it appeared important to look at the way in which Calvinism was understood and received in this particular context, in what was then the most far-flung corner of the British Empire. Theological and historical perspectives would need to complement one another. Attention would have to be given to Calvinism as an international phenomenon as well as one that become rooted in the soil of this region. The Scottish dimension was significant. There was agreement, too, that it would be good to accompany any academic symposium with events of interest to a much wider audience. Free public lectures by our keynote speakers were therefore planned, while a commemorative service in the iconic First Church of Otago incorporated elements of the traditional Genevan liturgy. Finally a rather remarkable Son et Lumiere performance was commissioned, of which more later.

One reason for making a special effort to attract the attention of the general public was that misconceptions about the impact of Calvinism in New Zealand abound. In the past rather romanticized representations of its sterling contributions have vied with iconoclastic denunciations of its malign influence. The hope, therefore, was that this commemoration of Calvin's birth might offer a more balanced perspective, avoiding both hagiography and mischievous caricature.

The scope of this volume is not limited, however, to the New Zealand scene. The first part of the book is concerned with Calvin the man—liturgist, preacher, pastor and scholar. Six chapters explore aspects of his ministry and of his thought. Part two then deals with Calvin's legacy, especially in New Zealand and Australia, but beginning with a snapshot of the Calvinism that had evolved in Scotland and that shaped in turn the 'new' life of the Scottish settlers as they sought to establish themselves in Australia and New Zealand.

For the academic symposium, which was gratifyingly well attended, we were extraordinarily fortunate in securing the services of two internationally renowned keynote speakers: the theologian, Randall Zachman, of Notre Dame University, and the historian Elsie McKee, of Princeton Seminary. They proved to be exceptionally gracious and accommodating participants in all the events as well as offering sparkling lectures and seminars. A feature of the papers offered by New Zealand scholars was the wide range of disciplines covered, literary and anthropological, as well as doctrinal and historical. A more human and pastorally oriented Calvin emerged.

A word is in place about Richard Huber's remarkable Son et Lumiére presentation in First Church. This brought together in evocative and haunting manner the aspirations of the first Scottish settlers, men and women, in Dunedin with the original concerns of Calvin. Spectacular light effects and original music from a talented choir accompanied the script, which was notable for a drum-beat of a few frequently repeated phrases. The 'voices' of the past came alive for the very appreciative audiences.

Generous support from many sides enabled this ambitious celebration to be so successful. The Synod of Otago and Southland offered extremely generous financial support. The Knox Centre for

Ministry and Leadership contributed both financial and logistical assistance. Enthusiastic backing was also given by First Church of Otago, the Mayor of Otago, and the University of Otago, especially its Department of Theology and Religion. Peter Matheson and Murray Rae would like in particular to acknowledge the manifold contribution of Graham Redding, both as Principal of the Centre for Theology and Ministry and as Moderator of the Presbyterian Church of Aotearoa New Zealand.

'In terms of this publication, I would like to acknowledge the eagle eye of our copy editor, Brett Knowles, the perseverance of Murray Rae in bringing it to print, and the warm cooperation of our publisher.'

Part I

The Man and His Thought

1
Medicine for Poor Sick Souls?: Calvin's Communion Service in Profile

Graham Redding

On the eve of the Calvin conference at which the papers in this volume were presented, a communion service was held at First Church of Otago, Dunedin. As far as possible, the pattern of Calvin's communion liturgies in Strasbourg in 1540 and Geneva in 1542 was replicated in the service.

Despite care being taken to explain the difference in context between Calvin's day and ours, and the inclusion of explanatory notes in the order of service, at the conclusion of the service several people voiced their dismay at the condemnatory tone of much of the liturgy and the underlying bleak view of the human condition. They said it reinforced their worst assumptions about Calvin and his theology.

The two liturgical segments that caused most offence and were singled out repeatedly for criticism are as follows. Firstly, a segment of the prayer of confession:

> O Lord God, eternal and almighty Father, we confess and acknowledge unfeignedly before thy holy majesty that we are poor sinners, conceived and born in iniquity and corruption, prone to do evil, incapable of any good, and that in our depravity we transgress thy holy commandments without end or ceasing: Wherefore we purchase for ourselves, through thy righteous judgment, our ruin and perdition.[1]

And secondly, the declaration of excommunication that followed the words of institution:

---

1. B Thompson, *Liturgies of the Western Church* (Cleveland: Meridian Books, 1961), 197.

> We have heard, my brethren, how our Lord observed His Supper with His disciples, from which we learn that strangers and those who do not belong to the company of His faithful people must not be admitted. Therefore, following that precept, in the name and by the authority of our Lord Jesus Christ, I excommunicate all idolaters, blasphemers and despisers of God, all heretics and those who create private sects in order to break the unity of the Church, all perjurers, all who rebel against father or mother or superior, all who promote sedition or mutiny; brutal and disorderly persons, adulterers, lewd and lustful men, thieves, ravishers, greedy and grasping people, drunkards, gluttons, and all those who lead a scandalous and dissolute life. I warn them to abstain from this Holy Table, lest they defile and contaminate the holy food which our Lord Jesus Christ gives to none except they belong to His household of faith.[2]

One could argue, of course, that the liturgy needs to be looked at as a whole rather than assessed according to its constituent parts, but that does not do away entirely with the objection. Neither does the argument that the criticisms say more about modern sensibilities than they do about sixteenth-century liturgical deficiencies. What is needed, I think, is a consideration of the theology that underpins and informs Calvin's communion liturgy.

The celebration of the Lord's Supper was integral to Calvin's understanding of worship. His belief here was shaped not only by what he perceived to have been the practice of the early Church, but also by biblical and theological conviction. Word and Sacrament form a unity. The Supper seals the covenant promises proclaimed in the Word;[3] and the Supper derives its virtue from the Word when it is preached intelligibly.[4]

---

2. *Ibid*, 205–6.
3. John Calvin, *The Institutes of the Christian Religion*, IV.xiv.6.
4. John Calvin, *Short Treatise on the Holy Supper of our Lord Jesus Christ*, 48. Theologia, http://www.hornes.org/theologia/john-calvin/short-treatise-on-the-holy-supper-of-our-lord-jesus-christ, accessed on 20 December 2010.

Even when the Genevan Council denied Calvin's proposal for more regular celebration of the Supper, his Sunday service remained an AnteCommunion, standing in anticipation of it. As Howard Hageman notes, with Calvin,

> ... we do not find, as with Zwingli or Farel, two separate services, one for preaching and the other for the Eucharist. There is but one service for the Lord's Day, rubricated to show at what point and in what manner it may be terminated whenever the Eucharist is not to be celebrated. In Strasbourg we are working with a very different theological background from that in Zurich or even in Geneva. Here the Eucharist is seen as a necessary part of the cultic act, so necessary that it must determine the structure of the service even when it is not celebrated.[5]

In the same year that he drafted his Strasbourg liturgy, Calvin wrote a *Short Treatise on the Holy Supper of our Lord Jesus Christ*, which was published a year later, in 1541. This document gives us a remarkable insight into Calvin's mind at that time and serves as a very useful theological commentary on his liturgy.

In his *Treatise*, Calvin repeatedly uses language of 'nourishment' and 'participation' to define the primary purpose of the Lord's Supper: It is *nourishment* for the soul, preserving and strengthening, confirming and fortifying us in the promises of salvation and the benefits of Christ's death on the cross and, at the same time, delivering us from condemnation. And it is an essential means of *participation* in Christ's humanity and eternal life.

These notions of nourishment and participation are brought together in the simple declaration that 'in order to have our life in Christ our souls must feed on his body and blood as their proper food'.[6]

The initiative here lies entirely with Christ, not with us. Through the Holy Spirit, Christ leads us to communion with Himself, whereupon we feed upon Him by faith with thanksgiving. There is nothing in ourselves, therefore, that merits our presence at the Table. As Calvin puts it:

---
5. H Hageman, *Pulpit and Table* (Richmond: John Knox Press, 1962), 26.
6. Calvin, *Treatise*, 13.

> Here, then, is the singular consolation which we derive from the Supper. It directs and leads us to the cross of Jesus Christ and to his resurrection, to certify us that whatever iniquity there may be in us the Lord nevertheless recognizes and accepts us as righteous, whatever materials of death may be in us he nevertheless gives us life, whatever misery may be in us he nevertheless fills us with all felicity. Or to explain the matter more simply, as in ourselves we are devoid of all good, and have not one particle of what might help to procure salvation, the Supper is an attestation that, having been made partakers of the death and passion of Jesus Christ, we have everything that is useful and salutary to us.[7]

This key passage in the *Treatise* anticipates a similarly key section in the 1556 edition of the *Institutes of the Christian Religion*, titled 'Union with Christ as the special fruit of the Lord's Supper', in which Calvin refers to the wonderful, or miraculous exchange:

> That, becoming Son of man with us, Christ has made us sons of God with him; that, by his descent to earth, he has prepared an ascent to heaven for us; that, by taking on our mortality, he has conferred his immortality upon us; that, accepting our weakness, he has strengthened us by his power; that, receiving our poverty unto himself, he has transferred his wealth to us; that, taking the weight of our iniquity upon himself (which oppressed us), he has clothed us with his righteousness.[8]

This notion of miraculous exchange only works if we recognise simultaneously the fullness of depravity that is in us and the fullness of life that is in Christ. There are two dangers. The first is to separate the two and to talk of human depravity without reference to the fullness of life in Christ. This leads inevitably to a despairing and unhealthy knowledge of the human condition. The second is to deny the truth of human depravity. This leads inevitably to a failure to rely on, and participate fully in the new life in Christ. As Calvin puts it:

---

7. *Ibid*, 9.
8. Calvin, *Institutes*, IV.xvii.2.

> If we consider our life to be placed in Christ, we must acknowledge that we are dead in ourselves. If we seek our strength in him, we must understand that in ourselves we are weak. If we think that all our felicity is in his grace, we must understand how miserable we are without it. If we have our rest in him, we must feel within ourselves only disquietude and torment.[9]

Calvin goes on to stress the importance of having a 'deep-seated conviction of our own misery, which will make us hunger and thirst after Him (Christ)'.[10]

It is here that Calvin's perspective on the human condition and the nature of confession is most at odds with the modern mindset. Significantly, in the Church of Scotland's 1994 *Book of Common Order* not a single one of the prayers of confession in the ten morning and evening orders of worship acknowledges fully the ontological nature of sin. The prayers of confession focus almost entirely on what we have done or failed to do; no mention is made of the state into which we are born.

Typical of the prayers of confession in the *Book of Common Order* is the following:

> Holy God, giver of light and grace, we have sinned against you and against fellow men and women, through ignorance, through weakness, through our own deliberate fault. We have belittled your love, and betrayed your trust. We are sorry, we are ashamed, we repent of all our sins. For the sake of your Son Jesus Christ, who died for us, forgive us all that is past, and lead us out from darkness to walk as children of light.[11]

Note the acknowledgement of sins committed, but not the state of sin; and the need for forgiveness, but not the need to be reconstituted. I have argued elsewhere that most often missing from post-Reformation liturgies in the Church of Scotland

---

9. Calvin, *Treatise*, 22.
10. *Ibid*, 23.
11. Church of Scotland, *Book of Common Order, 1994* (Edinburgh: St Andrew Press, 1994), 22.

> ... is an appreciation of the ontological aspect to both sin (it is something into which we are born, not merely something that we do) and the atonement (Christ does not merely forgive individual sins; rather, in the hypostatic union and through his vicarious life of obedience and faith he has healed and sanctified our sinful human condition.[12]

This failure can be traced back to the influence of seventeenth-century federal Calvinism and Puritanism, both of which tended to cast the atonement in forensic terms—Christ dying for our sins on the Cross—while understating the atoning significance of the Incarnation.

By way of contrast, Calvin's portrayal of the miraculous exchange requires us to recognise the filial and ontological dimensions of the atonement that has taken place in Jesus Christ.

The *filial* dimension testifies to the fact that the atonement is not about the wrath of God being appeased on the cross, but rather about the loving will of the Father to receive us as His children being fulfilled. It is about the outworking of a covenant relationship, not the satisfaction of contractual obligations. Calvin says as much when he opens his section on the Lord's Supper in the *Institutes* with the following declaration: 'God has received us, once for all, into his family, to hold us not only as servants but as sons'.[13]

The *ontological* dimension testifies to the atoning significance of the incarnation and ascension, so often overshadowed by our focus on the Cross. In the humanity of the Saviour, from Bethlehem to Calvary, God took hold of our rebellious humanity in a reconciling union; in the faith and prayerful obedience of the Son, our wayward humanity was redirected towards the Father; in Jesus' suffering and death, God penetrated the depths of human sin, guilt and god-forsak-

---

12. G Redding, *Prayer and the Priesthood of Christ in the Reformed Tradition* (Edinburgh: T&T Clark, 2003), 273–4.
13. Calvin, *Institutes*, IV.xvii.1. Similarly, in his *Treatise*, Calvin declares: 'Since it has pleased our good God to receive us by baptism into his Church, which he desires to maintain and govern, and since he has received us to keep us not merely as domestics, but as his own children, it remains that, in order to do the office of a good father, he nourishes and provides us with every thing necessary for life' (Calvin, *Treatise*, 3).

enness; in the resurrection, the shackles of sin and death were broken once and for all; and, now, in and through the ascension of our Lord our humanity has been lifted—healed, redeemed and sanctified—before the throne of grace. To live, therefore, is to live *in Christ*; to pray is to pray *in Christ*; to know ourselves is to know ourselves *in Christ*.

Understood in this context, the doctrine of justification refers to nothing less than the ungodly being clothed in Christ's righteousness. It is about being judged and acquitted, condemned and vindicated, exposed as guilty and made righteous, in and through Jesus Christ. All this takes place within our humanity, as Christ the Mediator and High Priest assumes the human nature that we all share, reconstitutes it from within, and by His Spirit unites us to Himself so that His humanity becomes ours. This is what sanctification refers to. So it is that Calvin declares in the *Institutes* that 'we or our prayers have no access to God unless Christ, as our High priest, having washed away our sins, *sanctifies us* and obtains for us that grace from which the uncleanness of our transgressions and vices debars us'.[14]

For Calvin, sanctification is grounded in the hypostatic union, in and through which the unholy human nature that we all share has been brought into a sanctifying union with the Son's holy nature. He insists that this applies to the whole life of Jesus, in which our conception, birth, childhood, youth, adulthood and death have all been sanctified.[15]

To grasp these deep truths and mysteries is to have awakened in us a deep and abiding hunger for the One who is our life:

> Now to have a good appetite it is not enough that the stomach be empty, it must also be in good order and capable of receiving its food. Hence it follows that our souls must be pressed with famine and have a desire and ardent longing to be fed, in order to find their proper nourishment in the Lord's Supper.[16]

This is precisely what Calvin's communion liturgy seeks to do—to reawaken in us that deep desire and ardent longing to be fed, and

---

14. Calvin, *Institutes*, II.xv.6 (italics mine).
15. *Ibid*, II.xvi.19.
16. Calvin, *Treatise*, 23.

to lead us to the place where our hunger might be satisfied. The severe words of confession and excommunication must be viewed in this context. Being in union with Christ, not merely following the example of Christ, is of crucial importance for Calvin. Being in union with Christ expresses the vitality of a process by which our humanity is progressively transformed by the humanity of the Saviour.

Thus, in Calvin's Exhortation to come to the Table, we are assured

> . . . that the sins and imperfections which remain in us will not prevent Him from receiving us and making us worthy partakers of this spiritual Table. For we do not come here to testify that we are perfect or righteous in ourselves: On the contrary, by seeking our life in Jesus Christ we confess that we are in death. Know, therefore, that this Sacrament is a medicine for poor sick souls, and that the only worthiness which our Lord requires of us is to know ourselves sufficiently to deplore our sins and to find all our pleasure, joy and satisfaction in Him alone.[17]

'Medicine for poor sick souls.' In these words we detect not only the doctrinal conviction of a theologian, but also the heart of a pastor, yearning for the people of God to be made whole and to live the fullness of life that God intends for them in Christ.

This helps us understand more fully the purpose of Calvin's declaration of excommunication. It does not mean that those subject to it are 'cast into outer darkness', and it does not profess to extend to the union of the soul with God; rather, it means that certain categories of persons should refrain from communicating in the Sacrament until such time as they have sought forgiveness and reconciliation, have made amends, and desire to be reconciled and reintegrated into the community of faith. Moreover, the Church is under obligation to work with them to restore their broken relationship with Christ, so that they may again join in the fellowship of the Lord's Table.

What Calvin is concerned to preserve here is the integrity of the Church as the holy, elect people of God. The Christian life has a certain shape to it. As Calvin states in his *Treatise*, in the supper we are

---

17. Thompson, *Liturgies of the Western Church*, 206-207.

reminded of our duty towards God[18] and we are given a 'most powerful incitement to live holily, and especially observe charity and brotherly love toward all'.[19] The Christian life, therefore, involves accountability and discipline.

While discipline proved to be one of the more controversial aspects of Calvin's reform of the city of Geneva, as Murray Rae points out, it should be remembered that

> . . . *discipline*, in a church context, is concerned with the formation of *disciples*, of people whose lives are ordered by the gospel. Nurture, encouragement, pastoral care and even correction, sensitively and prayerfully exercised, and determined always by love, are appropriate means of strengthening faith and forming disciples within the Christian community. The Scottish *Second Book of Discipline* explains that 'As the pastors and doctors should be diligent in teaching and sowing the seed of the Word, so the elders should be careful in seeking the fruit of the same in the people.' The eldership is conceived, therefore, as an instrument of God's transformative work, nurturing and encouraging the Church's participation in God's new creation.[20]

In conclusion, while it is indeed the case that Calvin's communion liturgy suffers from certain defects, including a verbosity, repetitiveness and didactic style that reveal the mind of a lawyer more than they do a liturgist, the liturgy embodies some significant doctrinal convictions about the nature of salvation and what it means to be human, which we moderns need to hear afresh. These might be summed up in the following terms: Although it is true that we are mired in sin, a deeper truth is that we are wired for praise. And it is as we share in the life of Christ that we are enabled truly and fully to join in the praise and worship that He offers God in our place and on our behalf.

---

18. Calvin, *Treatise*, 18.
19. *Ibid*, 19.
20. M Rae, 'A Brief Theology of Ordination', unpublished Doctrine Core Group report to the 2010 General Assembly of the Presbyterian Church of Aotearoa New Zealand. Emphasis as cited.

The Christian life is not so much a life of grim obedience as a life of joyful participation, at the centre of which stands this simple act of gathering around this Table where Christ is simultaneously the One who feeds us and the One upon whom we feed. Here Christ is both Host and Bread of Heaven. Here we receive medicine for poor sick souls. We gather by His invitation; we are fed at His hand; we are sent forth in His name.

2

John Calvin: Servant of the Word

Jason A Goroncy

Introduction

While the Church had known schism before, its sixteenth-century programme of reform led to its fragmentation the likes of which it had not known since the 'Great Schism' some five centuries earlier. The magisterial reformers were understandably concerned about the centrifugal force that their programme encouraged, and they did not dismiss lightly Rome's sharp indictment that disunity indicated defect. This concern is evident in one of the more 'catholic' of the Reformed confessions, the Second Helvetic Confession (1566) penned by Huldrych Zwingli's student Heinrich Bullinger: 'We are reproached because there have been manifold dissensions and strife in our churches since they departed themselves from the Church of Rome, and therefore cannot be true churches.'[1] In response, and by way of marking some distance from more radical wings of the reformation, the magisterial reformers reminded Rome of her own history of conflict and fragmentation, and, more substantively, addressed the question of what constitutes 'true church'. Their conclusion, précised by John Calvin, is well known: 'Wherever we see the Word of God purely preached and heard, and the sacraments administered according to Christ's institution, there, it is not to be doubted, a church of God exists.'[2] These two 'marks' function not as boundaries so much as

---

1. Heinrich Bullinger, 'A Simple Confession and Exposition of the Orthodox Faith: The Second Helvetic Confession of 1566', in *Reformed Confessions of the Sixteenth Century*, edited by Arthur C Cochrane (Louisville: Westminster John Knox, 2003), 264.
2. John Calvin, *The Institutes of the Christian Religion*, IV.i.9. Unless otherwise stated, this is the edition published by Westminster Press, Philadelphia, in 1977.

'directional signs that point to the core of faithful church life'.[3] They recall that no matter how frequently or intentionally the Church may engage in additional practices or activities, the most basic, indispensable and controlling hub of its life remains its witness to the Word of God from pulpit, font and table. Here we will be concerned mainly with the place that the former occupied in Calvin's ministry and thought, and ask what remains serviceable about Calvin's homiletic for those who preach—and for those who hear and taste—the Word of God today.

Peter Steinfel's recent piece in the *New York Times* recalls that 'Calvin is often imagined, if he is imagined at all, as the implacable snoop who enforced a prudish morality on the citizens of Geneva, a steely spinner of harsh theological doctrines about a depraved humanity and a fierce God predestining people to heaven or hell'.[4] The truth is that, as Marilynne Robinson has observed, 'People know to disapprove of [Calvin], though not precisely why they should'.[5] They also know that Calvin was 'an eighteenth-century Scotsman, a prude and obscurantist with a buckle on his hat, possibly a burner of witches, certainly the very spirit of capitalism'.[6] Bruce Gordon's recent work paints Calvin as not only 'brilliant, visionary and iconic', but also as one who 'intimidated, bullied and humiliated'.[7] But when Gordon comes to enquire what it was that made Calvin great, what made Calvin Calvin, he unequivocally concludes that it was Calvin's 'brilliance as a thinker and writer, and, above all, his ability to interpret the Bible'.[8] While today's preachers will not want to embrace every facet of Calvin's homiletical method, there remains, nonetheless, some abidingly valuable things that those who preach, and those who listen to, sermons can learn from Calvin. It is these more constructive elements that this essay will seek to highlight.

---

3. Joseph D Small, 'A Church of the Word and Sacrament', in *Christian Worship in Reformed Churches Past and Present*, edited by Lukas Vischer (Grand Rapids/Cambridge: Wm B Eerdmans, 2003), 312.
4. Peter Steinfels, 'Man of Contradictions, Shaper of Modernity. Age? 500 Next Week', *The New York Times*, 4 July 2009, A14.
5. Marilynne Robinson, *The Death of Adam: Essays on Modern Thought* (New York: Picador, 2005), 174.
6. *Ibid*, 206.
7. Bruce Gordon, *Calvin* (New Haven/London: Yale University Press, 2009), vii.
8. *Ibid*, viii.

James Nichols, among others, has argued that 'Whatever else it was, the Reformation was a great preaching revival, probably the greatest in the history of the Christian church'.[9] This reflects a conviction among the magisterial reformers that preaching (and so pastors[10]) is not only indispensable to Christianity, but that it is also the primary means by which Calvin and others (including the council of Geneva) expected God to transform the Swiss city and the known world.[11] But as central as preaching was to the 'man who spoke',[12] the ministry of the Word, for Calvin, comprises more than public speech, and includes catechism, private exhortation, authoring liturgy, as well as civic and ecclesiastical administration. Between 1555 and his death in 1564, and whilst racked by constant pain, ill health and grief, Calvin laboured to establish an education system, to arrange for the care of refugees, the aged and the poor, and to continue the revision of the city's governance—all of which he considered part of the ministry of the Word. We might understand Calvin's various ministries of the Word under a five-fold form: as writer, as public speaker, as advocate of church discipline, as minister to individuals, and as liturgist.[13]

Ministries of the Word

Calvin the writer[14]
While best known for the various editions of his *Institutes of the Christian Religion*, Calvin also wrote theological treatises such as the *Genevan Confession of Faith* (1536), the *Confession of Faith Concerning the Eucharist* (1537), the short *Treatise on the Lord's Supper* (1541), and

---

9. James Hastings Nichols, *Corporate Worship in the Reformed Tradition* (Philadelphia: Westminster Press, 1968), 29.
10. See the French (Gallican) Confession of 1559.
11. See Calvin, *Commentaries*, XIXb.424. Unless otherwise stated, *Commentaries* refers to the 22-volume set published by Baker Books between 1999 and 2003 and which were originally printed for the Calvin Translation Society. These have been variously translated by James Anderson, Henry Beveridge, Charles William Bingham, J King, John Owen, and William Pringle.
12. Bernard Cottret, *Calvin: A Biography* (Grand Rapids/Cambridge/Edinburgh: Wm B Eerdmans/T&T Clark, 2003), 288.
13. On Calvin as liturgist, see Wulfert de Greef, *The Writings of John Calvin: An Introductory Guide* (Grand Rapids/Leicester: Baker/Apollos, 1993), 126, note 8.
14. Here I follow Peter Adam, *Speaking God's Words: A Practical Theology of Preaching* (Leicester: Inter-Varsity Press, 1996), 61–6.

the *Catechism for the Church of Geneva* (1545). To these we might add his *Reply to Sadolet* in 1539. But it was not only theology that attracted Calvin's pen. He also wrote documents on church order such as his articles *Concerning the Organization of the Church and of Worship at Geneva* (1537), *Draft Ecclesiastical Ordinances* (1541), and the *Ordinances for the Supervision of Churches in the Country* (1547), all examples of Calvin's upholding of the centrality of the ministry of the Word in the Church. Thirdly, he wrote commentaries on most books of the Bible, many of which were conceived from his public teaching and preaching. Finally, Calvin wrote letters, not only to the kings of England, Denmark and Poland, and to the king and queen of Navarre, but also to fellow reformers in France, Switzerland, the Netherlands and England, to prisoners and martyrs, and to his friends. Jean-Daniel Benoît properly attests that Calvin considered his letter-writing a key aspect of his ministry of the Word.[15]

Calvin the public speaker
Calvin's focus during his first period in Geneva was lectures, but it was not long before he was 'elected pastor' and so began his two-fold work of lecturing and preaching.[16] He continued this pattern even when banished from Geneva in 1538 which led, from September, to his serving the French Church in Strasbourg where, in addition to his lectures on the New Testament (beginning with John's Gospel and 1 Corinthians) at the Strasbourg Academy, he preached, it would seem, four times a week.

From the time of Calvin's return to Geneva in 1541, his principal point of contact with Genevans was the pulpit. The expectation of Genevans during Calvin's time was that Sunday would begin with a

---

15. See Jean-Daniel Benoît, 'Calvin the Letter-Writer', in *John Calvin*, edited by Gervase E Duffield (Appleford: Sutton Courtenay Press, 1966), 67–101; Jean-Daniel Benoît, *Calvin in His Letters: A Study of Calvin's Pastoral Counselling, Mainly from his Letters* (Appleford: Sutton Courtenay Press, 1986).
16. *Ioannis Calvini Opera quae supersunt omnia*, edited by Guilielmus Baum *et al.* (Corpus Reformatorum; Brunsvigae/Berlin: Apud CA Schwetschke et Filium, 1863–1900), 21:58. [Hereafter *Opera Calvini*.] One recalls Heinrich Ott's claim that 'the separation between the duties of preaching and theological teaching is a purely practical technical division of labour'. Heinrich Ott, *Theology and Preaching: A programme of work in dogmatics, arranged with reference to Questions I–II of the Heidelberg Catechism* (London: Lutterworth Press, 1965), 23.

daybreak service comprising a one-hour sermon, be followed by a catechism class for children at midday, and conclude with another sermon at three o'clock. Sermons were also fixed for Monday, Tuesday and Friday mornings until, in 1549, they increased to every day of the week.[17] Speaking with few or no notes, though still prepared,[18] Calvin's practice was to preach twice each Sunday at Saint-Pierre's and once every day on alternate weeks. On Sundays his usual practice was to preach through the New Testament, with the exception of a few Psalms on Sunday afternoons. During the week, his sermons were almost always from the Old Testament.[19] As age and poor health restricted his movement, he requested to be carried to church in a chair in order to fulfill his pulpit responsibilities. In his fifty-five years, Calvin preached over 2,300 sermons (some forty-four volumes), including 200 sermons on Deuteronomy, 194 on 1 and 2 Samuel, 189 on the Acts of the Apostles, 174 on Ezekiel, and 159 on Job.

In addition to preaching, Calvin lectured to the Friday Congrégation and, later, before the Academy of Geneva, an institute dedicated to the study of theology and to the training of pastors. On Calvin's assessment, the quality of pastoral ministry in Geneva was in serious need of attention. Consequently, with his support, the period between 1541 and 1546 witnessed a drastic transformation of the pastoral ministry landscape, wherein local Genevan pastors were replaced by well-educated Frenchmen closely aligned to Calvin and eager to support his programme of reform. With the support of the Consistory and the Congrégation of Pastors, Calvin arranged for well-respected ministers who had a long-standing record of serving the French evangelical cause—such as Nicolas des Gallars, Reymond Chauvet, François Bourgoing, Michel Cop, and others—to come to Geneva and to play a leading role in Church reform.

Calvin spoke frequently at the Friday Congrégation which probably met at seven or nine in the morning after worship, which preceded the meeting of the Company of Pastors, and which afforded ministers

---

17. *Opera Calvini*, 10a:288. In 1549, the city council decreed that pastors would preach daily. Calvin, who was concerned that pastors would burn out, opposed this decree.
18. See *ibid*, 26:473–4.
19. The Reformation—and particularly its Calvinistic branch—marked the first step in many centuries of a genuine recovery of the Old Testament for the Church.

and some lay persons from Geneva and surrounds the opportunity to gather together for Bible study, mutual admonition, and worship.[20] These Congrégations (which began under Farel's leadership in Geneva from 1536, and which were modelled after the so-called *Prophezei* (school of the prophets) in Zurich) encouraged public discourse on the Bible, a radical concept but one which was quickly established as 'central to the life of the Reformed community in Geneva'.[21] Plainly, Calvin recognised that while circumstances dictated flexibility of approach, ecclesiastical reform 'depended on the ability of the ministers to teach true doctrine and administer the sacraments in a disciplined community'.[22] Consistent with this claim, in January 1537, the Genevan preachers presented the city council with their *Articles Concerning the Organisation of the Church*, a document possibly drafted by Farel which outlined the implementation of weekly celebration of Holy Communion, excommunication, the catechesis of young people, singing in worship, and the substitution of Roman marriage laws.

Calvin lectured three times a week. September 1536 saw Calvin begin a series of lectures (probably on St Paul's Epistle to the Romans) to a small group who gathered in the cathedral of Saint-Pierre. Still a year later he was lecturing daily on the New Testament at the Latin school just outside Geneva. Modelled on the Academy in Lausanne, the Genevan Academy was finally opened in 1559 under the rectorship of Theodore Beza. The Academy was 'a triumph of Christian humanism',[23] and the *schola publica* (upper school) welcomed Calvin as one of its two theological professors, Calvin being responsible for teaching Old Testament. He never taught theology as a separate subject. The creation of the Academy paralleled Calvin's conviction that pastors are fundamentally guides for the congregation's reading of Scripture. This required pastors skilled in reading the 'spectacles'[24] of faith themselves, and sponsored the ideal of educated pastors lit-

---

20. See Erik A de Boer, 'The Congrégation: An In-Service Theological Training Center for Preachers to the People of Geneva', in *Calvin and the Company of Pastors: Papers Presented at the 14th Colloquium of the Calvin Studies Society, May 22–24, 2003, the University of Notre Dame, Notre Dame, Indiana*, edited by David L Foxgrover (Grand Rapids: CRC, 2004), 57–87.
21. Gordon, *Calvin*, 71.
22. *Ibid*, 314.
23. *Ibid*, 299.
24. Calvin, *Institutes*, I.vi.1.

erate in Hebrew, Greek and Classical Latin. It also meant that Calvin was about forming an entire generation of pastors who would be concerned with the gospel rather than with fostering a Calvin cult. Indeed, some 'evidence of [Calvin's] success may lie in the fact that one can read very far into the voluble literature of his tradition—not a tradition inclined to spare citations or balk at footnotes—and never find him quoted or even alluded to'.[25]

The Academy served not only the members of the college, pastors and temporary residents in Geneva, but also students from all over Europe (mainly from France, but also from Scotland, Poland, Hungary and England), many of whom had come to Geneva to train as pastors with a view to returning to their native lands to evangelise and to plant churches. Little wonder then that Calvin's lectures on the prophets include as one of their *foci* the evangelistic mission of the Church. Calvin's contemporary, Peter Viret, estimated that by 1561 around one thousand people attended Calvin's lectures every day, the same year that the Venerable Company of Pastors in Geneva sent 151 ministers to serve Reformed churches in France, a number significantly short of the demand.[26]

Calvin as advocate of church discipline
For Calvin, the ministry of the Word extended to the implementation of a bible-informed church polity and pattern of life among Genevans. This found voice through his work on the *Church Ordinances* and through his membership of the Consistory. In his *Instruction in Faith*, where he treats the matter of the power of binding and loosing from Matthew 16:19, Calvin reminds pastors that

> . . . this power (which in the Scriptures is attributed to pastors) is wholly contained in and limited to the ministry of the word. For Christ has not given this power properly to these men, but to his word of which he has made these men ministers. Hence, let these pastors boldly dare all things by the word of God, of which they

---
25. Robinson, *Death of Adam*, 192–3.
26. See Peter J Wilcox, 'Restoration, Reformation and the Progress of the Kingdom of Christ: Evangelisation in the Thought and Practice of John Calvin, 1555–1564' (DPhil thesis, University of Oxford, 1993), 58–65.

have been constituted dispensators; let them constrain all the power, glory and haughtiness of the world to make room for and to obey the majesty of that word; let them by means of that word command all from the greatest to the smallest; let them edify the house of Christ; let them demolish the reign of Satan . . . but all through and within the word of God. Pastors who substitute their own fancies for the word are to be chased away as wolves. For Christ has commanded us to listen only to those who teach us that which they have taken from his word.[27]

Calvin as pastor to individuals
Although never 'ordained', Calvin was before all else a pastor, and one who carried the conviction concerning the pastoral task that 'the manner of teaching not only consists in public discourses, but also has to do with private admonitions'.[28] Or, as he penned elsewhere: 'As to the pastors, . . . their office is to proclaim the Word of God, to instruct, admonish, exhort and censure, both in public and private'.[29] So Randall Zachman observes:

> The bulk of Calvin's work as a preacher, unlike his work as a teacher, consists of applying that doctrine [gleaned from Scripture] to the lives of the members of his congregation, and exhorting them to be transformed by the power of the doctrine they are hearing, which is none other than the power of Christ working by his Spirit. However, such general preaching to the whole congregation is just the first step of the pastor's application of Scripture; the real work begins when the pastor visits every member of the congregation in private in order to apply scriptural doctrine specifically to them.[30]

---

27. Cited in John T McNeill, 'The Significance of the Word of God for Calvin', in *Church History* 28/2 (1959), 138.
28. Calvin, *Institutes*, IV.iii.6.
29. 'Draft Ecclesiastical Ordinances, September & October 1541', in *Calvin: Theological Treatises*, translated by JKS Reid (London: SCM Press, 1954), 58.
30. Randall C Zachman, *John Calvin as Teacher, Pastor, and Theologian: The Shape of His Writings and Thought* (Grand Rapids: Baker Academic, 2006), 65; compare

And Calvin's contemporary, Nicolas Colladon, describes Calvin's life and ministry thus:

> Calvin for his part did not spare himself at all, working far beyond what his powers and regard for his health could stand . . . He never failed in visiting the sick, in private warning and counsel, and the rest of the numberless matters arising out of the ordinary exercise of his ministry. But besides these ordinary tasks, he had great care for believers in France, both in teaching them and exhorting them and counselling them and consoling them by letters when they were being persecuted, and also interceding for them, or getting another to intercede when he thought he saw an opening.[31]

Again, the point here is simply to highlight the multifaceted shape of Calvin's comprehension of the ministry of the Word. We turn now to preaching.

The Function of Preaching

Preaching as divine accommodation

With some indebtment to Chrysostom,[32] Calvin contends that by employing human speech, God not only accommodates to the varying circumstances and 'customs of each age and nation',[33] but also, in Christ, 'God in a manner makes himself little, that he might accommodate himself to our comprehension'.[34] Chaperoned by the Spirit,

---

THL Parker, *Portrait of Calvin* (London: SCM Press, 1954), 80–1.
31. Cited in THL Parker, *Calvin's Preaching* (Edinburgh: T&T Clark, 1992), 62–3.
32. See John R Walchenbach, 'John Calvin as Biblical Interpreter: An Investigation into Calvin's Use of John Chrysostom as an Exegetical Tutor' (PhD thesis, University of Pittsburgh, 1974); Najeeb George Awad, 'The Influence of John Chrysostom's Hermeneutics on John Calvin's Exegetical Approach to Paul's Epistle to the Romans', in *Scottish Journal of Theology* 63/4 (2010), 414–36.
33. Calvin, *Institutes*, IV.x.30.
34. Calvin, *Commentaries*, XXIIb.54. In his sermon on Job 38:1–4, Calvin recalls God's gracious condescension to Job through Elihu so that Job would not be overwhelmed by God's immediacy but would receive God's Word in an accessible way. Calvin argues that this is how God continues to work by way of human ministers. Unfortunately, this approach, as Job's response illustrates, is not always

therefore, God's Word is 'suited to us'.³⁵ The divine decision to self-disclose extends to the human inscripturation of God's soteriologically-shaped engagement with creation in language available and apposite to us. So, 'the creatureliness of the Bible is no hindrance to hearing God's Word but rather the completely necessary condition' for so doing.³⁶ The sometimes crude and unrefined grammar of the Bible, and the protoscientific descriptions of God's creative activity, do not, for Calvin, undermine Scripture's authority but instead bear witness to the means by which God re-presents 'himself to us not as he is in himself, but as he seems to us'.³⁷

Preaching, for Calvin, represents a further example of divine accommodation, and this in (at least) three ways. First, through preaching God addresses us 'in human fashion through interpreters in order to draw us to himself, rather than to thunder at us and drive us away'.³⁸ Christ, Calvin contends, declares himself through his ministers in such a way that 'their *mouth* [is] to be reckoned as his *mouth* and their *lips* as his *lips*'.³⁹ 'God', Calvin writes, 'does not speak openly from heaven, but employs men as his instruments, that by their agency he may make known his will'.⁴⁰ When God speaks via servants it is, Calvin writes, 'as though he were nigh to us, face to face'.⁴¹ And again: 'God does not wish to be heard but by the voice of his ministers, who he employs to instruct us'.⁴²

---

    successful, in which cases God reverts to the opposite course—of overwhelming Job (and us) with his greatness and majesty: '. . . one will have some scruples, and some troubles in his conscience, another will be afflicted by illnesses, another will have other adversities'. Calvin, *Sermons from Job*, translated by LeRoy Nixon (Grand Rapids: Baker, 1980), 290–1. See also David F Wright, 'Calvin's "Accommodation" Revisited', in *Calvin as Exegete: Papers and Responses Presented at the Ninth Colloquium on Calvin and Calvin Studies, 1993*, edited by Peter De Klerk (Grand Rapids: CRC, 1995), 171–90.

35. Paul Helm, *Calvin: A Guide for the Perplexed* (London/New York: T&T Clark, 2008), 19.
36. THL Parker, *John Calvin: A Biography* (Louisville: Westminster John Knox Press, 2007), 102. See also Calvin, *Institutes*, I.xi.1; I.xiii.1; Calvin, *Sermons on the Ten Commandments*, edited and translated by Benjamin Farley (Grand Rapids: Baker, 1980), 153; Calvin, *Commentaries*, XVIIb.119.
37. Calvin, *Institutes*, I.xvii.13.
38. *Ibid*, IV.i.5.
39. Calvin, *Commentaries*, VIIa.381 emphasis Calvin; compare *ibid*, XVIIIb.553.
40. *Ibid*, VIIIb.172; compare *ibid*, XVIIb.106; and *ibid*, XXI.241.
41. *Ibid*, XVa.343.
42. *Ibid*, VIIIb.61; compare *ibid*, XVIIb.396–7.

Second, Calvin believes God uses pastors to train our humility. He writes:

> If [God] spoke from heaven, it would not be surprising if his sacred oracles were to be reverently received without delay by the ears and minds of all ... But when a puny man risen from the dust speaks in God's name, at this point we best evidence our piety and obedience toward God if we show ourselves teachable toward his minister, although he excels us in nothing.[43]

Implicit here is Calvin's conviction that in the face of human pride, it is appropriate that 'God purposely selects vile and worthless persons to instruct and warn us'.[44] Elsewhere, he writes, 'That the Lord ... should employ inconsiderable men in publishing his Word, may not be quite so agreeable to the human mind. But it tends to humble the pride of the flesh and try the obedience of faith; and therefore God approves of it.'[45] One might here recall Alan Lewis' words:

> The human brokenness of the Church and of her preachers—intellectual, moral and emotional—only highlights the mystery of proclamation. For it encapsulates the risk which entrusts the Word of God to the implausible and the impotent, and assigns solely to the reality of that Word's presence, any persuasiveness and creativity in the words of the church.[46]

---

43. Calvin, *Institutes*, IV.iii.1.
44. Calvin, *Commentaries*, XVIIb.387.
45. *Ibid*, XVIa.124; See Calvin, *Institutes*, IV.i.5; IV.iii.1; Calvin, *Sermons on Ephesians*, translated by Arthur Golding and revised by Leslie Rawlinson and SM Houghton (Edinburgh: Banner of Truth Trust, 1979), 376.
46. Alan E Lewis, 'Kenosis and Kerygma: the Realism and the Risk of Preaching', in *Christ in Our Place—The Humanity of God in Christ for the Reconciliation of the World: Essays Presented to Professor James Torrance*, edited by Trevor Hart and Daniel Thimell (Exeter/Allison Park: Paternoster Press/Pickwick Publications, 1989): 90-1; compare *Sermons of M. John Calvin, on the Epistles of S. Paule to Timothie and Titus*, translated by LT [Laurence Tomson] (London: G Bishop and T Woodcoke, 1579), 945-6.

Still, it is hoped that the preacher humbly submits to God. As Calvin so eloquently put it, 'It would be better for [the preacher] to break his neck going up into the pulpit if he does not take pains to be the first to follow God'.[47]

Finally, both pastor and proclamation serve as a bond of union between believers. If each person simply interpreted the Bible for themselves, then this would sponsor an individualism and arrogance indifferent to the gathered community. So Calvin: 'For neither the light and heat of the sun, nor food and drink, are so necessary to nourish and sustain the present life as the apostolic and pastoral office is necessary to preserve the church on earth'.[48]

Divine accommodation, therefore, recalls not only God's gracious determination to unveil before us, but also God's decision in freedom to descend to regions 'far beneath his loftiness' in order to do so. Borrowing an image from Augustine, Calvin contends that like a nurse with a young child in her arms, 'God is wont in a measure to "lisp" in speaking to us'.[49] It is such lisping that is so splendidly echoed by 'Calvin's great modern exponent',[50] Karl Barth, who draws attention to the 'intrinsic freedom of God, i.e., [God's] freedom to be unlike Himself': 'That God can become unlike Himself in such a way that He is not tied to His secret eternity and eternal secrecy but can and will and does in fact take temporal form as well'[51] gives to such *human* action as preaching the possibility that it may be employed as the Word of God.

Preaching as the Word of God

What is clear for the magisterial reformers is that the Word by and for which the Church lives is not the Church's own word, but is 'the outside word which is spoken to it, so that it cannot seize or possess or control that revelation'.[52] The Word is that whom the Church bows

---

47. *Opera Calvini*, 26:304; compare *ibid*, 27:537; 34:424; 54:286–7; 58:54.
48. Calvin, *Institutes*, IV.iii.2.
49. *Ibid*, I.xiii.1.
50. Robinson, *Death of Adam*, 181.
51. Karl Barth, *Church Dogmatics I.1*, edited by GW Bromiley and TF Torrance (Edinburgh T&T Clark, 2004), 320, 319.
52. Karl Barth, *Church Dogmatics I.2*, edited by GW Bromiley and TF Torrance (Edinburgh: T&T Clark, 2000), 545; compare Martin Luther, *Luther's Works, Volume 36: Word and Sacrament 2*, edited by Helmut T Lehmann and Abdel R Wentz

before, learns of, and participates in. For both Luther and Calvin, the *verbum Dei* (Word of God) refers not principally to Holy Scripture in itself but to the gospel concerning God's Son, the good news which creates the Bible and for which the Bible exists to bear witness. More specifically, the Word is the Son himself. So Calvin: '"Word" means the everlasting wisdom, residing in God, from which both all oracles and all prophecies go forth'.[53] The Word is that One by and in which the Church is birthed, lives, worships, is made one, holy and catholic, and serves God in the world. This Word is not only 'set before us in Scripture',[54] but is also reproclaimed through 'all who thereafter ministered the heavenly doctrine'.[55] To recognise this is to confess the gracious work of the Spirit.

Calvin believes that while preaching is not the only method of divine self-disclosure,[56] preaching remains 'the ordinary mode which the Lord has appointed for conveying his word'.[57] Made efficacious by the Spirit, preaching is, 'the instrument of faith',[58] the mother who produces faith, and faith is the daughter who ought not to forget her origin.[59] Calvin rebukes as ungrateful those who think that the Word's authority is 'dragged down by the baseness of [those] called to teach it . . . For, among the many excellent gifts with which God has adorned the human race, it is a singular privilege that he deigns to consecrate to himself the mouths and tongues of [people] in order that his voice may resound in them'.[60]

Calvin differentiates between the apostolic writings (the oracles of God) and the authority of those whose commission is to teach what is revealed therein and not to frame their own doctrines. If the preaching is faithful to Scripture, 'then it is God who is speaking and that precisely because [God's] teaching remains [God's] teaching irrespective of the purveyor of the teaching'.[61] So Calvin in Sermon XXII on 1 Timothy (3:2):

(Philadelphia: Fortress Press, 1959), 107.
53. Calvin, *Institutes*, I.xiii.7.
54. *Ibid*, I.xiii.7; I.vi.1.
55. *Ibid*, I.xiii.7.
56. *Ibid*, IV.xvi.19.
57. Calvin, *Commentaries*, XIX.398.
58. *Ibid*, XXIa.208; compare *ibid*, XXIc.91.
59. *Ibid*, XXb.397.
60. Calvin, *Institutes*, IV.xv; compare Calvin, *Institutes*, IV.iii.1.
61. Parker, *Calvin's Preaching*, 24.

> When a [person] has climbed up into the pulpit, is it so that [they] may be seen from afar, and that [they] may be pre-eminent? Not at all. It is that God may speak to us by the mouth of a [human being]. And [God] does us that favour of presenting himself here and wishes a mortal [human] to be his messenger.[62]

This underscores Calvin's confidence that the God who speaks in Scripture delights to go on speaking as 'the living voice . . . resound[ing] in His Church',[63] and that through 'the mouth of pastors'.[64] There is also here a clear conviction that proclamation is not 'the third-hand conveyance of fourth-rate opinions',[65] but is itself the Word of God, and this in a twofold sense. First, because the Word that was given to the human authors of Scripture is forwarded on by the proclaiming community; and second, because the same Spirit by whom the Word was so graciously given the first time continues to ensure (through the proclaiming community) that the Word shall find fertile soil in every generation. It is no accident that the reformers named the Church the 'creature of the word'. As Christoph Schwöbel notes:

> The church is called into being by the word of God, and the source of its life without which it would die is the divine word. The divine word reaches us through human words. The divine word calls human words into its service, making them the instruments of the communication of a message that could not be spoken by human means alone: the message of God's grace and truth for his creatures. God addressing us through the ordinary means of human communication—that is nothing less than the sanctification of human communication.[66]

---

62. *Opera Calvini*, 53:266; compare Calvin, *Sermons on Timothie and Titus*, 260–74.
63. Calvin, *Commentaries*, IIb.235.
64. Ibid, XXIIa.358.
65. Parker, *Calvin's Preaching*, 45.
66. Christoph Schwöbel, 'Introduction: The Preacher's Art: Preaching Theologically', in *Theology Through Preaching: Sermons for Brentwood*, by Colin E Gunton (Edinburgh/New York: T&T Clark, 2001), 3.

Upon this truth rests Section One of the *Confessio Helvetica Posterior* penned by Calvin's ally, Heinrich Bullinger, who (in 1562 and revised in 1564) publicised that 'The Preaching of the Word of God is the Word of God' (*praedictatio verbi Dei est verbum Dei*):

> Wherefore when this Word of God is now preached in the church by preachers lawfully called, we believe that the very Word of God is proclaimed, and received by the faithful; and that neither any other Word of God is to be invented nor is to be expected from heaven: and that now the Word itself which is preached is to be regarded, not the minister that preaches; for even if he be evil and a sinner, nevertheless the Word of God remains still true and good.[67]

God confronts us precisely in the weakness of human communication. To infer that this is an unfortunate burden for faith is to miss the point. For behind this Confession is the assumption that preaching is God's instrument for carrying God's Word to God's people. It is the act in which 'Christ continues to bear witness to himself through others, so that whoever hears them hears Christ... If Christ did not continue to speak through his witnesses, their testimony to him would have disappeared long ago.'[68] What becomes increasingly apparent is that, for both Luther and Calvin, the Word is the dynamic God in the free act of gracious self-unveiling through human speech and deed.[69] This revelation is made possible by the crucified Word himself, and is prolonged in the proclamation of those who direct us to Christ, as is so powerfully spoken in the underside image of Lucas Cranach's 1547 altarpiece in Stadtkirche St Marien in Wittenberg. What is remarkable about the magisterial reformers' language about preaching is that they ascribe to the proclaimed Word the muscle and efficacy that the Medieval Church credited to the seven sacraments. Hence Brian Ger-

---

67. Bullinger, 'Second Helvetic Confession', 225. On Calvin's relationship with Bullinger, see Machiel A van den Berg, *Friends of Calvin* (Grand Rapids/Cambridge: Wm B Eerdmans, 2009), 216–26.
68. Randall C Zachman, *The Assurance of Faith: Conscience in the Theology of Martin Luther and John Calvin* (Minneapolis: Fortress, 1993), 59.
69. See Dietrich Ritschl, *A Theology of Proclamation* (Richmond: John Knox Press, 1960), 67–8.

rish's observation that we may fairly extend Calvin's use of the term *verbum sacramentale* (sacramental word) to denote a proclamation that not only *makes* a sacrament but also *is* a sacrament.[70]

Not a few have likened Calvin the *theologian* and *pastor* to a Genevan version of the Apostle Paul, highlighting particularly Paul's relationship with the Christian community at Corinth. But when it comes to our image of Calvin the *preacher* we are given something more akin to an Old Testament prophet. Indeed, in a 1552 sermon on Ezekiel, Calvin cites his opponents by way of describing himself: 'There are some who say today, "There's Calvin who makes himself a prophet, when he says that one will know that there is a prophet among us. He's talking about himself. Is he a prophet?" Well, since it is the doctrine of God I am announcing, I have to use this language.'[71] And in a reference to Joel, Calvin stated, 'We also shall have the title of prophet, when we are true pupils of God'.[72] It was through such prophetic preaching, Calvin believed, that the congregation hears the Word *as God's*[73] and the preacher functions as God's ambassador. So, in his sermon on 2 Timothy 1:2, Calvin says: 'It is certain that if we come to church we shall not hear only a mortal man speaking but we shall feel (even by his secret power) that God is speaking to our souls, that he is the teacher (*maistre*).'[74]

For Calvin, the sermon's divine authority is 'an immediate authority' insofar as 'God is present to declare his will; it is not simply an authoritative message from one remote'.[75] To be sure, there is an important qualification here which concerns the words 'as if': in preaching, '[God] calls us to him *as if* he had his mouth open and we saw him there in person'. But what is being denied by this qualification is 'not the presence or the activity of God but only any sort of visible or audible perception of that presence or activity'.[76] Christ is present in preaching just as he is at the Supper; namely, by the Spirit. So God

---

70. Brian Albert Gerrish, *Grace and Gratitude: The Eucharistic Theology of John Calvin* (Minneapolis: Fortress Press, 1993), 85–6.
71. Cited in Max Engammare, 'Calvin: A Prophet without a Prophecy', in *Church History* 67/4 (1998), 649.
72. Cited in *ibid*: 647.
73. *Opera Calvini*, 58:54.
74. *Ibid*, 54:11.
75. Parker, *Calvin's Preaching* 42.
76. *Ibid*, 42. Italics mine.

rules the Church by the preaching of God's Word; hence Calvin's designation of the pulpit as 'the throne of God, from where [God] wills to govern our souls'.[77] And because God elects to be heard through pastors, believers ought to be cautious of criticising pastors, or of isolating themselves from those communities wherein the Word is proclaimed.

The Reception of the Word

The Word as exhortation
While there are times when Calvin's sermons take on a harsher tone—such as those sermons preached against the tumultuous backdrop prior to the reforms in Geneva around 1553, or those preached amidst the tense relationship between Geneva and Bern in which Calvin championed a ministry of reconciliation before the relationship was healed in 1557—these are more an exception than a rule. For what is alarmingly apparent as one reads Calvin's sermons is that they betray so little indication of the stressful storms in which this preacher ministered, and so much evidence of the 'calm, gentle, [and] reasonable'[78] Calvin's clear, persuasive and persistent call to frame our lives according to Holy Writ.

The other noticeable feature of Calvin's sermons is a consistency with which they are propelled toward exhortation, encouragement and edification: 'We come together in the name of the Lord. It is not to hear merry songs, to be fed with wind, that is, with a vain and unprofitable curiosity, but to receive spiritual nourishment. For God will have nothing preached in his name but that which will profit and edify.'[79] The preacher's task lay incomplete while the congregation is left without 'instruction on the framing of one's life'.[80] Indubitably, most preachers—and congregations—can testify that it is precisely with the *application* of Scripture that the real homiletical challenge lies. But Calvin is consistently fit for this task, embracing with due

---

77. *Opera Calvini*, 53:520.
78. John Updike, *In the Beauty of the Lilies* (London: Hamish Hamilton, 1996), 10.
79. Calvin, 'Sermon on II Timothy 2:16–18'. Cited in John H Leith, 'Calvin's Doctrine of the Proclamation of the Word and Its Significance for Today', in *John Calvin and the Church: A Prism of Reform*, edited by Timothy George (Louisville: Westminster John Knox Press, 1990): 222.
80. *Opera Calvini*, 52:384.

seriousness the claim that 'God does not intend there to be churches as places for people to make merry and laugh in, as if comedy were being acted here. But there must be majesty in his Word, *by which we may be moved and affected*.'[81] While Calvin's homiletical style has been described as 'usually grave, sedate, and unfocused—perhaps even ponderous',[82] his painstaking scholarship, his disciplined style, his determination to avoid speculation, his respect for original sources and vigilant attention to issues of translation and hermeneutics, and his extraordinary commitment to the exposition of Scripture was underwritten by a concern to be as practical as possible.[83]

The Word as event
In describing revelation's reception, Calvin employs the grammar of 'twice born'. The Word makes himself known through Scripture, and then reproclaims himself through the proclamation event. How this happens—and the fact that it happens—is, as Barth noted, 'God's affair and not ours'.[84] Moreover, the proclaimed Word is neither mere communication nor an action borne by human beings, but is an inherent part of the salvation event itself, defined by the uniqueness of that event in history and its consequent witness in Scripture.

Some of the themes upon which we have so far accentuated—on preaching as divine accommodation and exhortation—find specific locale in Calvin's conviction that the sermon is always a specific word to the particular congregation in which it is heard. Sermons are 'works of the moment',[85] examples of God's dynamic self-accommodation to this or that particular community at this or that particular time. Indeed, one of the most striking features of Calvin's preaching is that his sermons 'fit' not only the biblical text, but also the moment, the place, the people who heard and read them.[86] One might conclude that Calvin considered the exegesis of his congregation, society and

---

81. *Ibid*, 53:24. Italics mine; compare *ibid*, 54:287, 587.
82. Dawn DeVries, 'Calvin's Preaching', in *The Cambridge Companion to John Calvin*, edited by Donald K McKim (Cambridge/New York: Cambridge University Press, 2004), 121.
83. See, for example, Calvin's *Sermons on Timothie and Titus*, 419, 1199; *Opera Calvini*, 34:423; 54:292.
84. Barth, *Church Dogmatics I.1*, 109.
85. Cottret, *Calvin*, 289.
86. See *Opera Calvini*, 2:128-9.

time to be as much a feature of the preacher's task and attentiveness as that given to the Bible itself: The preacher must address the 'real and pressing concerns of the community whether or not the people wished to hear them. Not to do so amounted to neglect of the apostolic duty.'[87] Indeed, it was *because* of his attentiveness to the written text that he took the human context as seriously as he did.

The Reformed sermon, therefore, is not *preparation* for divine encounter (which then comes via the Supper) but is itself *decisive* encounter with God. Unlike the way that Dante (who is here representative of Rome's position) was required to change guides as he came near heaven, for the Reformed, the sermon is, as Heiko Oberman observes, an 'apocalyptic event' by which 'the doors of Heaven and Hell are put in motion . . . The sermon does not have to try desperately to be actual because it has the highest possible actuality.'[88] That the sermon is such an 'event' is one of the reasons for Calvin's reluctance to have his sermons published. As his publisher, Conrad Badius, notes: '[Calvin] desired that his sermons should not extend further than his pastorate; because they were preached especially for his sheep, to whose capacity he accommodated himself as best he could.'[89]

The Word and the hermeneutical community
The Word of God is God in God's revelation. In, through and by the Word inscripturated, God reveals God's self. The communication which is of the *esse* (being) of the triune life spills over, as it were, on to paper and out of the lips of those given to its public exposition. It is for this reason that Scripture 'enjoys the authority proper to God's communicative act' and why 'it is to be obeyed and trusted, but not worshiped.'[90] To preach, therefore, is to take up an invitation to 'hear' and to 'listen into' the eternal communication between Father, Son and Holy Spirit. Moreover, it is to confess that that speech may invite and sanctify our speaking and hearing. Christian worship cannot be reduced to hearing, and the Reformed liturgy sponsors a trialogue

---

87. Gordon, *Calvin*, 138.
88. Heiko A Oberman, 'Preaching and the Word in the Reformation', in *Theology Today* 18/1 (1961), 19.
89. Cited in 'Publisher's Introduction: John Calvin and his Sermons on Ephesians', in Calvin, *Sermons on Ephesians*, x.
90. Kevin J Vanhoozer, *The Drama of Doctrine: A Canonical Linguistic Approach to Christian Theology* (Louisville: Westminster John Knox Press, 2005), 65.

between God, God's creatures and God's creation. Put differently, we might think of the Triune God as a pulpit: of the Father who addresses, the Son who is the content of the Father's address, and the Spirit who listens to, celebrates and makes available the Word of the Father. And because the Spirit shares what is spoken and heard between the Father and the Son *with us*, we too are gathered up into this eternal conversation—into the pulpit, as it were—and in so being gathered, our speech too is sanctified.

The application of Scripture is, for Calvin, to be directed to the wider congregation. This does not mean that he is unconcerned to address current affairs taking place in Geneva (around the 1555 City Council elections, for example, or the threat of infiltration by the Turks, who were at this time allied with France), or of engaging in what is sometimes (to our ears at least) harsh and sarcastic antiRomanist, anti-Monarchic and anti-Anabaptist polemic towards those who would proffer what he calls a 'bastard Gospel'.[91] But, as Parker observes, Calvin's sermons are generally 'saved from fragmentation into addresses to particular groups, and the unity of the congregation is preserved, by continual generalisation'.[92] This does not mean that Calvin is unconcerned to address individuals. Indeed, Calvin insists that the Word *is* addressed to such, and, 'in the first place', to preachers themselves;[93] so Calvin's 'almost universal use of "we" and "us" and the rare address of "you"'.[94]

One of the most inviting features of Calvin's use of Scripture is what he coined *familière* (familiar), a reference to the responsibility of the preacher to bear witness to the reality that Scripture is personal and not simply a record of events far removed from us. 'We always try', he said, 'to make Scripture *familière*, so that we know that it is God that is speaking to us'.[95] Calvin the preacher 'deliberately adapts his style to the grasp of the common people in his congregation',[96] accommodating himself, as it were, to the congregation before him. Moreover, while Calvin 'seldom if ever tries to persuade by pleas-

---

91. *Opera Calvini*, 50:329, 399.
92. Parker, *Calvin's Preaching*, 117.
93. See *Opera Calvini*, 50:327; 53:257–8.
94. Parker, *Calvin's Preaching*, 116–17.
95. *Opera Calvini*, 53:18–19.
96. Parker, *Calvin's Preaching*, 148.

ing . . . he tries his utmost to keep the reader [and listener] awake'.[97] Perfecting his style while in Strasbourg, in Geneva Calvin reproved those preachers who 'babble in refined language',[98] even though on occasion he would remind the hearer (or reader) that he too was capable of such superfluity. Though he both lectured and preached direct (mostly) from the Hebrew and Greek text, for Calvin, this fidelity to public speech as *familière*—as employing the grammar of plain, colloquial but metropolitan French, and of the Bible itself—was aided by the fact that his preaching was extempore, reflecting an economy of time at his disposal.

But congregations, for Calvin, are not passive receptors of the preacher's labour; they are, rather, active participants and constituents in the proclamation and must work as hard as the preacher to hear and respond to God's Word. The congregation is indispensable to the gospel's enactment in the world, the assumption being that proclamation is a corporate action of the whole *ecclesia* (Church) and that listening is as much an act of faith as is speaking. In other words, God's Word is addressed to, and received by, a hermeneutical community. So in the 'Preface' to his 1539 commentary on Romans, Calvin writes: 'God hath never favoured his servants with so great a benefit, that they were all endued with a full and perfect knowledge in every thing; and, no doubt, for this end—that he might first keep them humble; and secondly, render them disposed to cultivate brotherly intercourse'.[99]

While Calvin never exhorted believers to study in advance those verses which would be preached upon, he frequently urged congregants to apprehend what the Church is claiming in and through this particular activity, and to 'come to God's school with burning desire, seeing that [God] seeks nothing but our welfare and salvation'.[100] The notion of church as school wherein all believers are both students and teachers under the Spirit's instruction is central to Calvin's ecclesiology: ' . . . all Christians ought to think, "Why do we come to the sermon? Why is there [this] order in the Church? It is so that God may

---

97. Quirinus Breen, 'John Calvin and the Rhetorical Tradition', in *Church History* 26/1 (1957), 8.
98. *Opera Calvini*, 53:19.
99. Calvin, *Commentaries*, XIXb.xxvii.
100. *Opera Calvini*, 54:287.

govern us and that we may have our Lord Jesus Christ as Sovereign Teacher, so that we may be the flock that he leads."'[101] Teachers who guide others in their reading of Scripture must also be willing to be taught themselves both by other teachers and by students.[102]

Calvin expects congregations to understand the sermon as the mode by which 'God rules his Church by declaring his will'.[103] The preacher is obligated to submit unreservedly to the Scriptures, and the *ecclesia* (Church) is obligated to listen carefully and to make sure that what is preached faithfully echoes the Word of God in Scripture and avoids embellishments. So Calvin's letter to Viret dated 19 May 1540:

> Zuingli [*sic*], although he is not wanting in a fit and ready exposition, yet, because he takes too much liberty, often wanders far from the meaning of the Prophet. Luther is not so particular as to propriety of expression or the historical accuracy; he is satisfied when he can draw from it some fruitful doctrine. No one, as I think, has hitherto more diligently applied himself to this pursuit than Œcolampadius, who has not always, however, reached the full scope or meaning.[104]

Preaching so understood is other than decanted propositions or overtures. Rather, it is Christ speaking to those 'sitting at his feet like Mary to hear his Word; and through it "the sheep rally to his voice and stand under his crook"'.[105] Both preacher and congregation must 'become a client of the Comforter in order to communicate the comfort to others'.[106] There is an expectation upon preacher and congregation alike to seek—and be pleased to receive—God's Word, and congregations ought to resist the temptation to make the preachers' task more difficult by appealing for competing words to be heard or by making preachers 'swerve aside' from the truth and feed God's flock with

---

101. *Ibid*, 25:647.
102. See Calvin, *Sermons on Ephesians*, 382.
103. Parker, *Calvin's Preaching*, 49.
104. *Letters, Part 1, 1528–1545*. Selected Works of John Calvin: Tracts and Letters, edited by Henry Beveridge and Jules Bonnet (Grand Rapids: Baker, 1983), 4:188.
105. Benoît, *Calvin in His Letters*, 187; compare John Webster, *Confessing God: Essays in Christian Dogmatics II* (London/New York: T&T Clark, 2005), 189.
106. Schwöbel, 'The Preacher's Art', 14.

'pleasing stories and buffoonery or "old wives' fables"'. Such demands, Calvin insists, constitute 'the cause of some preachers degenerating and disguising themselves and transforming God's teaching, which is as bad as destroying it'.[107]

Calvin also hoped—and anticipated—that the Word who engages the gathered congregation might continue to be received and wrestled with long after the benediction has been pronounced:

> How often do we remind ourselves of the content of the sermons in order to benefit from it? How do we talk about it at home? Most of them seem to think it is sufficient to hear one sermon on Sunday as a rule. When they return, they only talk about wicked and worldly plans, instead of considering what was said in the sermon, so that they better remember what the subject has dealt with. 'No, no, they say, it only makes us depressed to think about that; let us not agonize over it.' . . . They are mockers and despisers of God, enemies of Him and His Word who now mock and laugh in their homes. They enjoy breakfast more than the testimony of their salvation.[108]

Calvin's commitment to the hermeneutical community is likewise evident (as we have already had reason to indicate) in his sponsoring of the Genevan 'congregations' to gather for study on some prearranged passage of Scripture. The intent was to create space wherein the 'congregation' might wrestle in communal discourse in preparation for the preaching on the coming Lord's Day. 'For as long as there is no mutual exchange', Calvin writes, 'each can teach what he likes. Solitude provides too much liberty.'[109] The practice of an 'interpretative anarchy' was as much an anathema to Calvin as the 'interpretive monarchy' of the pope.

---

107. *Opera Calvini*, 53:371.
108. Calvin, 'Sermon on Acts 3:17–19'. Cited in Wilhelmus HTh Moehn, *'God Calls Us to His Service': The Relation Between God and His Audience in Calvin's Sermons on Acts* (Geneva: Droz, 2001), 204–6.
109. *Opera Calvini*, 13:433.

Words and 'the holy bread of heaven which gives us life'[110]

When Calvin returned to Geneva in 1541, he sought to make the Lord's Supper a defining centre of community life. His *Catechism of the Church of Geneva* (1545) articulates that the institution of the signs of water, bread and wine was fashioned by God's desire to communicate to us, and that God does this by 'making himself ours'.[111] The signs testify to divine accommodation, to God 'teaching us in a more familiar manner that he is not only food to our souls, but drink also, so that we are not to seek any part of spiritual life anywhere else than in him alone'.[112] But the signs are not only God's. They are also faith's testimony to the Church's cruciform identity in the world, to its belonging, its ontology. Moreover, font and table remain places of privilege where believers expect to see, taste, hear, touch and proclaim the Word's carnality in ways not expected elsewhere. In his *Short Treatise on the Lord's Supper*, written while in Strasbourg but with an eye on Geneva (where it was printed), Calvin further expanded themes introduced in his Strasbourg liturgy, notably a more christologically-determined epistemology and doctrine of assurance, and the claim that the 'substance of the sacraments is the Lord Jesus' himself.[113] Calvin contended that 'the singular consolation which we derive from the Supper' is that it 'directs and leads us' to Christ, attesting to the truth that 'having been made partakers of the death and passion of Jesus Christ, we have everything that is useful and salutary to us'.[114]

Calvin, likewise, begins his *Summary of Doctrine concerning the Ministry of the Word and the Sacraments* with the statement that 'The

---

110. The reference to 'the holy bread of heaven' is from Calvin's eucharistic Great Prayer of Thanksgiving. See Bard Thompson, *Liturgies of the Western Church* (Cleveland: Meridian Books, 1961), 204.
111. 'Catechism of the Church of Geneva, Being a Form of Instruction for Children in the Doctrine of Christ', in *Tracts and Letters, Volume 2: Tracts, Part 2*. Selected Works of John Calvin: Tracts and Letters, edited by Henry Beveridge and Jules Bonnet (Grand Rapids: Baker, 1983), 89.
112. *Ibid*, 91.
113. 'Short Treatise on the Supper of our Lord, in which is shown its True Institution, Benefit, and Utility', in Beveridge and Bonnet, *Tracts and Letters, Volume 2: Tracts, Part 2*, 169.
114. *Ibid*, 168; compare Calvin, *Institutes of the Christian Religion, 1536 Edition* (Grand Rapids: The HH Meeter Centre for Calvin Studies/Wm B Eerdmans, 1975), IV.i.

end of the whole Gospel ministry is that God, the fountain of all felicity, communicate Christ to us who are disunited by sin and hence ruined, that we may from him enjoy eternal life'.[115] And Calvin proceeds to outline that this communication is made possible because of God's desire to 'communicate himself to us', and involves us being joined to Christ our Head, 'not in an imaginary way, but most powerfully and truly, so that we become flesh of his flesh and bone of his bone'.[116] This union is effected by the Holy Spirit who 'uses a double instrument, the preaching of the Word and the administration of the sacraments'. Moreover, Calvin imagines that the *unio Christi* (union with Christ) involves 'two ministers, who have distinct offices'. There is (i) the 'external minister' who 'administers the vocal word' which is 'received by the ears' and 'the sacred signs which are external, earthly and fallible'; and (ii) there is the 'internal minister', the Spirit who 'freely works internally' to truly communicate 'the thing proclaimed through the Word, that is Christ'.[117] Clearly, for Calvin, the sacraments are essentially another form of the Word. They are, after Augustine, the *verbum visibile* ('a visible word'), 'God's promises as painted in a picture' and set before our sight.[118] They confer neither more nor less than the Word, and they have the same function as the Word preached and written—to offer and present Christ to us. They are, just as preaching is, the 'vehicle of Christ's self-communication', pledges of Christ's 'real presence' and the 'media through which Christ *effects* his presence to his people'.[119]

The separation of pulpit, font and table, and the prioritising of 'words' over the proclamation activities of baptism and eucharist, betray a failure by Christian communities to understand how these three particular activities might inform—and be informed by—theories of semiotics, ritual, dramaturgy and the sociology of knowledge.

---

115. 'Summary of Doctrine concerning the Ministry of the Word and the Sacraments', in Read, *Calvin: Theological Treatises*, 171.
116. *Ibid*, 171.
117. *Ibid*, 173.
118. Calvin, *Institutes*, IV.xiv.6.
119. Brian Albert Gerrish, *The Old Protestantism and the New: Essays on the Reformation Heritage* (Chicago: The University of Chicago Press, 1982), 111. Emphasis Gerrish; compare Trevor A Hart, 'Calvin and Barth on the Lord's Supper', in *Calvin, Barth, and Reformed Theology*, edited by Neil B MacDonald and Carl Trueman (Bletchley: Paternoster, 2008), 41–2.

It is also, and more urgently, a failure to understand the nature and witness of the Word in the Church's 'two marks', and of the way the Spirit functions to create faith in us and to make us 'living members of Christ'.[120] This has, consequently, sponsored both disproportion between word and sacrament, and a tendency towards binitarianism, both to the detriment of Christian worship and ecclesiology. As Joseph Small has noted:

> If word and sacraments together are the heart of the church's true and faithful life, neglect of one leads inexorably to deformation of the other, for when either word or sacrament exists alone it soon becomes a parody of itself . . . Reformed neglect of the sacraments has led to a church of the word alone, a church always in danger of degenerating into a church of mere words.[121]

While Calvin argued that 'it would be well to require that the Communion of the Holy Supper of Jesus Christ be held every Sunday at least as a rule',[122] forlornly, many Reformed churches have propagated a situation wherein the pulpit and its associated wordiness have eclipsed the sacraments, sponsoring an arid intellectualism which has reduced the worshipping community into 'a class of glum schoolchildren'.[123] It is not uncommon to witness Baptism's reduction to little more than a welcoming ceremony, for the Supper to be celebrated infrequently, and for fonts and tables to be discarded in favour of a pulpit which stands unbefriended in the centre of the chancel. In more appalling cases, the pulpit has joined font and table as relics on the sidelines, casualties of modernity's techno gods and replaced by the 'sacraments' of personality and PowerPoint. Calvin, conversely, placed sacrament and word together at the heart of the community's life not because he was a dreary traditionalist or obstructionist but because he 'regarded as a settled principle that the sacraments have the same office as the Word of God: to offer and set forth Christ to us, and in him the treasures of heavenly grace'.[124]

---

120. 'Ministry of the Word and the Sacraments', 173.
121. Small, 'A Church of the Word and Sacrament', 315.
122. 'Articles concerning the Organization of the Church and of Worship at Geneva 1537', in Read, *Calvin: Theological Treatises*, 49.
123. Gerrish, *Grace and Gratitude*, 82.
124. Calvin, *Institutes 1536*, IV.vii; Calvin, *Institutes*, IV.xiv.17.

By way of conclusion

When, in 1950, the city of Hamburg celebrated the anniversary of the death of Johann Sebastian Bach, Paul Hindemith recalled that:

> In the two hundred years since [Bach's] death each rising generation has seen him differently; his creations have been analyzed and criticized, performed and deformed, used and abused; books and pamphlets, paintings and plaster busts have made him a common household article; in short he has finally been transformed into a statue. It seems to me that having this statue constantly before our eyes has impaired our view of the true stature of Bach, both of the man and of his work.[125]

A similar assessment might be offered regarding Calvin. While this essay paints a largely positive—perhaps too positive—portrait of Calvin, I confess to being entirely uninterested in emboldening a Calvin cult. I began with a basic question: what remains serviceable about Calvin's homiletic for those who preach—and for those who hear and taste—the Word of God today? Does Calvin's theology and practice of preaching have some purchase in recalling what the Church is called to in an age and culture so radically removed from sixteenth-century Geneva? Calvin encourages the Church to return to its ground, centre and end in the Word of God; to embrace with confidence its missional life in light of that Word; to repent of the godless banality and trivialisation of its worship and to recover its nutrition in the Spirit's gifts of Bible, font and table; to recognise that while the Church is concerned with the publication of God's Word, the copyright remains with the author; to reject self-veneration and be given over to service of the Word fleshed out in the living documents of congregations; that *ecclesia reformata, semper reformanda est secundum Verbum Dei* (the reformed Church must be always reforming according to the Word of God) is a call to being reformed by the Spirit and the Word rather than an invitation to an 'endless cycle of idea and action, endless invention, [and] endless experiment'[126] for its own sake; to

---

125. Cited in Michael Steinberg and Larry Rothe, *For the Love of Music: Invitations to Listening* (New York: Oxford University Press, 2006), 117.
126. TS Eliot, 'Choruses from "The Rock"—1934', in *Collected Poems, 1909–1962* (New York: Harcourt, Brace & World, 1963), 147.

celebrate God's desire to be known and God's making apposite accommodation to that end; to recall that while God's principal apostle and prophet is Christ himself, proclamation still demands a lot of both preacher and congregation; that there is gospel-logic in making the training of ministers of the Word a priority for the Church's time, energy and budget; and to live in hope that the One who addresses his priesthood in the event of faithful preaching is the very Word of God, and that that address occurs so that the first fruit of a new reconciled and reconciling humanity might know that its very life, diet, and future, remain in God alone.

3
The Grateful Humility of the Children of God: Knowledge of Ourselves in Calvin's Theology[1]

Randall Zachman

Many of the themes that Calvin addresses—for example, our corruption, our depravity and our sinfulness—are usually seen as characteristic of his theology. These form subsidiary motifs in what could be called 'the knowledge of ourselves in Calvin's Theology'. The intriguing thing about Calvin's thought is that he always addresses themes that are discrete but are also indissolubly related to each other. Thus, for him, the knowledge of God and the knowledge of ourselves are distinct but inseparable: one cannot know God without knowing oneself, and at the same time, one cannot know oneself, without knowing God. There is a rhythm between the two: if one thinks one knows God, and this does not lead to knowledge of oneself, then this is not a real knowledge of God. Similarly, if one thinks that one knows oneself, and that does not lead to or reinforce the knowledge of God within oneself, then one probably does not know oneself. Calvin sees this self-knowledge as being equally (or even more) difficult to achieve than the knowledge of God. The danger of not knowing ourselves accompanies all of us throughout our lives.

In this paper, I will address the ways in which these two aspects (knowledge of God and knowledge of ourselves) are related, and will go on to discuss three aspects of Calvin's description of how we come to know ourselves. Firstly, there is the knowledge of ourselves as created, which endures in some sense even after the fall into sin, and which enables us still to appreciate the endowments with which we were created. Then, there is the knowledge of ourselves as fallen and

---

1. This chapter is adapted from the recording of an open lecture given by Professor Zachman for the Department of Theology and Religion, University of Otago, Dunedin, on 10 September 2009.

sinful (this is where Calvin's thinking becomes most familiar), and what the ramifications are for that, which should then lead us to faith in Christ. But the third (and most insightful and helpful) aspect is the knowledge of ourselves as allegedly faithful Christians. Calvin does not let us 'off the hook' once we get to faith in Christ. He sees (rightly, I think) that we are at our most dangerous precisely at that point, and all the way through his thought is the concern for what he calls, 'blind self-love'. By this he means that we are enamoured of ourselves almost completely, and therefore it is very hard for us to learn the truth about ourselves, because all we want to do is be flattered. We just want to hear good things about ourselves and we want others to think well of us. Consequently, we develop all manner of strategies to try to feel good about ourselves, usually at others' expense. Calvin tries to overcome this 'blind self-love' so that we can come to know ourselves even as faithful but self-deceptive people.

Gratitude and humility in Calvin's theology

It is interesting how quickly Calvin gets to the themes of gratitude and humility in his *Institutes*. He develops both of them in the opening paragraph. In the very first sentence he says, 'Nearly all wisdom we possess, that is to say true and sound wisdom, consists of two parts; the knowledge of God, and of ourselves'.[2]

It should be noted that while Calvin talks objectively about the knowledge of humanity in the third person, he also talks about true and sound wisdom in the contexts of knowing ourselves and of being so attentive to ourselves that we do not devalue other people. Similarly, there is a necessary connection between the knowledge of God and the knowledge of ourselves. He says,

> But, while joined by many bonds, which one precedes and brings forth the other is not easy to discern. In the first place, no one can look upon himself (or herself) without immediately turning his thoughts to the contemplation of God, in whom he 'lives and moves' [Acts

---

2. Calvin, *Institutes*, I.i.1. The editions used are *Ioannis Calvini opera selecta*, edited by Peter Barth, Wilhelm Niesel and Dora Scheuner (Munich: Chr. Kaiser, 1926–52); and *Calvin: Institutes of the Christian Religion*, edited by John T McNeill and translated by Ford Lewis Battles (Philadelphia: Westminster, 1960).

> 17:28]. For, quite clearly, the mighty gifts with which we are endowed are hardly from ourselves; indeed our very being is nothing but subsistence in the one God. Then, by these benefits shed like dew from heaven upon us, we are led as by rivulets to the spring itself.[3]

This is a remarkable statement with which to begin. Calvin begins with gratitude for what everyone can experience in herself, namely that she has life. Your enjoyment of life, of existence, should lead to the source of your life, which is God. So the very first theme that Calvin emphasises (in terms of knowledge of ourselves) is gratitude. Everything we have, everything we are and everything we will become, we owe to God. One can trace the benefits one receives to the source from which they flow, in the same way that one might trace the path of a stream to its source. It is therefore very significant that the opening of the *Institutes* sounds the theme of gratitude, since this is one of the ways we know that we know ourselves. If we are grateful to God for everything that we have received, genuinely grateful, then we know ourselves, but then we also know God. Calvin then goes on:

> Indeed our very poverty better discloses the infinitude of benefits reposing in God. . . . Each of us must, then, be so stung by the consciousness of his own unhappiness as to attain at least some knowledge of God. Thus, from the feeling of our own ignorance, vanity, poverty, infirmity, and—what is more—depravity and corruption, we recognise that the true light of wisdom, sound virtue, full abundance of every good, and purity of righteousness, rest in the Lord alone.[4]

The theme of gratitude leads to a second theme, that of humility. This is not the product of a teaching or of our assent to a doctrine or idea; nor is it an end in itself, a point where Calvin is often misinterpreted. For Calvin, this humility is grounded in our awareness of our poverty, our ignorance, our vanity, our infirmity, our depravity and of our corruption. The awareness of our poverty should lead us immediately to

---

3. Calvin, *Institutes*, I.i.1.
4. *Ibid.*

the one who can replace all these evil things with the good things that we lack, for in the abundance of God's goodness we find all that we need. As Calvin sees it, the awareness of our poverty will lead us to the fountain of every good, just as the awareness of the good things we receive from this fountain will lead us to the fountain itself.

> To this extent we are prompted by our own ills to contemplate the good things of God; and we cannot seriously begin to aspire to [God] before we begin to become displeased with ourselves... For what [person] in all the world would not gladly remain as he is—what [person] does not remain as he is—so long as he does not know himself, that is, while content with their own gifts, and either ignorant or unmindful of his own misery? Accordingly, the knowledge of ourselves not only arouses us to seek God, but also, as it were, leads us by the hand to find [God].[5]

So there is this rhythm in Calvin's thinking, that on the one hand the mighty gifts of which we were endowed do not come from ourselves; rather, they come from God, and we should follow these gifts to the source and be grateful. On the other hand, we are impoverished and we lack good things. Our consciousness of our poverty, our lack and our infirmity, should lead us to seek in God what we lack in ourselves. This consciousness forms the basis of human humility, which is rooted in our sense of poverty. These are the two themes with which Calvin begins the *Institutes*. The awareness of our gifts and the awareness of our poverty are the two elements that underlie the grateful humility of God's people. These are the two elements of human life.

Knowledge of ourselves as originally created

Calvin thought a great deal about how we come to know ourselves. In order to know how we were originally created and thus to know ourselves, we must first know ourselves as we no longer are but once were. We therefore need to know ourselves as we would have been if Adam and Eve had not fallen into sin. This is a very significant

---

5. *Ibid.*

move on his part. Calvin does this quite deliberately, because he is aware that one of the things that we do is to blame God. What Calvin wants to do, above all else, is to stop this blaming of God, whether for things that go wrong, for things that seem corrupt or amiss or defiled, or whenever our lives don't work out the way that we think they should. He sees this blaming of God as a very pervasive thing, within both Christian and pagan writings. One way of stopping this is to show that we were originally created in a very different state from the one in which we are now. It should be noted that this is the point at which Calvin's theology gets more difficult if one no longer adopts an understanding of original sin and of the fall of Adam and Eve into sin at a particular point in time (which, for Calvin, happened about six thousand years ago). But Calvin thinks we need to contemplate our original creation in order to see that humanity's predicament is our own doing; we were not created to be this way, but have made ourselves this way. On the other hand, there are an amazing number of things that remain after our fall into sin, for which we need to be grateful and for which we owe gratitude to God. He says,

> We must now speak of the creation of [humanity]: not only because among all God's works here is the most noble and most remarkable example of God's justice, wisdom, and goodness; but because . . . we cannot have a clear and complete knowledge of God unless it is accompanied by a corresponding knowledge of ourselves. This knowledge of ourselves is twofold; namely, to know what we were like when we were first created, and what our condition became after the fall of Adam.[6]

To understand how we were originally created, Calvin looks to the restoration of humanity in Christ, for our restoration should reveal to us how we were originally created.[7] Since Paul says that Christ restores the image of God in us (and especially in righteousness, holiness and innocence), Calvin takes that to be a clue as to what we were originally created to be. The restoration points back to what we were intended to be: that is, to be upright, to have integrity, to be righteous,

---

6. *Ibid*, I.xiv.1.
7. *Ibid*, I.xv.4.

to be holy and to share in the nature of God. Human beings were to be the image of God. By this, Calvin means that we were to be the self-portrait, in creaturely form, of the nature of God. As a consequence of humanity's renewal and restoration in the grace of Christ, human beings will become, at the end of time, completely like God and will see God face to face. This goal reveals what we were originally created to be. Calvin says, quite succinctly, that 'The highest human good is therefore simply union with God. We attain it when we were brought into conformity with his likeness.'[8] The goal of human beings is to become more and more like God, so that at the end of time, we will be united to God. Note that Calvin does not say that we will united to *Christ*, but rather that we will be united to *God*. Calvin, following Paul in 1 Corinthians 15, thinks that Christ will hand the kingdom over to the Father so that God will be all in all. Union with God is the goal; we were created in the image of God so that we would be capable of being united to God.

Calvin thinks that this image of God, in which we were created, shines throughout the whole human body. As he saw it, human beings were created upright so that they could contemplate the eternity of the heavens; this distinguishes human beings from other creatures. Our upright frame, the way we walk around upright, rather than on all fours, is, for Calvin, a sign that is part of being the image of God. Significantly, this turns humanity's gaze up and raises our faces upward. But he thought (and indeed was quite insistent on this) that the real seat or location of the image of God is the soul. This was a very important issue for Calvin: the soul, for him, is created, but it is essentially immortal and it will live on when what he calls the 'prison house of the body' dies. However, Calvin also insists that the bodies of the faithful will be recreated to become like the glorified body of Christ. So Calvin does not think that the soul will be disembodied forever, but he was always insistent that the soul survives the death of the body. The very first book he wrote was on this issue. This was an issue in which he may have been at odds with Luther. Calvin directs his thinking on this subject against the Anabaptists, but Luther actually taught, as a good Aristotelian, that the soul is a form of the body and therefore when the body dies the soul sleeps with it. Consequently Luther thought he would be lying in a grave in Wittenberg, waiting

---

8. Calvin, *Commentary on Hebrews* 4:10, *Opera Calvini* 55:48B.

to be restored body and soul by Christ on the last say and he had no expectation that the soul would exist independently of his body. Calvin thought this was absolutely abhorrent, and so he addressed this error right away. For Calvin, once the godly come to know the love of God in Christ, they can never be separated from that love, and the only way this is possible is if the soul is immortal. This was a major element of his thinking. For Calvin, we can only know ourselves if we know our immortality, if we know that we were destined for union with God, if we know that the existence of our soul will outlive our body. Calvin does consistently call the body (as also do Plato and Cicero) 'a prison house'. On the other hand he does also talk about the resurrected body, the glorified body on the last day.

So the image of God is rooted primarily in the soul, and is primarily understood by Calvin as our participation in the goodness of God, the wisdom of God, the power of God, the holiness of God, the righteousness of God, and (especially) the life of God. This image should lead us, then, to contemplate eternal life. If we are created in the image of God, we are destined for eternal life. Consequently, if all you think about is this life, earthly happiness and about making this world a better place (as important as that may be), you do not know yourself and therefore you do not know God, according to Calvin. Thus knowing yourself, as you were created in the image of God, should make you long, from the depth of your being, for eternity, to be united to God; and the degree to which you seek to be united to God is the degree to which you are a human being. To the degree to which that is not important to you, to that degree you are more like a beast. This theme has very strong implications for Calvin, for even after the fall into sin, he wants this driving force, deep in our soul, to be at work within us. He wants us to long for something that we now cannot attain, to strive and seek something that we can no longer find. Our goal as creatures is eternity. We are not created for this world (although this world is important); for Calvin ultimately what matters is union with God. In my view, this theme has largely disappeared from Christian theology, proclamation and hope. Eternity is gone and the focus is now on this life. Now that may be a good thing. But to the degree to which we do not long for eternity and for union with God beyond death, a union that triumphs over death and restores the broken body into the glory of the body of Christ, to that degree Calvin is utterly alien from us, and we really have nothing in common with him. For Calvin, this is quite important. If you know yourself, you know that you were destined for eternity; and if you know yourself and the way you were originally created, then you also know that God gave us everything that we needed to attain that goal. If we cannot attain that goal, it is our fault, not God's fault.

Knowledge of ourselves as fallen in Adam

While Calvin at times says that we only come to know ourselves when we know God and we only know God when we know ourselves, he also talks about knowing ourselves as fallen and says that we only come to know this by comparing our present state with the way we were originally created. Knowledge of ourselves as fallen comes from knowledge of ourselves as created. And of course, for Calvin, the knowledge of ourselves as fallen is radically different from the knowledge of ourselves as created; we are not in fact in the state in which we were created. He says,

> But knowledge of ourselves lies first in considering what we were given at creation and how generously God continues his favour toward us, in order to know how great our natural excellence would be if only it had remained unblemished; yet at the same time to bear in mind that there is in us nothing of our own, but that we hold on sufferance whatever God has bestowed upon us. Hence we are ever dependent on him. Secondly, to call to mind our miserable condition after Adam's fall; the awareness of which, when all our boasting and self-assurance are laid low, should truly humble us and overwhelm us with shame.[9]

The awareness of what we have become compared to the way we were originally created should not only lead us to gratitude, but also to genuine humility and to shame, and should undermine all of our self-assurance and our boasting, which are obviously two major problems that we have, according to Calvin.

---

9. Calvin, *Institutes*, II.i.1.

Now the fall into sin is one of the most notorious or infamous elements of Calvin's theology. We all know that Calvin thinks we are totally depraved and utterly wretched, and he does say all these things, but it is more interesting to me that Calvin realises that he overstated the extent of this depravity in his early theology, and spends the rest of his career retracting his position. Elsewhere in this volume Elsie McKee explains that Calvin does in fact change his thinking over time. This is one of the most important areas in which he changes his thought. Initially, in his 1536 *Institutes*, Calvin says that when Adam fell into sin, the image of God was completely obliterated and deleted in him. One thinks these days of an e-mail that you delete, and this is the same meaning Calvin has in mind. The image was there when Adam was created, but it is no longer there once he falls into sin. But within a year we see Calvin qualifying this statement, in light of the passage in Genesis in which God prohibits the shedding of human blood because we are created in the image of God, something that takes place after the expulsion from the garden. Calvin realises that if the commandment not to murder is rooted in the fact we are still in the image of God, there must be something of that image left, so he starts to tease out what that image could be. So when we come to know ourselves as fallen, we are to try to discern how much of the image of God still remains in us. This also has consequences for our relationships with others, especially our relationship with our enemies, because our enemies are made in the image of God, and in this sense the image of God cannot be eradicated, it cannot be obliterated. So Calvin builds a more comprehensive and detailed portrait of the image of God that remains in everyone. No matter how much we may fall into sin, we are still created in the image of God, and we must honour, respect, and love all those in whom the image of God is to be seen, for we cannot harm that person without harming God. 'Undoubtedly God would have the remains of his image which still shines forth in people to continue in some estimation, so that all might feel that every homicide is an offence against him.'[10] The most fully developed portrait of the remnants of the image of God occurs in Calvin's comments on Psalm 8:

---

10. Calvin, *Commentary on Deuteronomy* 5:17, *Opera Calvini* 24:611C.

> The reason with which they are endued, and by which they can distinguish between good and evil; the principle of religion which is planted in them; their intercourse with each other, which is preserved from being broken up by certain sacred bonds; the regard to what is becoming, and the sense of shame which guilt awakens in them, as well as their continuing to be governed by laws; all these things are clear indications of pre-eminent and celestial wisdom.[11]

These are the distinguished endowments which clearly manifest the image of God even in fallen human beings. We see the image of God in our reason, our conscience, in the seed of religion God plants in every person, in our communication with each other in society, our sense of what is becoming, and our being governed by laws. Calvin thought that every human being has a sense of equity, by which we all judge what is fair and just. Every human being knows when a law is framed to serve justice, and when a law serves our own interests against those of others. Calvin thought that the greatest crimes are often enacted into law; hence just because something is legal does not mean that it is fair or just. Thus every human being, be she pagan or Christian, has a natural sense of equity, so that she knows when something is oppressive, she knows when something is wrong, she knows when something is unfair, and she has the right and obligation to make this known. So part of the image of God is the sense of equity, which is related to conscience and reason. Every human being is endowed with these gifts, and when we come to know ourselves we should acknowledge our intellect and our conscience and our sense of equity as gifts of God, that remain after the fall into sin, for which we should be grateful and without which our lives would be monstrous. Calvin knew that there are people who so harden themselves in sin that they lose all sense of conscience, and he called such people the 'malicious'. We would call such people sociopaths. Such people lack conscience, and they are monsters, for they have no sense of shame, no sense of guilt, no sense of wrong, and therefore they are capable of anything. If God had not preserved the image of God in all people, we would all devolve into such monsters, as one sees in stories such as

---

11. Calvin, *Commentary on Psalms* 8:5, *Opera Calvini* 31:92B.

The Lord of the Flies. So we should contemplate the good things that remain in fallen human nature, and should thank God for them, for it is only due to the mercy of God that any of the image of God remains in us. We should see the image of God in every human being, which makes them worthy of our love, respect, and honour, and we should be advocates for the just treatment of every human being by the sense of equity within us. This is a considerable correction of his early statements about the obliteration of the image of God.

Moreover, the Holy Spirit bestowed gifts on some of the pagans that were to be of direct benefit for the ordering of our lives on earth, which comprise the mechanical and liberal arts, including law, literature, and medicine. Calvin fully supported the recovery and teaching of these arts that was taking place in his day, and defended them over against those who thought they were sinful since they came from the wisdom of the pagans. Calvin insisted that all of these things are gifts from God, for which we should be grateful, even though the people from whom they come to us were not believers.

> If we regard the Spirit of God as the sole fountain of truth, we shall neither reject the truth itself, nor despise it wherever it shall appear, unless we wish to dishonour the Spirit of God. For by holding the gifts of the Spirit in slight esteem, we contemn and reproach the Spirit himself.[12]

If you denigrate the liberal arts, you are denigrating the Holy Spirit. That is a pretty amazing statement. 'What then? Shall we deny that the truth shone upon the ancient jurists who established civic order and discipline with such great equity?'[13] Calvin goes on to the philosophers who describe nature, and who gave us the arts, medicine, and mathematics. 'Shall we consider them the ravings of madmen? No, we cannot read the writings of the ancients on those subjects without great admiration. We marvel at them because we are compelled to recognize how preeminent they are.'[14] So you should not overstate the fall into sin to the point where you say the philosophers and the

---

12. Calvin, *Institutes*, II.ii.15.
13. *Ibid.*
14. *Ibid.*

teachers of the classical world are fundamentally corrupt, for if you do so, you are disgracing the gifts of the Holy Spirit, and you are actually ungrateful for the gifts that God wants to give humanity. Those of us who see ourselves as Christian educators need to think more about this than we do, for what we call education—mathematics, science, literature, *et cetera*—comes from people who were not believers. They were neither Jews nor Christians. Calvin insists that we owe them a huge debt of gratitude, which should ultimately be directed toward God. So there is a surprising amount of goodness left in creation, even after the fall, and the children of God should be grateful for all the gifts they receive from God, even if these gifts come from people who were not children of God themselves. I think this is a remarkable claim on his part.

But there is no avoiding the fact that the knowledge of ourselves should not only concern what we still have, but should also make us personally aware of all that we lack. We only truly know ourselves when we have a deep and inward awareness of our sin, our evil, our corruption, as well as our poverty and nothingness. Calvin knows that this is the hardest thing for us to do, because the way we seek to know ourselves on our own is by comparison to other people. Whenever we see something displeasing in ourselves, we immediately try to make ourselves feel better by comparing ourselves to others that we deem to be worse than we are. I may have a hard time with my anger, but at least I don't have a hot-headed temper like my brother. I may drink too much on occasion, but at least I'm not a drunk like my sister. Calvin knows that when we come to know ourselves by comparison with others, we will always come out better than they will. 'For, such is the blindness with which we all rush into self-love that each one of us seems to himself to have just cause to be proud of himself and to despise all others by comparison.'[15] So if you feel heavy, if you feel overweight, you can always comfort yourself by finding someone heavier than you, so that you can feel superior to him. And if you feel foolish, it is very reassuring to come across someone who does not know what you know, so you feel better about yourself by looking down on her. That is why we love it when the press catches a prominent person in adultery, isn't it? The press seems to live off of our need to feel better about ourselves by comparing our lives with

---

15. *Ibid*, III.vii.4.

the train-wrecks celebrities have made of their own. This is what blind self-love does, according to Calvin. So as long as we attempt to know ourselves by comparing ourselves to others, we will continue to delude ourselves. One of the worst periods of my life was when I tried to judge my own theological career by comparing myself with John Calvin. Then I became aware of all the work he did in Latin, Greek, and Hebrew, and how he committed so much Latin and Greek literature to memory throughout his career, and I felt as though the car I was following pressed the turbo button, and suddenly all I could see were two tail lights receding in the distance. I was trying to assess my own abilities by comparing myself to him, and of course it was totally defeating. But then I learned to comfort myself in another way, in the thought that at least I understand him better than other people do! I may not be Calvin, but I understand him quite well, thank you very much, and I can show you that actually I understand him better than most people do. You see, the academic life operates entirely by this kind of comparison, but I think the ecclesial life works this way as well. You may not think your life is going very well, but then you comfort yourself with the thought that at least you go to church, unlike other people you know, and so you must be a better person than they are. So this kind of comparison happens all the time. We assess our place in the world and our understanding of ourselves by comparing ourselves to other people.

Calvin is a very keen social psychologist on this point, and he knows that this is our problem. We operate by comparing ourselves to others, and we will never know ourselves the way we ought to so long as we do that. But how then do you lead people to stop comparing themselves to others, so that they can finally come to know themselves? Calvin developed several different strategies to solve this problem because it is really hard to do. We are so good at deluding ourselves, we are so good at fooling ourselves—indeed, we excel at this! We are really good at fooling others, too. I often ask my students, 'When you are late for a meeting, or late handing in a paper, how many false excuses can you create, and how quickly can you do so?' It seems to me that I can create about twenty in just a few seconds. 'I was on my way to work and the train came, and then I ran out of gas. . . . ' It really is incredible—why don't I just tell the truth? Because it would make me look bad. So we lie to look good, and if we are willing to do that when we are just late handing in a paper or late for a meeting, imagine what we could do for the really significant things in our lives, how capable we are of lying to ourselves and others. Calvin knows that we are very slippery people, who deceive others and deceive ourselves. So he thought a great deal about how to get us to stop doing this, to come to know ourselves, and his favourite solution was, to summon us alone in conscience before God. I will only come to know myself when I stop comparing myself to others, and when I am brought in solitude and silence before the judgment seat of God. The conscience for Calvin is quite a remarkable faculty, which as we have seen is part of the image of God remaining in every human being. He thinks that the conscience is our awareness of God's judgement of us.[16] God already knows us, from the inside out. God works intuitively, even though we think God works deductively. We think that God starts with appearances, and then works from there to try to discover the reality concealed behind the appearance. Thus I try to create a façade of which God will approve, in the hope that God will not look any further into my heart, for my heart does not look nearly as appealing as the façade I try to create.

But for Calvin, God works in exactly the opposite way, God works from the inside out. God begins by seeing us in light of the inmost affection of our hearts, and then looks to see how the rest of our lives express that affection. God's knowledge of me in this way is made known to me in my conscience. So to be alone in conscience before God allows me to begin to know myself the way God already knows me. I personally think that this is a very terrifying thought, that the thoughts I harbour and have kept to myself are already known to God, the defects that I can hardly glimpse myself are already fully known to God, and his judgement of me is being made known to me in my conscience, if I just pay attention to it. So Calvin tells us that we can come to know ourselves the way God already knows us, by descending into ourselves, and by summoning our conscience before the face of God.

> Indeed, it is easy, so long as the comparison stops with [human beings], for anyone to think of himself as having something that his fellows ought not to despise. But

---
16. *Ibid*, III.xix.15.

> when we rise up toward God, that assurance of ours vanishes in a flash and dies.[17] [Calvin adds,] Let us not be ashamed to descend from this contemplation of God and look upon ourselves without flattery, without being blinded by self-love.[18]

Although a person may flatter himself on account of the outward mask of righteousness that he wears, the Lord weighs on the scales the secret impurity of the heart. So this is how God is judging us. God is not judging by the mask we create before the world, God is seeing us in light of the secret thoughts of our hearts, and that is what we need to come to know, for this is how we come to know ourselves in truth. So to be alone before God in conscience and in honesty is for Calvin the way we come to true self-knowledge. This is a terrifying thing to do, which is why we avoid doing it. But for him, without this there is no knowledge of ourselves, and consequently no genuine humility. There may be a feigned humility we adopt so as not to appear too proud to others, but there is no genuine feeling of humility, rooted in the feeling of your own nothingness. There is not the awareness of who you really are. This for Calvin is the problem, we need to become aware of who we really are, but solely so that we are led from the depth of our conscience to seek the good things in God that we now clearly know we lack in ourselves, as well as to ask God to remove the evil in us that we are powerless to eradicate. So the good news is that this knowledge of ourselves in conscience makes us 'capable' of receiving God's mercy. We only have access to God's mercy when we admit to ourselves who we really are. This is different for each one of us, which is why each one of us should examine our conscience alone before God. A general confession of sin is of no use in this context, for we can hide from ourselves and from God even as we echo the words of confession with the congregation. What makes us capable of grace is the deep, inward, personal knowledge of ourselves rooted in our awakened conscience, and if we do not have that, then we do not know ourselves; and if we do not know ourselves, then we cannot know God.

---

17. *Ibid*, III.xii.2.
18. *Ibid*, III.xii.5.

But once we do know ourselves, we should be led to seek in Christ what we lack in ourselves, so that we can be pardoned for the sin and evil within us, and so that we can be renewed in the image of God which we so little resemble. Our awakened conscience will lead us to seek forgiveness and renewal in Christ, and will cause us always to hunger for the benefits Christ alone can give. Our sin leads us to seek reconciliation in Christ, our impotence leads us to seek newness of life in Christ, and our poverty leads us to seek all that we lack in Christ. By turning to Christ, the conscience terrified by its sin will be consoled, and the conscience accusing us of living badly will begin more and more to testify to our integrity, as we seek to confirm our adoption as children of God in newness of life. Even though we always need forgiveness, we also know that we really are living as children of God, following the example of Christ our Redeemer.

But this hardly means that we are out of danger, and indeed a new danger arises that did not exist before. For my conscience tells me that I truly seek forgiveness, and it also tells me that I am striving to lead a new life. So the danger now arises that I will begin to look around yet again, and start to compare myself with others now that I belong to Christ. And when I look around, I can comfort myself with the thought that I am a much better person than the sinners by whom I am surrounded. I see an unrepentant sinner over here, an unsanctified person over there, a disobedient person to my right, a person who never worships to my left. And so I start to compare myself to other people again, only now on the basis of my faith in Jesus Christ. I start to become proud of myself, and to feel complacent about myself, and most damaging of all, I start to feel like I am finally safe. I become convinced that my faith has made me safe, so unlike those ungodly people out there whose children die, or whose partners leave them, or who become unemployed, God will protect me, so that nothing bad can reach me. For Calvin, this is the greatest mistake that a Christian can make, for this is the most pernicious form of self-love! This is why Scripture often encourages the faithful to examine themselves in solitude, with only God as their witness, so that they might be able to distinguish genuine faith from pride. 'If, not content with having to do with God only, we turn our eyes to men, it is almost impossible to prevent pride from insinuating itself into the room of faith.'[19]

---

19. Calvin, *Commentary on Psalms* 91:9, *Opera Calvini* 32:4C.

God knows that even the godly are tempted by this kind of self-love, and so God does yet one more thing to teach us to know ourselves. God sends affliction to us, to the faithful, to those who know their poverty, to those who know their sin, to those who flee to Christ for refuge. God makes our lives miserable, while the lives of the ungodly around us prosper, to see where our hope is, to see where our heart is, to see if we really know ourselves.[20] Once we believe in the love of God, God afflicts us to see if our hearts really trust in God's love, or in their own security. One of his favourite lines is from Psalm 30, where David, says, 'I said in my heart I am secure, I shall not fall' and of course immediately, he fell. Calvin says that God does this to teach David to remember that he is really nothing, and is not exempt from the common lot of humanity. Faith is not about security, faith is not about safety. Faith is about trusting in God alone, in spite of everything.

And so Calvin wants the faithful to remember people like Joseph. God loved Joseph, yet his brothers tried to kill him. They threw him into a pit, and then sold him into slavery, and he was taken as a captive to Egypt. Once there he is falsely accused of trying to rape his Egyptian master's wife, and is thrown into prison. He makes a friend there who says he will remember him, but he is forgotten. This is what it means to be loved by God? Joseph is an exemplary person for Calvin, for in the midst of all of his affliction, he never loses his confidence in the presence of God, and he never stops trusting in God. Therefore the whole time he is afflicted he has patience, and he is always compassionate to others. He does not lash out when he is accused of rape, and he does not hate his brothers when they sell him into bondage. Instead, he forgives them, and tells them though they intended all this for evil, God intended it for good. If you know yourself, and trust in God in genuine humility, you will be as patient and merciful in adversity as Joseph showed himself to be, and you will never lose hope. Calvin saw a similar pattern of affliction in Jeremiah. Jeremiah faithfully follows his calling from God, but it only leads him from bad to worse, as his own family betrays him and seeks to have him killed, and his king has him thrown into a cistern. At the end of the book, Jeremiah tells people that they are better off going to Babylon, for if they go to Egypt, God will destroy them. And the last time

---

20. Calvin, *Institutes*, III.vii–viii.

we see Jeremiah, the people to whom he made this prophecy kidnap him and take him off with them to Egypt. So it just goes from bad to worse to much worse. Calvin sees this pattern above all in Jesus, the beloved Son of God, whom God seems to afflict beyond measure, till he cries out that God has forsaken him. For Calvin, God uses affliction to teach the godly to know themselves, lest they become deluded by comparing themselves to others yet again, for God knows that we can mistake faith for security, and we can think that God will protect us because God favours us. But God is our refuge, not our faith; God is our rock, not our creed or our doctrine. God will take everything away from us to teach us to take refuge in God alone, and not in ourselves in comparison to other people.

The children of the world may deceive and be deceived, but the self-deception of the godly is the most pernicious threat we face, for our relationship to God seems to give us every excuse to compare ourselves favourably to our godless neighbours, and to trust that God will keep us safe. We come to know ourselves the most truly by how we respond to adversity, by how we respond to affliction. Thus Calvin would have us pose a series of questions to ourselves, so that we might truly know the state of our own hearts. For instance, do we exercise patience when we suffer adversity, or do we blame God? 'How could God do this to me? I can't believe in God anymore—I lost my job; I can't believe in God anymore—I lost my wife . . . ' We hear this all the time, and I'm sure pastors will have been through this many times with members of their congregations. Do we have patience when we suffer adversity, or do we lash out in blame? Do we renounce ourselves when things do not go our way?

Are we silent when we are reviled for doing something good, when we are hated for doing something out of love, when someone reproaches us for doing something right? I do not know about you, but that makes me crazy, I want vindication and I want it now, because I have an undying need to be in the right, and for everyone to know I am in the right. For anyone to think I am in the wrong drives me crazy, and this reveals me to myself, that I am proud, not humble. I am not trusting in God and casting myself on God in prayer, I am trusting in myself, and in my superiority to those who falsely accuse me. That is what this kind of affliction is telling me.

And how do I respond to those who are being afflicted? Do I secretly blame her for her situation, even as I seek to help her? Do I think in my heart, 'You know, if you had quit smoking, you would not have got lung cancer in the first place; but I will still help you, even though I will not be able to help blaming you somewhere along the way'. If we exercise our compassion with a feeling of superiority, or with a feeling of contempt toward the very people we say we are helping, then we do not know ourselves, and we do not really love the people we are helping.

And so we have to ask another question, are we content with God's blessing, or when we suffer poverty do we long for riches and power? When we experience poverty, do we suffer joyfully, or do we suffer it unwillingly, still longing for the things we have lost, still bitter that we have lost these things. These are really hard things to go through, but this kind of affliction is what really reveals us to ourselves.

Finally, and this is where Calvin himself obviously falls down as much as we do, what about our enemies, what about those who seriously wrong us, what about those whose main objective in life is to do us harm, to betray our trust, to betray our confidence, to betray our love, to try to destroy us? What about them? Do we bless them when they curse us? Do we love them when they hate us? Do we pray for them when they persecute us and utter all kinds of slander against us? How do we deal with our enemies? And it is here, actually that I think he is the most helpful, for you simply cannot love your enemy if you do not know yourself; you cannot love your enemy if you do not know your own nothingness; you cannot love your enemy if you are not genuinely humble. On the other hand, think of the violent passions we experience when we are wrongly accused, or when someone seeks to do us harm though we are innocent—the rage, the pain, the despair. This is a theme that has almost completely disappeared from Christianity, and yet it is the litmus test for knowing ourselves. If you want to know yourself, ask yourself how you respond to your enemy? Do you bless those who curse you? Do you love those who hate you? Do you pray for those who persecute you? And if you do, then you are a humble and grateful child of God. And if you do not, then you have a lot of work to do, as I do.

4

A Week in the Life of John Calvin

Elsie McKee

Everyone has heard of Calvin the dictator of Geneva, the one who executed Servetus and ruled the people which harsh discipline, but like many popular stereotypes of famous figures, this picture is as much interpretation as fact and says as much about the reporters as about the actors. Many people have heard of Calvin the systematic theologian, the polemical writer who fought with a sharp and cruel pen, but again this image is shaped by selective and ahistorical reading. This is not the place to deal with distinguishing fact from fiction, but the objective is to present a view of the daily work of Calvin as a way to provide a perspective 'from below', that is, as his colleagues, parishioners, and neighbours knew John Calvin.

The time chosen is a month early in the year 1556, chiefly because the wealth of sources allows for a fuller picture than some other periods of the reformer's life. These sources include dated transcripts of Calvin's sermons, of the acts of the Company of Pastors and the Consistory and the city council, information drawn from marriage and baptismal records, Calvin's correspondence and other materials from his writings.[1] This time was also chosen to coincide with preparations

---

1. Jean Calvin, *Sermons sur le V. livre de Moyse nommé Deutéronome* (Genève: Thomas Courteau, 1567). *Registres de la Compagnie des Pasteurs de Genève au temps de Calvin. Tome II. 1553–1564*, edited by RM Kingdon (Genève; Droz, 1962); *Tome I. 1546–53*, edited by J-F Bergier (1964). *Registres du Consistoire* and *Registres du Conseil* are not yet edited for the 1550s but the *Registres du Consistoire* have been transcribed by RM Kingdon and his group, and excerpts of the *Registres du Conseil* are cited in the *Annales* in volume 21 of the *Opera Calvini*, edited by G Baum, E Cunitz and E Reuss, 59 volumes (Brunsvigae: A Schwetschke et filium, 1879). Calvin's letters are found in several volumes of the *Opera Calvini*; for 1556 it is volume 16 (1877). Information about Calvin's writings is found in *Bibliotheca Calviniana. Les oeuvres de Jean Calvin publiées au xvi*

for Easter. The four celebrations of the Lord's Supper were the most important liturgical high points of the year, and Easter was arguably the most intense because it was preceded by the annual house-to-house visitation by teams of pastors and elders.[2] In an effort to make the story more fluent without sacrificing authenticity, the chronological sequence has been maintained but the details have been limited. For example, usually there is only passing reference to the texts of sermons, or topical listings for correspondence or for actions of the consistory or the company of pastors. As each institution or feature of Calvin's daily life is presented, a brief introduction to that activity and its place in the life of Geneva and/or the wider European world will be given. Otherwise, the text follows Calvin through each day for one complete week, beginning on Sunday, 1 March 1556, and then an abbreviated sketch of a second.

Preaching and teaching formed a very large part of Calvin's life, and his sermons and lectures established a regular rhythm in his daily work. One of the major religious reforms characteristic of Protestants was an insistence on regular Biblical exposition as a part of every Sunday worship service, and weekday preaching was also introduced as frequently as possible, especially in the urban centres where the population density made that feasible. There were considerably more sermons in late medieval Latin Europe than Protestant polemic might lead one to think, but they differed from Protestant ideals in two ways: they were not essential to worship (sacramental liturgies were complete without preaching) and they did not have to be based on the Bible. So, for example, in catholic Geneva parish priests had not been expected to preach regularly, although friars were often invited to give a series of sermons in Lent or other special occasions. The first Protestants in Geneva, William Farel, Pierre Viret and John

---

siècle. I. Ecrits théologiques, littéraires et juridiques [volume I] 1532–1554, edited by Rodolphe Peter and J-F Gilmont (Genève: Droz, 1991), and volume II. 1555–64, edited by Peter and Gilmont (1994). [Hereafter Peter and Gilmont, Bibliotheca Calviniana, with volume and number of text.] The baptismal and marriage records of Geneva begin in 1550; particular citations are found in the Annales, others in EA McKee, 'Calvin and His Colleagues as Pastors: Some Insights into the Collegial Ministry of Word and Sacraments', in Calvinus Praeceptor Ecclesiae, edited by Herman J Selderhuis (Genève: Droz, 2004), 9–42.

2. See Christian Grosse, Les rituels de la Cène. Le culte eucharistique réformé à Genève (XVI-XVII siècles) (Genève: Droz, 2008).

Calvin, had changed that. By 1556 most long-term residents of the city would have become accustomed to the new system of preaching services—four times on Sundays and at least once and sometimes twice on each week day. All except one of the services would be focused on exposition of a particular book of the Bible; the exception was the catechism lesson at noon on Sundays. Reformed preachers believed that scripture itself should determine not only the content but also the order of exposition, and thus preachers worked their way through a single book, verse by verse, in the fashion known as *lectio continua*, continuous reading. Normally each minister would be explaining a different book, although there was apparently no specific rule and two might be preaching on the same book in different contexts or parishes.

Calvin's Geneva had three parishes, and by 1556 each parish had at least three of the four Sunday services, and two had all four. There were weekday services, Monday–Saturday, in two parishes, and services at two times on Mondays, Wednesdays, and Fridays. This multiplication of sermons presented a considerable challenge for the seven or eight city pastors whom Calvin had organised to work in pairs, according to patterns which the Company of Pastors proposed and city council approved. For many years, Calvin's alternate had been Abel Poupin, but the latter became seriously ill in 1553 and his work load had been reduced, so other colleagues were obliged to compensate. Usually pairs of alternates preached in designated places at given times, but individuals could be shifted around; especially the newer additions to the group might move from one parish to another during the week, according to the specific needs of the day. Calvin's main assignment was in the older and larger part of the city where the two parishes of St Pierre and Magdeleine functioned in a kind of symbiosis.[3] (These churches were in close geographic proximity on one side of the river which divided the city, and the third parish, St Gervais, was a smaller part of Geneva on the other side of the river.) The full complement of Sunday and weekday services was available on each side of the river, but in the old city these were held sometimes in both St Pierre and Magdeleine, more often in one or the other; on

---

3. Although for many years he probably preached at least semi-regularly in the third parish of St Gervais on Sunday afternoons, by 1556 he was working almost exclusively in the other part of the city.

weekdays the choice depended at least in part on the size of the crowd expected to attend, since St Pierre was much larger than Magdeleine.[4]

On Sunday morning, 1 March 1556, Calvin went as usual to St Pierre for the service at eight o'clock ('mid-morning' by the early modern clock). This was the second sermon in St Pierre, because one of his colleagues had preached at five o'clock. Calvin's text was 1 Cor. 6:9-10 (sermon #37), that is, he picked up the exposition of First Corinthians where he had left off the previous Sunday afternoon.[5] His practice was to take the Greek text (or Hebrew, if he was preaching on the Old Testament) into the pulpit and translate into French the number of verses he thought he could explain in approximately an hour (or slightly less). While he was in the pulpit Calvin might well have announced the banns for couples seeking to marry. The rule was that a man and woman who had promised marriage and received the approval of the council (that is, the equivalent of a marriage license), should have the announcement of their intent to wed spoken from the pulpit three times over the course of three to six weeks, in both parishes if they came from different ones, so that anyone who knew of any impediment might bring it to the proper authorities.[6] Since Calvin would be marrying two couples that afternoon, he could have made the third announcement of their banns in the morning service. By 1556 one of his younger colleagues had taken over the noon catechism. Therefore on this day Calvin's next task was preaching again at the three o'clock service, taking up where he had stopped in the morning, so his text was 1 Cor. 6:11-13. Before beginning the regular liturgy, however, he married the two couples: they were required to come before the service began in order to be ready for the marriage liturgy which would be celebrated at the beginning of the worship time, and the wedding party had to stay for the whole service.[7]

---

4. For schedules, rotation, parish plans, see McKee, 'Calvin and His Colleagues as Pastors'.
5. The sermons on chapters 1-9 of First Corinthians are among the manuscripts which are being edited for the *Supplementa Calviniana*. I am the editor for this volume, which is still in process. The liturgy, 'La forme des prieres' (1542) is found in *Opera Selecta*, edited by Peter Barth and Wilhelm Niesel; and *Opera Selecta*, Volumen II, edited by P Barth and Dora Scheuner (Monachii in Aedibus: Chr. Kaiser, 1952), 11-58. The Sunday service is at 18-26. For English see *John Calvin: Writings on Pastoral Piety*, edited by EA McKee (Mahweh, NJ: Paulist, 2001), 111-34.
6. 'Ecclesiastical Ordinances', *Opera Selecta* II.345, 348-9.
7. *Annales*, *Opera Calvini* 21:629; marriage liturgy in *Opera Selecta* II.50-6.

This week was not Calvin's turn to preach at the daily service but on Monday March 2 he would have been at the Magdeleine at seven o'clock to attend worship led by a colleague, his alternate. Probably a good part of the rest of the morning would be spent in preparation for his two o'clock lecture on Hosea, the book through which he was then working his way, verse by verse.[8] While he preached in French, of course, Calvin lectured in Latin, to anyone who wished to attend, though naturally most of his hearers were his fellow ministers and any educated residents or visitors to the city who were interested. By 1556 the latter would include a number of religious refugees, for example the theological leaders of the Italian and English-language congregations as well as the more numerous French refugees. Also by 1556 the lectures were being held in the chapel of Our Lady the New, now called the Auditoire, next to St Pierre. This had been decommissioned at the Reformation (along with several other church buildings which were not needed in the consolidated parish organization), but had recently been re-opened for worship to provide space for refugee congregations like the Italians and English. For this purpose, the usual equipment of a Protestant church had been installed: a pulpit and benches.[9]

Lecturing on the Bible to prepare ministers to preach was one of the most influential tasks of the leading reformers, and the source of many of the commentaries which Protestants began to publish with great energy. In his teaching as in his preaching Calvin skipped nothing, but his exposition was also distinguished from that of some of his colleagues by its more 'practical' character, in that he tried to give what he considered the essential points for understanding each verse, without citing everything he knew. The point was to provide what a pastor would need to know both to explain scripture to his congregation and to defend Biblical teaching against misinterpretation. In typical humanist fashion, Calvin dealt with linguistic points on how best to interpret particular words, using Erasmus for the Greek and Sebastian Münster for the Hebrew. The explanation normally included a concise survey of disputed issues in the exegetical history of the verse, especially if there were points of controversy based on patristic comments or arguments between Roman and Protestant

---

8. See Peter and Gilmont, *Bibliotheca Calviniana* II.#57/3, 622–4.
9. *Annales, Opera Calvini* 21:619, 620 (November 14 and 25, 1555).

theologians. Calvin's first commentaries (on New Testament books vital to the Protestant understanding of the gospel, like Romans or Galatians, the Gospel of John or Hebrews), had been both spoken to students and written down and polished by the reformer himself. Gradually it became clear that the busy pastor did not have time to do it all himself so a new system had to be found and his colleagues were eager to help him. They would copy down what he said in his lectures as fully as possible; often several would collate their notes to prepare a text for Calvin to correct and polish before publication. By 1556 it had become too much for him even to do this polishing; the Hosea lectures would be the first to be published still in the lecture format as he had spoken them, complete with the prayers with which he began and ended his lessons.[10]

Before or more likely after his lecture on March 2, Calvin wrote a long letter to the Lutheran church leaders in Frankfurt about several rather delicate issues of potential friction between Lutheran and Reformed Protestants. Since he did not personally know the men to whom he wrote, Calvin excuses himself for addressing them but appeals to the concern for the church which they and he shared and then explains two matters which he requests them to consider. One is the publication in Frankfurt by the (rather extreme) Lutheran theologian Joachim Westphal of a book against Calvin's doctrine of the Lord's Supper; since some of the Frankfurt church leaders also rejected Calvin's teaching, he offers to travel to Frankfurt to talk with them in person. The other issue he treats is the state of the recently-arrived Reformed congregation, as he intercedes on their behalf. Frankfurt, like most of Germany, was Lutheran, but they were willing to accept religious refugees when they were assured by some of their own leaders that these people were theologically acceptable. This was the case with a French-speaking Reformed congregation—originally from Strasbourg but coming now from exile in England. The problem was that there were internal disagreements in the Reformed congregation which Calvin feared might jeopardise their welcome and he

---

10. See Peter and Gilmont, *Bibliotheca Calviniana* I.#52/3, 442 for Acts written as commentary; #51/6, 404–5, for Des Gallars' explanation of how he produced the first edition of the commentary on Isaiah from his notes but in his own style; Calvin was not satisfied and in a number of ways revised the text in 1559; #57/3, 622–4 for Hosea.

asks the Lutheran leaders' forbearance with the faults of their refugee guests.[11] The strife over Westphal was a theme throughout the mid-1550s, and recurs repeatedly in Calvin's correspondence. The matter of the French church in Frankfurt was a different kind of problem, which would personally occupy Calvin for many months of this year. Thus the themes of this letter reflect ways that the pastor in Geneva continued to interact with the larger European church scene in the midst of the daily duties which occupied most of his time.

Tuesday March 3 was much like Monday: attending worship, seeing to other duties and preparation for the lecture at two o'clock. In addition part of the day was spent writing more letters to Frankfurt, this time to members of the French church itself, people whom Calvin knew personally and for whom he felt a special responsibility because this community was a part of the congregation he had served during his years in Strasbourg. The problem Calvin needed to address was internal arguments about the choice of a new minister after the recent death of one of the church's two pastors, complicated by irregularities in the election of the other surviving pastor. As the French church's senior counsellor, he writes to attempt to move this situation in the direction of mutual understanding and resolution as well as to offer them help in finding a replacement for their deceased minister.[12] Along with his other specific tasks, Calvin would also have spent some times during these days visiting his dying colleague Abel Poupin, joining with fellow ministers in Geneva to pray with their friend and his family through his last hours.[13] Prayers and exhortations, Psalms and edifying conversation, pastors and family present with the dying man—Pastor Abel would have them all, as his colleagues gathered or took turns at his bedside during these last hours.

---

11. See *Opera Calvini* 16:53–4, letter #2401.
12. See *Opera Calvini* 16:55–6, letter #2402.
13. Something of this pastoral scene can be found in the long letter which Calvin had written in April 1549 describing the deathbed of a French refugee in Geneva, Mme de Normandie. This includes the dying woman's words of confession of faith (sense of sin and confidence in Christ's grace) and her counsel to her servant to cling to the gospel, her husband's loving encouragement to her despite his own sorrow, exhortation and comfort by the ministers present, her own recitation of the French metrical Psalm 51 and Calvin's exposition of it, and further prayers by the gathered company. See *Opera Calvini* 13:244–8, letter #1179, 29 April 1549; English in McKee, *John Calvin: Writings on Pastoral Piety*, 301–5. See also instructions for pastoral care of the sick and dying in the liturgy, *Opera Selecta* II.56–8.

Wednesday March 4 was another full day for Calvin. Usually weekday services were composed of sermons and prayers, but Calvin had developed a distinctive practice (begun by Martin Bucer) of a remarkable service called the day of prayer held every Wednesday. This day was the high point of the weekday worship, with its own liturgy which included the congregational singing of Psalms (something otherwise practiced only on Sundays). Services were held at two times on Wednesdays, to ensure that everyone might have an opportunity to come to worship, and more people attended than on other work days. Although usually the daily service in the old city was held in the smaller church of Magdeleine, on Wednesday it was transferred to St Pierre to accommodate more people, so, on both sides of the river, at St Pierre and St Gervais, the special prayer liturgy took place at five o'clock and again at eight o'clock. The service was focused on the church's situation in its concrete historical time and place, and had several purposes: one was repentance, one was intercession and one was thanksgiving. In keeping with the Biblical idea that various kinds of afflictions can be chastisement to turn sinners back to the right way, the day of prayer gave particular attention to the connection between asking forgiveness for sins and interceding for those who are afflicted. The long central prayer after the sermon included both more general petitions and the names of specific individuals, especially the sick. If the pastors did not already know who the sick were, the *dizeniers* (civic officials of each district) would alert them. Because the day of prayer was so important, the Company of Pastors wanted to insure that the best preachers were in the pulpits. In 1553 when Poupin fell ill, they asked Calvin to take the service on the day of prayer every week, and the person who was serving as his alternate in place of Poupin would do the Saturday of Calvin's regularly assigned week.[14]

Thus on the morning of Wednesday March 4 as he walked to St Pierre for the service at eight o'clock, Calvin might have been reminding himself of the names of the sick, including Pastor Abel, to be included in the day's intercessions. Although the liturgy of the day

---

14. Liturgy in *Opera Selecta* II.26–30; English in McKee, *John Calvin: Writings on Pastoral Piety*, 159–77. For fuller discussion, see EA McKee, 'Calvin's Day of Prayer: Origins, Nature, and Significance," in *Calvin und Calvinismus – Europäische Perspektiven*, ed. Irene Dingel & Herman Selderhuis. (Göttingen: Vandenhoeck & Ruprecht, 2011), pp. 315-32.

of prayer was distinctive, the sermon was usually a continuation of the book which Calvin was expounding during the week. In 1556 he had been working his way through Deuteronomy, verse by verse, for many months. On March 4, his text was Deut. 27:16–23 (sermon #151), taking up where he had left off the previous Friday. Normally when he preached on a week day Calvin would not be lecturing also, but because of the change in schedule so that he could do the sermon on the day of prayer every week, there were times when he did both. Thus, two o'clock found Calvin back in the Auditoire lecturing on Hosea—his second Biblical lesson of the day, though the audiences and languages were different. Then he would go again to Poupin's bedside.

March 5 began with Poupin's death at seven o'clock, with at least some of his colleagues—likely including Calvin—gathered around him. Before his burial the church still had its regular business to do, and so by later in the morning all the ministers and the city elders were gathered for the regular consistory meeting. The word 'consistory' immediately brings to mind the old legends about Calvin's harsh discipline and juicy stories of sexual scandals where everyone is excommunicated. Recent studies based on the wonderful transcriptions and editions which Prof. Robert Kingdon and his students have been producing reveal a different institution.[15] Since this body had a very significant role in social as well as religious life, the degree of its autonomy had long been a source of dispute in Geneva, as Calvin worked to persuade the citizens and especially the leaders that ecclesiastical oversight must be distinguished from civil. By 1556 those elected to the city council were convinced of the right of the consistory to make judgments about specifically church matters, including suspension from the sacraments, so the cooperation between consistory and council was much smoother.[16]

---

15. For an overview of the consistory, see Robert M Kingdon, *Adultery and Divorce in Calvin's Geneva* (Cambridge, MA: Harvard, 1995), chapter 1 'The Institutional Matrix'; see also other articles, for example, Robert M Kingdon, 'Calvin and the Establishment of Consistory Discipline in Geneva: The Institution and the Men Who Directed it', in *Nederlandsche Archief voor Kerkgeschiedenis* 70 (1990): 158–71. Edited volumes of The *Registres du Consistoire* now published go through the year 1552.; the rest of the registers for Calvin's lifetime have been transcribed and are in process of being edited. I am very grateful to Professor Kingdon and the HH Meeter Center for Calvin Studies for access to the transcriptions.

16. The arguments about the authority of the consistory are well known; for one recent discussion of the political developments, see William Naphy, *Calvin and*

The consistory was made up of all the pastors plus twelve lay men whom Calvin called 'elders',[17] one of whom served as moderator. Ordinarily it met once a week, although sometimes a second meeting was scheduled (just before a celebration of the Lord's Supper) or might be called for a particular cause. About one-third of the consistory's business involved learning the facts about and reconciling quarrels within families or between neighbours.[18] Only known conflicts would come before this body, and then only if the first effort at resolution by those immediately at hand did not succeed. As soon, however, as a quarrel affected the community, something had to be done by the authorities, and in the tightly-packed social situation of an early modern city, household quarrels rarely remained private affairs.

On this March 5,[19] the most time-consuming business before the consistory was a continuing investigation into the behaviour of Guillaume Lecointe, sire de Boiville, and a number of witnesses: servants, neighbours, and others, gave accounts of what they knew about his blasphemy and sexual improprieties. The case was not resolved until much later in the year, but at this point one of the women involved with M. de Boiville was judged to be guilty of fornication; she was suspended from taking the Lord's Supper until she manifested repentance, and remanded to the city council for punishment because her behaviour was contrary to civil moral laws. A minister and an elder, Calvin and Guillaume Chicand, were charged to convey this decision to the council and at the same time to request permission for the annual preEaster house-to-house visitation. (Council authoriza-

---

the Consolidation of the Genevan Reformation (Manchester, UK: Manchester University Press, 1994; reissued by Westminster/John Knox, 2003).

17. Calvin took the name from the New Testament and explained their origin according to specific NT passages. Since in the NT, which showed the ideal model church, there had not been any Christian magistrates/princes, Calvin was convinced that the offices of the church must be distinct from civil offices, though he was very happy for the two forms of divinely established rule to cooperate. See Elsie Anne McKee, *Elders and the Plural Ministry. The Role of Exegetical History in Illuminating Calvin's Theology* (Genève: Droz, 1988), part one.

18. For the fullest discussion, in the context of city practice, see Grosse, *Les rituels de la Cène*, chapters 6–8; one-third of cases conflicts, 513; questions of conflict, see graphs, 513, 537. See also John Witte, Jr. and Robert M Kingdon, *Sex, Marriage, and Family in John Calvin's Geneva, volume 1: Courtship, Engagement, and Marriage* (Grand Rapids: Wm B Eerdmans, 2005), note 21, *infra*.

19. *Registres du Consistoire*, transcription of XI:2, 5v–7v.

tion was necessary as a matter of policy but also because the civil officers of each district, who knew everyone in their area, must accompany the ecclesiastical representatives.) After the business with de Boiville, several shorter cases were heard: a husband and wife who were fighting, a conflict between two brothers and their mother also involving 'blasphemy' (speaking against God's word), a couple who had promised marriage but wanted to dissolve the engagement, and guards who were fighting. (The last was referred to the appropriate civil authority.)

In the case of the couple who were fighting, the problem had almost certainly been causing tensions in their neighbourhood for some time; the rebellious sons and the complaints of their mother would also have been common knowledge. What Kingdon aptly calls 'a compulsory counseling service',[20] the consistory worked to bring communal harmony to Geneva, in a context in which the common good took precedence over individual freedom. The case of the young man and woman asking to be freed from their engagement involved the presentation of evidence that they had not consummated their union and both wanted to dissolve the tie between them. Arguments over marriage promises were not uncommon and frequently appeared on the consistory's agenda. The reason was that a promise to marry, made in the presence of witnesses, constituted a legally binding contract. Traditionally a betrothed couple would begin to live together but Geneva required other preliminary forms, including official recognition that there was no impediment, proclamation of the banns, and the marriage service.[21] Quite often the problem was a breach of promise claim by the woman, when the man denied having made a promise. In this case, the matter was simpler, and the consistory agreed that the promise could be withdrawn and the two young people would be free of any obligation.

Calvin's day was far from over. The burial of Pastor Abel Poupin took place that afternoon. In reaction against the great focus on the dead and elaborate funeral and mourning practices of the late medi-

---

20. Robert M Kingdon, 'Calvin and the Family: The Work of the Consistory in Geneva', in *Calvin's Work in Geneva*, edited by RC Gamble (New York: Garland, 1992), 96.
21. 'Ecclesiastical Ordinances', *Opera Selecta* II.348. For full discussion with texts, see Witte and Kingdon, *Sex, Marriage, and Family in John Calvin's Geneva*.

eval church, Protestant reformers cut away much of the theology and practice common in the middle ages; there were no more prayers or Masses for the dead, no more teachings about purgatory or burial in hallowed ground. Reformed leaders were particularly austere in this regard, and eliminated funeral services as such.[22] By Genevan law, burials must take place within twenty-four hours of death, in a decent fashion, but there was no church service.[23] By general custom friends and neighbours and (in the case of pastors) parishioners would visit the home of the deceased before the procession to the gravesite, and in some places ministers might speak of the faith of the person being buried, but there are no explicit records of this for Geneva. Naturally, however, a great part of the city turned out to accompany the ecclesiastical and civil leaders who went with the family to bury 'Pastor Abel'.[24]

Still Calvin's day was not over. Probably in the evening, tired though he might be, if he had a messenger waiting Calvin would push himself to complete his correspondence for Frankfurt. This time he wrote letters to individuals: one to the Lutheran merchant Johannes Clauburger, a leading layman who had befriended and protected the French congregation, the other to Valeran Poullain, the irregularly elected minister of the congregation who was a part of the controver-

---

22. Calvin speaks briefly of the importance of respectful burial in his discussion of the resurrection of the body (John Calvin, *The Institutes of the Christian Religion*, III.xxv.5 and 8), rejects purgatory (*ibid*, III.v.6–7). For burial practices, see Bernard Roussel, '"Ensevelir honnestement les corps": funeral corteges and Huguenot culture', in *Society and Culture in the Huguenot World 1559–1685*, edited by Raymond Mentzer and Andrew Spicer (Cambridge: University Press, 2002), 193–208.
23. The 'Ecclesiastical Ordinances' prescribe decent burial, leaving the organization of the process to individual discretion but insisting that there be no superstition and the hour should be appropriate, not less than twelve hours after death and not more than twenty-four ('Ecclesiastical Ordinances', *Opera Selecta* II.355). In this case the appeal to appropriateness apparently trumped the regulation about specific hours, since Poupin was buried less than twelve hours after death, in order that this might be during daylight.
24. For practice in Reformed Strasbourg, see the records of burial for Matthew Zell, in Elsie Anne McKee, *Katharina Schütz Zell. Volume One. The Life and Thought of a Sixteenth-Century Reformer* (Leiden: Brill, 1999), 125–9; and McKee, *Volume Two. The Writings: a Critical Edition* (Leiden: Brill, 1999), chapter 4. Geneva's burial of Abel Poupin is briefly recorded in the *Registres de la Compagnie des Pasteurs*, II, 66.

sy (some members supported him, others did not). Both letters were part of ongoing correspondence, and the one to Poullain responded to his praise for Calvin's most recent book against Westphal (*Second Defense*, January 1556).[25] In both letters Calvin gives counsel about the church conflict.

Friday March 6 began with worship as usual. The next thing on the schedule was the *congrégation*, a kind of practice-preaching Bible study held every Friday by the ministers and open to the public. One of the purposes was to give ministers practice in expounding Biblical texts in the vernacular; all their theological education was in Latin, but they must preach in French. In addition, this study and preaching session provided a chance for them to critique each other, since one person would explain a chosen text, followed by others who would offer their shorter comments, and normally Calvin would then give his exposition (almost another sermon). Finally lay people might also speak, usually to ask questions; they did not attempt to explain the text. In 1556 the book being expounded was probably a continuation of the Psalms begun in the previous year.[26]

After the Friday *congrégation*, the pastors would retire from the public room and meet together as the Company of Pastors. Generally the meeting was occupied with the business of organization, for example, making preaching assignments for specific ministers to be in specific pulpits at specific hours, or proposing and examining candidates for the ministry, attending to matters of overseeing the schools, mutual corrections, correspondence with ecclesiastical leaders in other places, and so forth.[27] On this day there is no explicit record of the agenda but it is almost certain that, besides the remembrance of Poupin, one topic would have been the problem with Pastor Jean Fabri which had reached a crisis point. Saturday March 7, after worship at seven o'clock, the consistory gathered for an extraordinary

---

25. *Opera Calvini* 16:58–65 for letters #2404 and #2407. For information about the *Second Defense*, see Peter and Gilmont, *Bibliotheca Calviniana* I.#57/4, 608.
26. See Erik de Boer, 'The Congrégation: An In-Service Training Center for Preachers to the People of Geneva', in *Calvin and the Company of Pastors*, edited by D Foxgrover (Grand Rapids: CRC, 2004), 57–87. Also Erik de Boer, 'The Presence and Participation of Lay People in the Congrégations of the Company of Pastors in Geneva', in *Sixteenth-Century Journal* 35/3 (2004): 651–70.
27. See 'Ecclesiastical Ordinances', *Opera Selecta* II.332–5 for institution, and *Registres de la Compagnie des Pasteurs* for ongoing activities.

session to discuss the case of Fabri. There were public claims of his having made sexual advances to, if not actually seduced, a married woman, and gossip accused him of getting his serving girl pregnant (something which was apparently only gossip). The consistory dealt with witnesses and Fabri regarding the relationship with the married woman (who also testified), and despite his denials of wrongdoing Fabri was deposed and dismissed.[28] Along with the death of Poupin, meant that the city was short two pastors. Poupin had been unable to preach except occasionally for some time, so the pastors had already doubled-up their duties, but a more permanent solution was needed now that two places were vacant.

The next week can be sketched more briefly, giving a simple overview of Calvin's activities to illustrate the continuation of the daily activities.

Sunday March 8, at St Pierre, eight o'clock, he was preaching on 1 Cor. 6:13–17, and in the afternoon at three o'clock on the following verses, 1 Cor. 6:18–20.

Monday March 9, at the Magdeleine at seven o'clock Calvin did the daily sermon, this time on Deut. 27:24–6. At eight o'clock, he and elder Chicand went to the regular meeting of the city's governing council to lay before them the consistory matters discussed on the previous Thursday.

Tuesday March 10, at the Magdeleine at seven o'clock he preached on Deut. 28:1–2.

Wednesday March 11, at St Pierre at eight o'clock he preached on Deut. 28:2–8.

Thursday March 12, at Magdeleine at seven o'clock he preached on Deut. 28:9–14, then attended the Consistory meeting.

Friday March 13, at the Magdeleine at seven o'clock Calvin preached on Deut. 28:15–24; this was followed by the Bible study/practice-preaching *congrégation*, and then the Company of Pastors meeting, organizing the visitation. As soon as practical (probably within a couple of days) the teams of pastors and elders, with the *dizenier* of each district, would begin their visits to each household.

---

28. Transcription of *Registres du Consistoire*, XI:2, 7r–v. For gossip, XI:2, March 31st, 12v–14v. Report to council and decision, *Annales*, *Opera Calvini* 21:630; *Registres de la Compagnie des Pasteurs*, II, 66.

Saturday March 15 after worship Calvin may have spent in study or reading, dealing with correspondence, and doing visitation. On Friday the council had given him a copy of his colleague Nicholas Cop's exposition of Proverbs, which as senior minister Calvin was asked to examine and approve before it could be published.

The rest of the month followed much the same pattern, continuing sermons on 1 Corinthians on Sundays and weekday sermons on Deuteronomy or lectures on Hosea, with the regular meetings of consistory, *congrégation* and the company of pastors, plus other pastoral duties such as performing marriages and the busy visitation schedule. In fact March 1556 was not an unusual time; it is simply better documented than some others. What it reveals is the reformer of Geneva—an exile and resident alien—doing the ordinary work of a pastor and preacher, with colleagues and civil leaders and the people of a busy and crowded city-state, fitting the academic theology for which he is best known around the schedule of sermons and pastoral visits and frequent committee meetings of a parish . . . this is the way his colleagues and neighbours and parishioners knew Calvin, and it may provide modern readers with a practical balance to the legends.

Stepping back a little it is possible to raise some contemporary questions about the relationship between Calvin's working life and that of later Reformed ministers. Two things should be remembered, however. One is that Calvin's practice was not unique to him nor did he create it; there were a significant number of figures who shared in moulding the Reformed pastorate, and some very influential ones were chronologically senior to Calvin. Although relations between ecclesiastical and civil authorities differed somewhat in the various situations, the vision of pastoral ministry as practiced by Calvin was essentially patterned on his first generation predecessors like Martin Bucer, Matthew Zell and Wolfgang Capito in Strasbourg or Ulrich Zwingli and Heinrich Bullinger in Zurich or Johannes Oecolampadius in Basel or William Farel in Geneva.

The other factor which is vital to remember is the great differences in historical context between the sixteenth century and the modern world, perhaps especially in terms of popular literacy but also in terms of religious culture and theological education. Even the new Protestant ministers had to be re-trained by their learned colleagues. It was no surprise that Calvin was the most highly regarded preacher in Geneva, especially in the early years, since his pastoral counterparts were in fact also usually his students, and the citizens were quite prepared 'to vote with their feet' when they did not respect a preacher.[29] What may seem very unbalanced in the early Protestant ideal of a pastor and the specific work of Calvin is largely shaped by the situation the reformers inherited and their convictions about the means of salvation and pastoral care.

The primary task of the Reformed pastor was preaching: day in and day out, *lectio continua* style through books of the Old Testament as well as the New. Indeed, the Reformed became known for their regular preaching on the Old Testament; this had not been the practice before but it became a distinctive trait of the Reformed tradition. Preaching was not simply an intellectual matter nor was it only for the sake of the ignorant. As Calvin repeated to his congregation, even when they had heard the content of the gospel they needed repeated exhortation—and he included himself and other preachers in the number of those who must continue to learn all their lives.[30] Even when people were able to read the Bible for themselves, they still needed guidance to understand what, for most laity, was virtually a new book. Equally important was the fact that preaching was understood as a key part of pastoral care, because Protestants were convinced that knowing the Word of God was essential for the health of the soul. Becoming a follower of the gospel meant unlearning much old piety such as petitions to the saints or pilgrimages to miracle-working shrines or multiplication of Latin prayers; Protestants were convinced that trusting in these human activities was not only wrong but led to insecurity about one's salvation: 'have I done enough?'! For those who broke with the old theology, the new 'gospel' teaching was the way to assurance of God's grace and peace of heart through Christ alone.

Although Calvin clearly wanted to have the Lord's Supper celebrated very frequently—at least once a month—and he conceived of the ideal Sunday service as Word and Sacrament, it is important to remember that he did not expect ideal conditions at all times. Participation in the Supper required higher standards of knowledge and behaviour than could be readily achieved by the whole commu-

---

29. See McKee, 'Calvin and His Colleagues as Pastors', 36.
30. One example in *ibid*, 11.

nity and, according to Reformed understanding, all communicants should partake whenever the sacrament is offered. Under such conditions, re-educating and re-forming the Christian faith and practice of a large city whose people had grown up in the late medieval tradition was a considerable task. Calvin set very high standards and he approximated them more closely than many of his contemporaries thought feasible, but he was also a practical reformer; he could compromise when necessary. To protect the integrity of the sacraments as God's gift to the whole church (not just those who felt qualified to come) he would accept a less frequent administration of the Supper than he wanted.

To Calvin and his fellow Reformed leaders, proclamation of the Word of God through words and sacraments was their fundamental calling. Implied in this vocation was teaching both the people and future pastors, and sharing with lay elders in forming every member of the church—including the civil authorities—to witness to the gospel. Part of the formation was local 'discipline' and welcoming refugees and teaching foreign students to send new preachers back as evangelists. Part was linking the whole body of the visible church together through prayer and correspondence and mutual support among the local worshiping communities such as Geneva and Frankfurt, Lyons and Zurich, London and Budapest, St Andrews and Emden, and beyond, and working to extend the preaching of the gospel as far as possible through books and preachers, both local and international.

Over the centuries, the literacy level of Reformed congregations grew, the catechesis took effect, and the nature of pastoral care was redefined in various ways. In some ways the different situation in which modern pastors find themselves is at least partly the fruit of the success of the preaching and teaching of Calvin's generation. The reformers might say, not 'copy us', but 'do as we did' in proclaiming God's good news in your time and place.

5

Calvin on the Authority of Scripture

Murray Rae

When Karl Barth gave a series of lectures on the theology of Calvin to his students at Göttingen in 1922, he began by advising the students that one did not become a Calvinist merely by repeating Calvin's formulations. The aim in studying Calvin is to enter into dialogue with him. Good students of Calvin may, in the end, say something very different from Calvin but they will have learned it through engagement with him. That advice seems especially apposite in respect of Calvin's biblical hermeneutics. Reading Calvin's commentaries we come across passages and formulations that few biblical scholars are likely to repeat today, yet that does not mean that nothing can be learned through the careful study of Calvin's commentary upon Scripture. It behoves us to penetrate beyond the surface of Calvin's sometimes astonishing claims about what a biblical author intended to the theological framework from which Calvin's claims arise. We will find in that framework, I suggest, a far more profound and robust conception of Scripture than that which informs some of our hermeneutical choices today.

Before developing that suggestion, however, let me offer just a few examples of the kinds of claims Calvin makes that biblical scholars today are reluctant to make. Consider, for instance, Calvin's comments on the opening verse of Isaiah 49. The verse reads: 'Listen to me, you islands; hear this, you distant nations: Before I was born the LORD called me; from my birth he has made mention of my name.' Contemporary commentators explain, rightly enough, that the one 'called by the Lord' is Israel. The context is Israel's exile in Babylon and this verse identifies the basis of Israel's presumption that she is the rightful occupier of the land of Palestine. Israel reminds the 'distant nations', those currently occupying Palestine, that her claim upon the land is based upon Yahweh's call.[1] Contrast that account with Calvin's comment on Isaiah 49:1, which says:

> After dealing with the future deliverance of the people, Isaiah comes now to Christ, under whose guidance the people were brought out of Babylon, as they had earlier been brought out of Egypt. The earlier prophecy must have been confirmed by this doctrine because they would scarcely have hoped that the Lord would deliver them if they had not looked to Christ, by whom alone desponding souls can be comforted and strengthened; from him they ought not only to expect eternal salvation but ought equally to expect temporal deliverance. Besides, when the prophets are talking about the restoration of the church they commonly bring Christ into view, not only because he wants to be the minister of the church, but because on him was founded the adoption of the people.[2]

Without feeling the need of any explanation, Calvin simply assumes here that when Isaiah speaks of the one 'called by the Lord', he is referring to the very same one who Christians refer to when they speak of Jesus Christ. He further supposes, again without feeling the need to provide any warrant, that Isaiah is concerned here with 'the restoration of the church'. 'When the prophets are talking about the restoration of the church', Calvin says (as though that is straight-forwardly what Isaiah is doing), 'they commonly bring Christ into view'. He also credits Israel with remarkable Christological insight: 'they would scarcely have hoped that the Lord would deliver them if they had not looked to Christ'.

The christological and ecclesiological assumptions evident here continue to inform Calvin's commentary upon the subsequent verses and pervade, indeed, the whole of his treatment of Isaiah. I take the commentary on 49:4 as further example. The verse reads: 'But I said,

---

1. See, for example, John DW Watts, *Word Biblical Commentary: Isaiah 34–66* (Waco: Word Books, 1987), 187.
2. John Calvin, *Isaiah: The Classic Crossway Commentaries*, edited by Alister McGrath and JI Packer (Wheaton, IL.: Crossway Books, 2000), 299.

"I have laboured to no purpose; I have spent my strength in vain and for nothing. Yet what is due me is in the LORD's hand, and my reward is with my God.'" Calvin writes in explanation:

> The prophet here brings forward a grievous complaint in the name of the church, but he does so in such a manner that we must begin with the Head. Christ complains along with his members, then, that it seems as if his labor were thrown away . . . he introduces the church as complaining that her labors are fruitless because [and here is further exegetical novelty] people do not repent at the preaching of heavenly doctrine.[3]

A representative contemporary commentator, by contrast, reads the lament of verse four as Israel's 'self-serving sigh of pseudo-piety'.[4] The contemporary scholar will have nothing to do with Calvin's christological and ecclesiological reading, although, as an aside here, it seems clear that for the contemporary commentator too the interpretive task is informed by assumptions drawn from somewhere outside the text itself. It is not obvious from the immediate context that this is Israel's 'self-serving sigh of pseudo-piety'. The point of difference between Calvin and the contemporary scholar then, is not that one operates with an interpretive framework shaped by convictions arising from beyond the text while the other does not. The point of difference, rather, concerns the nature of the convictions that each brings to the text and that constitute, therefore, the interpretive framework within which each does his or her hermeneutical work.

My intent in this paper, however, is not particularly to draw comparisons between Calvin's biblical hermeneutics and that of contemporary scholars, but rather to investigate Calvin's interpretation of Scripture on its own terms and then to consider whether there might be an enduring validity in the theological convictions and hermeneutical strategy that shape his reading of Scripture. We will begin with an account of what Calvin takes Scripture to be, before then considering how it is to be read.

---

3. *Ibid*, 300.
4. Watts, *Isaiah 34–66*, 187.

It is clear that Calvin is well aware of the human provenance of the scriptural texts and that they are shaped, in part at least, by particular historical circumstances and occasional interests. 'There are many passages of Scripture', he says, 'the sense of which depends on the circumstances connected with them'.[5] Something along the lines of historical criticism would seem to be important, therefore, to the task of biblical interpretation, but discernment of the circumstances connected with the production of a biblical text is, in Calvin's view, a very slight part of the hermeneutical task. The major part and the true end towards which the reading of Scripture ought to be directed is attentiveness to what God communicates through the biblical text.

The expectation of Calvin that God addresses us through Scripture is an expectation born of his experience that that is so. The authority of Scripture in this regard simply reveals itself, or, more particularly, is revealed by the Spirit under whose inspiration Scripture was formed. II Timothy 3:16–18, is the straightforward expression of what Calvin holds to be true: 'All Scripture is inspired by God, and is useful for teaching, for reproof, for correction, and for training in righteousness, so that everyone who belongs to God may be proficient, equipped for every good work.'[6] Commenting on this text, Calvin explains: 'Our religion is distinguished from all others in that the prophets have spoken not of themselves, but as instruments of the Holy Spirit; and what they have brought to us, they received by heavenly commission.'[7] In the *Institutes*, Calvin explains that Scripture is given by God to facilitate a true understanding of himself and as a safeguard against human error.

> For, if we consider the mutability of the human mind,—how easy its lapse into forgetfulness of God; how great its propensity to errors of every kind; how violent its rage for the perpetual fabrication of new and false religions,—it will be easy to perceive the necessity of the heavenly doctrine being thus committed to writing, that

---

5. John Calvin, *The Institutes of the Christian Religion*, IV.xvii.23.
6. This and all scriptural quotations are taken from the NRSV unless contained within citations of Calvin himself.
7. *Calvin: Commentaries*, Volume XXIII, edited and translated by Joseph Hartounian (London: SCM Press, 1958), 84.

> it might not be lost in oblivion, or evaporate in error, or be corrupted by the presumption of men. Since it is evident, therefore, that God, foreseeing the inefficiency of his manifestation of himself in the exquisite structure of the world, hath afforded the assistance of his word to all those to whom he determined to make his instructions effectual,—if we seriously aspire to a sincere contemplation of God, it is necessary for us to pursue this right way. We must come, I say, to the word . . .[8]

It is a mistake to consider the divine inspiration of Scripture to be a presupposition of Calvin's hermeneutics. It is certainly both the starting point and the framework within which Calvin's reading takes place, but, on Calvin's own terms, the doctrine of divine inspiration is *given* rather than presupposed. That the scriptural text is for us the very word of God is not known through human conjecture or supposition but is itself revealed. It is vital to understand this distinction; for Calvin takes pains to point out that the authority of Scripture is a self-authenticating authority. 'For the Scripture exhibits as clear evidence of its truth, as white and black things do of their colour, or sweet and bitter things of their taste.'[9] Thus the authority of Scripture is not bestowed upon it by some human authority but is in faith simply recognised and received. Calvin's view is thus distinguished from those accounts of scriptural or canonical authority, that suppose that the authority of the canonical texts is a product of the church's collection of these texts and not others to be its authoritative scripture. Calvin resists this claim, precisely because it makes the authority of scripture subordinate to that of the church:

> . . . when the Church receives [scripture], and seals it with her suffrage, she does not authenticate a thing otherwise dubious or controvertible; but knowing it to be the truth of her God, performs a duty of piety, by treating it with immediate veneration.[10]

---

8. Calvin, *Institutes*, I.vi.3.
9. *Ibid*, I.vii.2.
10. *Ibid*, I.vii.2.

The point had to be secured, of course, in the context of Reformation polemics—if Scripture was not an authority over the Church, then it could not be appealed to in cases where the Church had strayed into error. The antecedent and superior authority of Scripture is a principle of Reformed theology, however, that challenges those of our age too who wish to subject all truth claims to the authority of human judgement. Calvin might just as well have had the postenlightenment sceptic in view when he wrote,

> . . . with great contempt of the Holy Spirit, they inquire, Who can assure us that God is the author of [the scriptures]? Who can with certainty affirm, that they have been preserved safe and uncorrupted to the present age? Who can persuade us that this book ought to be received with reverence. . . [11]

Calvin's answer, not to the sceptic but to the faithful, is simply this: It is God who offers assurance, it is God who affirms, and it is God who persuades. He writes,

> The same Spirit who made Moses and the prophets certain of their calling, has now testified to our own hearts that he used them as his servants for our instruction. It is not surprising that many have doubts as to the author of Scripture. For even though the majesty of God is displayed by it, only those illumined by the Spirit have the eyes to see what should be evident to all men, but in fact is seen only by the elect.[12]

Here I have quoted from the *Commentaries* but Calvin repeats this hermeneutical principle in numerous places, including the *Institutes*. There he writes, '. . . the testimony of the Spirit is superior to all reason. For as God alone is sufficient witness of himself in his own word, so also the word will never gain credit in the hearts of men, till it be confirmed by the internal testimony of the Spirit.'[13]

---

11. *Ibid*, I.vii.1.
12. Calvin: *Commentaries*, XXIII.85.
13. Calvin, *Institutes*, I.vii.4.

It may be objected that Calvin's argument does not advance us very far. Assurance that God's word is to be heard through Scripture is attained through the word of God spoken to our hearts. That explanation will not help the sceptic at all, but we must note again that the explanation is not directed to the sceptic.[14] It is directed to the believer who is eager to read Scripture and to discern God's word therein. Calvin here encourages in readers of Scripture a particular disposition, a disposition of trust and humility before Scripture. He encourages readers to set aside the pretentious demand that the Word of God be subjected to the authority of human judgement. 'It is godless profanity', he says, 'to set up our own acumen as capable of understanding Scripture, which contains mysteries of God hidden to our flesh and sublime treasures of life which are far beyond our powers.'[15] Assurance of such mysteries can come only from God. Thus,

> . . . being illuminated by him, we now believe the divine original of the Scripture, not from our own judgement or that of others, but we esteem the certainty, that we have received it from God's own mouth by the ministry of men, to be superior to that of any human judgement, and equal to that of an intuitive perception of God himself in it. We seek not arguments or probabilities to support our judgement, but submit our judgements and understandings as to a thing concerning which it is impossible for us to judge. . .[16]

Post-enlightenment epistemologists are unlikely to be impressed by such a claim but it is not for that reason untrue. There is no compelling reason to suppose, and much reason to doubt, that the authority of the eternal and ineffable God should be answerable to the provisional judgement of finite and limited human beings. If Calvin is right that in addition to being limited and provisional, human judgement

---

14. Calvin dismisses all attempts in this matter to defeat the sceptic with human argument. 'But those persons betray great folly, who wish it to be demonstrated to infidels that the Scripture is the word of God, which cannot be known without faith.' *Ibid*, I.viii.13.
15. *Calvin: Commentaries*, XXIII.88.
16. Calvin, *Institutes*, I.vii.5.

is distorted by sin, there is even more reason to reject the view that divine authority must submit to the scrutiny of human reason. The suggestion that human judgement is distorted by sin is not popular, of course, but it may evoke less indignation if we translate a little. Our judgements are shaped, we might say, by self-interest, by deep-seated prejudices, by cultural assumptions and circumstances that render us insensitive to the plight and the perspectives of others. Likewise, we often read what we want to read in order to confirm our prejudices or to avoid uncomfortable truths. Put this way, we might begin to recognise the wisdom in Calvin's insistence that our human logic is a fickle thing and has no power to stand in judgement over the logic and logos of God. The divine Word sounded in Scripture and made flesh in Jesus Christ ought to be seen as calling into question our cherished assumptions, our vested interests and our reluctance to concede that the world as we see it, may not be the world that is.

For the same reason, the reason of our propensity to interpret Scripture in conformity with our own perspectives and interests, Calvin insists that the assurance of the Spirit given to readers of Scripture does not make the devout and well-meaning individual a hermeneutical authority unto him or herself. The testimony of the Spirit does not license private interpretations. Drawing upon 2 Peter 1:20, Calvin advises that 'it is not godly for [readers of Scripture] to come out with something out of their own heads'.[17] 'We must test doctrines', Calvin says, 'in a twofold way, private and public. By private testing, each one establishes his own faith, and accepts only the teaching which he knows to be from God.'[18] That is to say, individuals must satisfy themselves that interpretations of particular texts, their own or by others, are agreeable with Scripture as a whole. That is the first but not yet sufficient condition of faithful reading. What must follow is that theological claims be publicly tested according to 'the common consent and polity of the church'. In the face of 'fanatical men', 'believers should seek a remedy by coming together and reasoning their way to an honest and godly agreement'.[19] Beyond that, *and above all*, the safeguarding of the church against error rests in the hands of God. 'It is a marvellous work of God', Calvin says, 'that, overcoming all our

---

17. *Calvin: Commentaries*, XXIII.88.
18. *Calvin: Commentaries*, XXIII.87.
19. *Ibid*, XXIII.87–8.

perversity, he makes us of one mind, and unites us together in the pure unity of faith.' This claim too might evoke some incredulity. Are those in the church of one mind, and held together in the pure unity of faith? Our answer may depend on whether or not we think that the gospel has been preserved in the church. Does there exist across the vast diversity of Christian communities a gospel, testified to in Word and Sacrament, which obliges us to recognise one another as a sister in Christ, a brother in Christ, whatever shape our individual perversities may take? Are we agreed, in spite of all else, that in Jesus Christ, God is reconciling the world to Godself? Wherever that gospel is preached and heard and received, there is a unity of faith, sustained by the miracle of God's grace, sustained in spite of all the church's disagreements and disputes. Calvin was very far from being naïve about the fragmentation and disunity of the church, but he could trust nevertheless that despite the perversity of individual Christians, God sees to it that the gospel is not lost; the gospel is preserved and the church survives wherever the Word is truly preached and heard and the sacraments are rightly administered. Wherever that takes place, the sinful remnant of God's people are gathered together in the pure unity of faith.

I have attempted so far to give a brief account of what Calvin takes Scripture to be, namely the word of God which is recognised as such only through the testimony of the Spirit. It is time now to make explicit a further aspect of Calvin's doctrine of Scripture, namely the testimony Scripture gives to Christ. For Calvin, as was evident in his exegetical remarks on Isaiah noted at the beginning of this paper, the whole of Scripture has to do with Christ. He is the Word heard in Scripture, and the one to whom all Scripture points. 'We ought to read the Scriptures', Calvin says, 'with the express design of finding Christ in them.'[20] While Calvin held that the gospel of Jesus Christ is manifest with a great deal more clarity in the New Testament than in the Old,[21] it is the gospel of Christ nevertheless that is conveyed through the law and through the prophets. Calvin maintained, therefore, a very high view of the Old Testament and sternly resisted the likes of

---

20. Commentary on John 5:39 in Calvin, *Commentary on the Gospel according to John*, translated by William Pringle (Edinburgh: The Calvin Translation Society, 1857), 218.
21. See, for example, Calvin, *Institutes*, II.ix.4.

Servetus who regarded the Old Testament as virtually worthless so far as the gospel was concerned.[22] While Calvin said things about the Jews that offend contemporary sensibilities he regarded them, nonetheless, as 'partakers with [Christians] of the same inheritance' and consistently upheld both the divine authority of Israel's Scripture and the continuing importance of the law and the prophets in the drama of God's self-revelation.

Calvin's insistence on this point is both remarkable and instructive, and the implications for Scriptural hermeneutics are profound. Calvin wants to be very clear: 'The covenant of all the fathers [of Israel]', he says, 'is so far from differing substantially from ours that it is the very same; it only varies in the administration.'[23] In explanation of this claim Calvin outlines three principles, the third of which is of most interest here, namely, that the Jews 'both possessed and knew Christ as the Mediator, by whom they were united to God, and became partakers of his promises.'[24] Calvin offers a number of arguments in defence of the view that Israel knew Christ, ahead of time, as it were. 'The whole substance of the [Old Testament covenant] terminates in Christ', he writes. 'Who then dares to represent the Jews as destitute of Christ,—them with whom we are informed the evangelical covenant was made, of which Christ is the sole foundation.'[25]

Calvin does not contend here that the Jews of the Old Testament knew Jesus of Nazareth explicitly, but they understood the logic of the covenant relationship with God and they knew themselves to be a people who were called into being, commissioned and sustained by the Word of God. Therefore, according to Calvin's reasoning, they knew the Word who was to become flesh in Jesus. And that in turn gives license for Christian readers of Israel's Scripture to identify the Word of God in the Old Testament as the very same Word now sounded in Jesus Christ. It is therefore legitimate, theologically, and indeed exegetically, Calvin supposes, to give to the Word of the Lord revealed in the Old Testament the same name by which he identifies himself in the New, that is, the name, Jesus Christ. Kathryn Greene-McCreight thus observes that 'while it would not be entirely accurate

---

22. See *ibid*, II.x.
23. *Ibid*, II.x.2.
24. *Ibid*.
25. *Ibid*, II.x.4.

to say that Calvin believed that Isaiah [for example] predicted Christ in any detail, he clearly did understand Isaiah to preach the gospel about Jesus in advance'.[26]

The so-called servant songs in Deutero-Isaiah are the texts most obviously amenable to Calvin's line of argument. Indeed, in June 1558, Calvin preached a series of seven sermons on Isaiah 52:13–53:12 later published under the title, *Sermons on Isaiah's Prophecy of the Death and Passion of Christ*.[27] Remarkable, in these sermons, once more, is the alacrity with which Calvin interprets Isaiah in explicitly Christological terms. Here is a sample: 'Now the Prophet shows that without the wounds of our Lord Jesus Christ, there is nothing in us but death . . . '[28] Or again, 'This is why the Prophet calls here to each of us and says, "You poor people, Look at what you are until God declared his mercy to you in our Lord Jesus Christ His Son."'[29] A final example among many that might have been chosen illustrates Calvin's confidence that his own Christological reading of Isaiah conforms straightforwardly to the author's intention: 'Even more let us learn that all of our desires are corrupt and that we will look for evil in place of the good until our Lord Jesus Christ corrects and reforms us and until he has placed in us the proper desire to obey Him. This is what the prophet wished to state.'[30] Modern commentators concerned to respect authorial intention (so far as it may be discerned) might struggle with such claims, but I want to suggest, in the time remaining, that there may be more exegetical merit and coherence with authorial intention in Calvin's treatment of Isaiah, for example, than may appear to be the case at face value.

---

26. 'Selections from John Calvin's Sermons on Isaiah translated and introduced by Kathryn Greene-McCreight', in *The Theological Interpretation of Scripture: Classic and Contemporary Readings*, edited by Stephen E Fowl (Cambridge, MA.: Blackwell Publishers, 1997), 186–98, at 187.
27. Greene-McCreight reports that the sermons have been published in two modern English translations: *The Gospel according to Isaiah: Seven Sermons on Isaiah 53 Concerning the Passion and Death of Christ, by John Calvin*, translated by Leroy Nixon (Grand Rapids: Eerdmans, 1953); and *Sermons on Isaiah's Prophecy of the Death and Passion of Christ, by John Calvin*, translated by THL Parker (London: James Clark and Co., 1956). See Greene-McCreight, 'Selections from John Calvin's Sermons on Isaiah', 188.
28. Greene-McCreight, 'Selections from John Calvin's Sermons on Isaiah', 191.
29. *Ibid*, 192.
30. *Ibid*, 194.

In defence of that claim let me begin with Calvin's insistence that the true sense of Scripture is the plain and literal sense, for Calvin's christological reading of Isaiah 53 does not obviously conform to that exegetical advice. We are more likely to be persuaded that the plain and primary sense of the so-called servant song has to do with Israel's situation in exile and the longing for one who will restore Israel's fortunes. Calvin's account of the plain sense of this text is not so plain to us, who have learned to read with an historical-critical eye. But, we must hear Calvin out.

Calvin's appeal to the plain sense of Scripture was directed against the tradition of allegorical reading, going back at least as far as Origen. Commenting on Galatians 4:22, Calvin writes,

> Origen, and many others along with him, have seized this occasion of twisting Scripture this way and that, away from the genuine sense (*a genuino sensu*). For they inferred that the literal sense is too meagre and poor and that beneath the bark of the letter there lie deeper mysteries which cannot be extracted but by hammering out allegories.[31]

A large part of Calvin's suspicion of allegorical readings of Scriptural texts is the high demand made by such readings upon the ingenuity of the reader. Calvin expects God to communicate straightforwardly with his people, making himself understood to the humble rather than imparting his truth in a manner accessible only to the clever.[32] 'The light which shines in [Scripture] comes only to the lowly', he says.[33] Allegorical reading, however, assumes precisely the opposite:

---

31. John Calvin, *The Epistles of Paul The Apostle to the Galatians, Ephesians, Philippians and Colossians*, translated by THL Parker (Grand Rapids: Eerdmans, 1965), 84.
32. In fact, Calvin thinks that all of us stand in need of a simple manner of speech. God 'has lowered himself to the level of our ignorance', he writes. 'When we find God prattling to us in the Bible in an uncultivated and vulgar style, let us remember that he does it for our sake . . . Anyone who cannot bear to lay hold of God as he comes down to him will still less soar up to him beyond the clouds.' Calvin, *Commentaries*, XXIII.90.
33. *Ibid*, XXIII.88.

> For many centuries [Calvin says elsewhere] no man was thought clever who lacked the cunning and daring to transfigure with subtlety the sacred Word of God. But this was undoubtedly a trick of Satan to impair the authority of Scripture and remove any true advantage out of the reading of it. God avenged this profanation with a just judgement when he suffered the pure meaning to be buried under false glosses.[34]

Calvin has no time for flights of exegetical fancy. He is determined to discern the meaning given in Scripture itself and to 'set aside as deadly corruptions, those pretended expositions which lead us away from the literal sense (*a literali sensu*)'.[35]

> Scripture, they say, is fertile and thus bears multiple meanings. I acknowledge that Scripture is the most rich and inexhaustible fount of all wisdom. But I deny that its fertility consists in the various meanings which anyone may fasten to it at his pleasure. Let us know, then, that the true meaning of Scripture is the natural and simple one (*verum sensum scripturae, qui germanus est in simplex*).[36]

We return once more to the problem at hand; how is Calvin's insistence on the plain sense of Scripture to be reconciled with his christological readings of the Old Testament that seem far from being natural and simple. To read Isaiah as referring straightforwardly to Jesus Christ, or to read him as admonishing the church, seems to take us some distance beyond the plain or literal sense—unless Calvin means something different by the plain and literal sense than the mere verbal sense such as a naïve, literal reading might yield. There is abundant evidence in fact, that Calvin does not intend Scripture to be read in a naively literal way. To begin with, Calvin is very clear that the content of Scripture can be understood only under the guidance

---

34. Calvin, *The Epistles of Paul The Apostle to the Galatians, Ephesians, Philippians and Colossians*, 84.
35. *Ibid*, 85.
36. *Ibid*, 84–5.

of the Spirit. 'We should not rush at reading Scripture rashly, trusting our own wits; because the Spirit who has spoken by the prophets is his own interpreter.' The plain sense, then, is not the sense that may be evident to any uninspired and unenlightened reader. It is rather to be understood as the sense disclosed by God, who 'by the light of his Holy Spirit . . .opens an entrance into our hearts for the word . . . which otherwise would only strike the ears and present [itself] to the eyes, without producing the least effect upon the mind'.[37]

Further rejection of a naively literal reading of Scripture is found in Calvin's polemic against the Anthropomorphites who imagined God to be corporeal, because the Scripture frequently ascribes to him a mouth, ears, eyes, hands and feet. Even the 'meanest capacity' Calvin writes, should understand 'that God lisps, as it were, with us, just as nurses are accustomed to speak to infants? Wherefore such forms of expression do not clearly explain the nature of God, but accommodate the knowledge of him to our narrow capacity . . .[38] Clearly the meaning of Scripture transcends, in these instances, what *we moderns* usually mean by the literal sense. Again it is evident that Calvin does not mean, in commending the literal or plain sense, that Scripture makes no use of metaphor or of other figures of speech. We need to pay attention to the subtleties of meaning and truth conveyed by different linguistic techniques. Inspiration by the Spirit does not entail that Scripture's truth is conveyed in a single linguistic or semantic mode.

So far we have learned that the plain sense of Scripture is not evident to us unless we are tutored by the Spirit. We have learned also that preference for the plain and literal sense does not require us to be naïve about how language corresponds quite variously to reality, sometimes, for instance, through metaphor. But an important third indication of what Calvin does and does not mean in commending the plain sense of Scripture is given in the Preface to the *Institutes*. There Calvin explains that,

> . . . my design in this work has been to prepare and qualify students of theology for the reading of the divine

---

37. Calvin, *Institutes*, IV.xiv.8.
38. *Ibid*, I.xiii.1.

words, that they shall have an easy introduction to it, and be enabled to proceed in it without any obstruction. For I think I have given such a comprehensive summary, and orderly arrangement of all the branches of religion, that, with proper attention, no person will find any difficulty in determining what ought to be the principal objects of his research in the Scripture and to what end he ought to refer anything it contains.[39]

The hermeneutical implications of these remarks are far-reaching, not the least of them being that to understand Scripture, to understand the *plain sense* of Scripture, students need to be tutored; they need to be prepared and qualified. Discernment of the plain sense requires something more by way of hermeneutical skill than the mere capacity to read the words on the page and to understand their verbal sense. The reader needs as well a sound appreciation of the scope and content of Christian doctrine. Or, to put it otherwise: in order to understand the plain sense of Scripture the reader needs to know the broad scope of God's creative and redemptive purpose for the world. A systematic exposition of that purpose is precisely what Calvin offers to his reader in the *Institutes of the Christian Religion*. He offers it, let me repeat the point, so that 'students of theology may be prepared and qualified for the reading of the divine words'. Knowledge of the divine economy, from the law and the prophets through to the definitive gift of God's Word in Jesus Christ, is the necessary condition, Calvin suggests, for the reading of Scripture, and the indispensable context for the understanding of Scripture's plain sense.

Although we must be cautious in doing so because, for Calvin, Scripture itself provides the rule of faith, we may suggest here that Calvin's intent in the *Institutes* is to serve readers of Scripture in just the same way that the rule of faith was held to do in patristic exegesis and in much exegesis since. The rule of faith, that is to say, a more or less extensive, confessional, doctrinal summary of God's work in creation and through redemption, provides the conceptual framework within which Scripture can be understood on its own terms, and therefore, rightly.

---

39. Calvin, *Institutes*. I have quoted from the 'Author's Preface' of 1559, but much the same wording appears in the 1536 edition.

We must be clear, however, that Calvin did not wish to *impose* a theological framework upon Scripture; rather the rule of faith is drawn from Scripture itself. There is of course a circularity here, but it is an entirely defensible circularity. It is a matter of common, everyday experience that we understand a thing by attending to its parts, but as well, we understand the parts in light of some conception of the whole. Calvin's Scriptural hermeneutics does not at this point require any special pleading on Scripture's behalf. What is required, however, is some account of the unity of Scripture, some account that enables us legitimately to speak of Scripture as being a singular whole. Without at all denying the rich variety of Scripture, the multiple authorial perspectives and the diversity of insight and conviction represented in the biblical texts, Calvin's hermeneutical strategy clearly requires that the texts of the Christian canon possess a unity more fundamental than the mere fact of their having been bound together in a single book. It did not occur to Calvin to provide an account of this unity in terms that would satisfy our own much greater awareness of the diversity of the biblical texts and the complicated story of their production, redaction and transmission. For us however, I suggest that the unity of Scripture may be defended on two counts, pertaining respectively to what we might call the two natures of Scripture, the human and the divine.

At the level of human authorship we may say that the texts constituting the Christian canon are unified by the intent of their authors to bear witness to the divine economy. In some cases that intent is inferred, while in others it is made quite explicit. Luke provides a paradigmatic example of the latter:

> Since many have undertaken to set down an orderly account of the events that have been fulfilled among us, just as they were handed on to us by those who from the beginning were eyewitnesses and servants of the word, I too decided, after investigating everything carefully from the very first, to write an orderly account for you, most excellent Theophilus, so that you may know the truth concerning the things which you were instructed.[40]

---

40. Luke 1:1–4.

In the Old Testament, the constant refrain as numerous authors offer their account of Israel's story is, 'This is what the Lord did . . . ' or 'Thus says the Lord . . . ' The intent to bear witness to the divine economy, is, at the level of human authorship, then, a unifying feature of the biblical texts. At the same time as they are witnesses to the divine economy, however, the biblical writers may also be understood as instruments of that economy, called forth, and guided in their witness by the Holy Spirit of God. That accords with the view of Scripture set forth in II Timothy 3:16–18, which, of course, Calvin accepts, and that instrumentality is what the church claimed to have recognised in Scripture when it settled upon its canon. On both levels, the human and the divine, an account may thus be given of the unity of the Scriptural texts. If such an account is true, then we have every reason to observe Calvin's principle that Scripture is its own interpreter, and to read the parts of Scripture, the individual texts, in light of the whole. Calvin considers such a principle to be entirely commensurate with the authorial intentions of the Old Testament writers. When Calvin says, after an extensive Christological treatise, that 'this is what Isaiah meant to say', he means simply that Isaiah's teaching, Isaiah's inspired witness to the nature and purposes of God, is, as Calvin puts it, 'understood more fully and shines more brightly now that the gospel has been added to it'.[41]

Returning then to Calvin's account of Scripture's plain sense, the plain sense is the sense that appears in the light of all else we know of the divine economy, all else that we have learned through reading Scripture as a whole. This, I suggest, is the hermeneutical principle underlying Calvin's insistence that we read the Scriptures with the express design of finding Christ in them. God is not duplicitous. He speaks with one voice, and so the Word made flesh, the Word spoken through the Son, is the very same Word who in many and various ways was given to 'our' ancestors by the prophets. It is a claim utterly coherent and reasonable, therefore, that the Word Christians hear sounded in Jesus Christ should also be heard in the prophets Isaiah and Ezekiel and Micah, for example, and in the books of the law as well. That is what Calvin believes and gladly affirms in his exposition of II Timothy. '*All Scripture* is given by the inspiration of God, and is profitable for doctrine, for reproof, for correction [and] for

---

41. Calvin, *Commentaries*, XXIII.86.

instruction in righteousness.' The plain sense of such Scripture is not, we repeat, the sense apparent to anyone who understands the verbal sense of the words. It is the sense apparent to one who has learned the story that Scripture tells, who has been tutored by the Sprit, and who recognises in Jesus of Nazareth the one in and through whom the God of Israel gives himself to be known.

We may not find in modern commentaries, nor be inclined to offer ourselves, a repetition of Calvin's exegetical formulations. But, to return to Barth's point referred to at the beginning of this paper, we do not become true followers of Calvin merely by repeating what he said. We may need to say something very different from Calvin in our own hermeneutical work, but there are, nevertheless, things we may learn through engagement with him. Let me conclude by suggesting one thing in particular that we may learn.

If Scripture is properly described along Calvinist lines as the instrument of God's self-communication; if it is both inspired and illumined by the Spirit, then, as Calvin himself puts it, 'You will never come to it well prepared to read it, unless you bring reverence, obedience, and teachableness with you . . . reverence comes from the knowledge that it is God who speaks to us and not mortal men.'[42] To bring teachableness with you to the reading of Scripture, to bring reverence and obedience, is to come, not with the desire to master the text, but with a readiness to be transformed.

---

42. *Ibid*, XXIII.88.

6

Calvin's Interpretation of Scripture[1]

Randall Zachman

I propose to consider in this chapter the overall framework in which Calvin understands the interpretation of scripture and hopefully draw in some surprising things to tease our imaginations.[2] I have framed this paper in terms of a series of questions. The first question would be, 'By whom is scripture written?' The second question is, 'For whom is scripture written?' And then the third question 'Does God only give Scripture to us, or does God also give us interpreters of Scripture?'.

Let us begin with the first question. In order to interpret a text, Calvin thinks it is important to know who the author is, and so the question is '*by whom is scripture written?*' This seems very straight forward, in that everyone knows that Calvin would say that the author of scripture is God. Indeed, the divine authorship of scripture is a very important principal to which Calvin repeatedly returns. So when he interprets scripture, he is basically interpreting it in light of what God wishes to teach us. Since scripture contains all that God wishes to teach us, the church should study this book together as though it were a school. So it is not surprising that Calvin calls the church the school of Christ, and in fact John Knox described Geneva as the most perfect school of Christ that had ever existed on earth. So, Knox picked up on this idea that the Church is a school, which studies a text and the text that it studies is in fact, scripture. However, Calvin is also aware, as we are now even more so, that people wrote

---

1. This chapter is adapted from the recording of a seminar paper given by Professor Zachman in the Department of Theology and Religion, University of Otago, Dunedin, on 9 September 2009.
2. See Randall C Zachman, *John Calvin as Teacher, Pastor, and Theologian: The Shape of his Writings and Thought* (Grand Rapids, MI: Baker Academic, 2006).

scripture, and the human authors of scripture wrote over a vast period of time, in vastly different historical and cultural contexts and languages. So he takes that fact very seriously, that people are also the authors of scripture. And one of the reasons he takes this seriously is that it shows us how God accommodates God's-self to human capacity in order for us to come to know God. Since God is spiritual and invisible, we could never come to the knowledge of God as temporal creatures, even without sin, if God did not accommodate God's-self to our capacity, and one of the primary ways God does this is by speaking to us through human beings who are just like us. So the authors of scripture are very familiar to us, in fact, in some ways they are overly familiar to us. I mean, everyone has an opinion about Paul, for he has his own distinct personality, as does Moses. So, Calvin takes the human element of scripture very seriously, because in order for God to teach us, God has to use human beings, and so the humanity of the authors of scripture is essential to understanding their message. And so, even though the divine context never recedes from view, the human context is absolutely critical to Calvin, in terms of when they wrote, for whom they wrote, etc. Taking them seriously is taking the divine author seriously. So he will say, 'This is what Moses intended to say, that is, what the Holy Spirit had in mind', so that in his interpretation he will have these two authors in mind.

Another important consideration—and I actually find this to be one of the most interesting things I have discovered in Calvin—is that scripture was not the original form in which the teaching of God found in scripture was delivered. In other words, the doctrine found in scripture was not originally written down. Scripture is the written codification of a prior oral tradition, and a very old oral tradition, at that, one that stems from the oracles delivered directly to the patriarchs in dreams and visions.[3] This is quite unlike Luther, for instance, who insisted against the heavenly prophets, especially Carlstadt, that everyone received doctrine from another human teacher. Luther was very suspicious of this kind of immediate teaching of the Spirit and of visions and oracles. Calvin actually emphasises these phenomena, claiming that they are the foundation of scripture. God originally

---

3. Randall C Zachman, 'Oracles, Visions, and Oral Tradition: Calvin on the Foundation of Scripture', in *Interpretation: A Journal of Bible and Theology* 63/2 (April 2009), 117-129.

revealed heavenly doctrine to the matriarchs and patriarchs by oracles and visions. For instance, in the narratives of Genesis, Abraham heard oracles in dreams and visions, and sometimes he had visions in a dream, as in Genesis 15. Far from being made nervous by such phenomena, Calvin thinks that these visions and dreams actually give divine authority to the oracles that they receive, as is indicated by the statement of God in Numbers 12:6 that he speaks to prophets in visions and dreams, in contrast to Moses, to whom God speaks face to face. Once the patriarchs and matriarchs received these oracles, confirmed as divine by the accompanying visions and dreams, they hand them on orally to others, especially to their children. So the original form of what is taught in scripture is oral tradition, and the source of the oral tradition is the visions and dreams of the patriarchs and matriarchs. Calvin sees the two sources of this oral tradition as being Adam on the one hand and Noah on the other. And you can see why that would be the case: Adam is the source of the tradition of our creation and fall. Thus, when sceptics ask, *'How would Moses know about creation? He was not even there!'* Calvin replies that this comes from an oral tradition that was handed down from Adam through the fathers right down to Moses, and Moses is just writing this tradition down. 'Therefore, we ought not to doubt that the creation of the world, as here described, was already known through the ancient and perpetual tradition of the fathers.'[4] Noah is important because of the deluge and the obliteration of all of humanity except him, and so the tradition from Adam only survived through Noah, and without him that tradition would have been lost. So Noah is a major transmitter of this tradition as well.

The other thing that is interesting to note about this oral tradition that comes to be recorded in scripture is that there are elements of that oral tradition that never got written down. They are handed on orally right through the entire history of Israel, right down to the epistle to the Hebrews. My dear friend Rabbi Michael Singer used to ask me, 'What is the reason for the Christian obsession with Melchizedek?' He would tell me that the Rabbis could not care less about Melchize-

---

4. *Commentary on Genesis Argumentum, Ioannis Calvini opera quae supersunt omnia*, edited by Wilhelm Baum, Edward Cunitz and Eduard Reuss (Brunswick: A Schwetschke and Son (M Bruhn), 1863–1900), Volume 23, 7–8A; henceforth *Opera Calvini* 23:7–8A.

dek, the king and priest of God Most High, who blesses Abram after he defeats the kings who oppressed Lot (Genesis 14:18). But for Christians, he is a central figure, at least for those who give a prominent place to the epistle to the Hebrews, as Calvin did, because Christ is a priest according to the order of Melchizedek, and not of Aaron or the Levitical priesthood. Calvin actually thinks that the insight that Melchizedek is a type of Christ is an oral tradition handed on from the fathers, right through David, who mentions this in Psalm 110: 'You are a priest forever according the order of Melchizedek'. This is the only other time that he is mentioned, before finally showing up in Hebrews, which expands quite a bit on how Melchizedek is a type of Christ. Calvin knows that scripture does not tell us that Melchizedek is a type of Christ. He therefore appeals to an oral tradition to explain how David knew this, and also why this typology appears in Hebrews.[5] In fact, Calvin thinks that an oral tradition taught the Israelites and Jews throughout their history that all of the symbols of the Law symbolised and referred to Christ. 'But since no clear and, as they say, literal evidences of his death and resurrection exist in the Law, there is no doubt that they had teaching handed down from the fathers, from which they learned to refer all figures to Christ.'[6]

The other form of oral tradition that never gets codified in writing regards burial rites. Calvin was fascinated with burial customs, as we can see from the fact that he refused to allow his place of burial to be known. Calvin thought that burial rites apply only to the dispensation of the Law, for they set forth the hope of the resurrection, which has been fully disclosed in Christ. Hence in the Christian dispensation, such burial rites would be a denial of the resurrection of Christ. So the elaborate funereal practices we have, with huge marble monuments and things like that, would be regarded by Calvin with dismay, as being ungodly denials of the resurrection of Christ. On the other hand, patriarchs, Israelites, and Jews observe elaborate burial rites, right on down to the times of John the Baptiser and Jesus, and these for Calvin are all divinely instituted symbols of the resurrection. Burial tells the people yet alive that the one they are burying died in the hope of life beyond death. If you have been to Jerusalem and you have been on the mount of Olives, you will know that that is one of

---

5. *Commentary on Genesis* 14:18, *Opera Calvini* 23:201C.
6. *Commentary on Acts* 26:22, *Opera Calvini* 48:545–6.

the prime places for certain kinds of orthodox Jews to be buried, for they are facing the temple, and hence will be among the first to be raised by the Messiah when he returns. They are buried with their feet facing the temple mount, so that when the Messiah comes, they can rise and face him. So it is very interesting; you would think they would be face-first toward the temple out of reverence, but they are feet first so that they can rise. Calvin knows of the elaborate attention the Jews gave to burial rites, and he also knows about Egyptian burial rites, which are far more elaborate. For Calvin all of this could only be explained by an oral tradition coming from Adam, teaching that burial is a symbol of the resurrection, and is therefore to be practiced with great conscientiousness and reverence. But you never see this in scripture, not even in the New Testament.[7] Burial is never described as a symbol as the resurrection. But every time scripture mentions somebody being buried, Calvin will say, 'Now we know that the rite of burial was a symbol of the resurrection', and we will say, 'Well, how does he know that?' Calvin replies by assuring us, 'This is in oral tradition' and in this case it is an oral tradition that extends from Adam to the time of Christ.

The other element of this is that the oral tradition handed on from Adam and Noah is transmitted to every culture, and not just to the Jews. The oral tradition that comes to be written down in scripture is found in literature outside of scripture, which only makes sense, since in Calvin's view of history every human culture descends from Adam and Noah. In other words, the oral tradition recorded in scripture is ubiquitous. Every culture is transmitting it. The question is how accurately they are transmitting it. For instance, Calvin knew that every culture offers sacrifices to their gods. This practice is not unique to the Jews or to Israel, quite the contrary. 'The custom of sacrificing has always been in use among all nations, and its origin is doubtless to be traced to the ancient fathers.'[8] Indeed, if any people from that time were to be asked to go with us to worship our god, they would wonder why we were not taking them to the local temple to see the offering of sacrifices. If all they saw were pews, a pulpit, and an organ, they would be deeply puzzled, and would ask us, 'Where is the temple?' 'Where is the blood?' 'Where is the fire?' 'Where is the sac-

---

7. Ibid, 9:37, *Opera Calvini* 48:218B.
8. *Commentary on Exodus* 29:38, *Opera Calvini* 24:489.

rifice?' 'Where is the priesthood?' Every culture had a temple, where sacrifices were offered. Every culture offered sacrifices of propitiation for the atonement of sins. Calvin would account for the universality of this practice by claiming that is all comes from the oral tradition handed on from Adam and Noah, the same tradition from which scripture comes. The difference is that the Gentiles practice these things without knowing the purpose of sacrifices, whereas the Jews preserve the whole of the oral tradition in scripture, and hence know that sacrifices are not meaningful in themselves, but only as they refer to the death of Christ. The fact that they offer sacrifices and the fact this practice is ubiquitous reveals to Calvin an oral tradition that goes all the way back to the fathers. Scripture is embedded in an oral tradition that completely surrounds Jewish people. And in that sense scripture is the normative expression of this oral tradition. So the ones that have scripture can look around at these other forms of oral tradition and judge them, as to their adequacy. This is a major reason that Calvin thinks that God wanted this tradition written down by Moses. Calvin thinks that Moses wrote the book of Genesis, along with the four other books of the Pentateuch, on the top of Mount Sinai, at God's dictation, but what God is dictating to him, through the Spirit, is the accurate version of the prior oral tradition. By the time of Moses, so much time had elapsed in the transmission of this tradition that major mistakes or distortions could make their way into it, as we see in the way this tradition is transmitted in the literature outside scripture. 'Yet, since nothing is more easy than that the truth of God should be so corrupted by men, that, in a long succession of time, it should, as it were, degenerate from itself, it pleased the Lord to commit the history to writing, for the purpose of preserving its purity.'[9]

So he interprets scripture in light of this larger tradition surrounding it, and sometimes he cites it approvingly, and sometimes he cites it disapprovingly. For instance, Ovid in the *Metamorphoses* has stories that sound a lot like Lot's wife being turned into a pillar of salt, and Calvin thinks that Satan introduces this story to discredit the reliability of Moses, to make the histories Moses narrates sound like the fables invented by Ovid.[10] This would be an example of the larger tradition being portrayed negatively. But there is another example he

---

9. *Commentary on Genesis Argumentum, Opera Calvini* 23:7–8A.
10. *Commentary on Genesis* 19:26, *Opera Calvini* 23:278B.

gets from Horace having to do with the teaching that the disorder of the natural world is a result of human sin. Calvin says,

> This has been celebrated in poetical fables, and was doubtless handed down, by tradition, from the fathers. Hence that passage in Horace:
>
> > 'When from heaven's fane the furtive hand
> > Of man the sacred fire withdrew,
> > A countless host—at God's command—
> > to earth of fierce diseases flew;
> > And death—till now kept far away—
> > Hastened his step to seize his prey.'[11]

Horace agrees with the teaching of Moses in Genesis, stating that all sorts of awful things evolve on earth, including death, as a result of human sin. But where did Horace learn this? Calvin's answer is that he learned it from the same oral tradition that Moses recorded in scripture. This is a very interesting example of how seriously Calvin takes this tradition. He is always examining the writings outside of scripture to see if there are echoes of this tradition, either confirming or undermining the credibility of the accounts in scripture. This means then, that Calvin interprets scripture within the context of the religious life of the world. Now again, the world got a lot bigger at the beginning of the nineteenth century, with the *Golden Bough* and the discovery of the rich religious traditions of China, India, Africa, and the Americas. But Calvin pursued his knowledge of this wider context as far as he could, because the sacred rites of every culture reflect in their own way the oral tradition from which scripture itself comes, going all the way back to the origin of humanity in Noah and Adam. I think it is very important to appreciate the way Calvin views scripture within this larger context outside of itself. So the author of scripture is God, but the divine source of scripture really comes from oracles and visions, which are then handed on in an oral tradition, which comes to be accurately recorded in scripture, even as it is also less accurately transmitted in non-scriptural traditions.

---

11. *Ibid*, 3:19, *Opera Calvini* 23:75B.

The second question is, '*For whom is scripture written?*' God may be the author of scripture, even as the source of scripture is oral tradition, but for whom is scripture written? This question forms one of the central disagreements Calvin had with the Roman Church. The Roman Church defended its use of images in worship by means of a statement of Gregory the Great, that such images are 'the books of the unlearned'. Gregory was understood to mean by this that since the great majority of Christians could not read, the church told the stories of the faith in paintings, murals, statues, and other images, so that they could 'read' them in this way. Calvin of course knows that the majority of people in his own day cannot read. It is estimated that roughly five per cent of the population of Europe could read any language at the time of Calvin, and only a tiny fraction of these could read Latin, let alone Greek and Hebrew. But Calvin insists that Gregory the Great and the Roman Church are wrong: images are not the books of the unlearned, rather scripture is the book of the unlearned. Scripture adapts its method of teaching so that it can be understood by the most unlettered, unlearned person. The replacement of scripture with images is responsible for two of the major problems created by the Church of Rome: first, they took scripture away from the very people for whom it is written; and second, they led the people into idolatry by placing images in places of worship. Why did they not teach their people how to read the book that God had written specifically to teach them? Why did they not guide them in their reading of that book? Why did they leave them illiterate, so that they couldn't read the book that was written specifically for them? The dedication and tireless energy Calvin exhibited in trying to return scripture to its rightful audience is truly humbling. I remember the effect it had on me when I first discovered how important this issue was for him. Here I was, a scholar in a major university, writing learned articles and books for other learned scholars of the Reformation, which is a very small community. And then I discover that the man I was studying in this learned way to impress the elites of the scholarly world worked tirelessly to help to teach the unlearned how to read scripture for themselves, so that they might profit from its instruction. It was very embarrassing to me to discover this, and my chagrin became even worse when I imagined putting in my curriculum vitae anything like the objective Calvin set for himself. Imagine my saying, 'In my writing and teaching I seek to edify the most unlearned, uneducated, unlettered people, and it is them alone whom I serve'. I would be scorned, and would never be either hired or promoted! And if I boasted that I considered myself to have most succeeded when the most unlearned person understood what I said, I would be laughed out of the room! But that is how Calvin understood his work. If scripture is written for the unlearned, and I am not teaching the unlearned how to read it, then I am a catastrophic failure'. Now Calvin knows that he cannot reach that audience directly, at least as a teacher, because he seeks to train pastors to be faithful guides of their unlearned congregations, teaching them how to read scripture for themselves, so they might apply it to their lives. These pastors must be learned, for they have to read scripture in its original languages, and must be well versed in the principles of sound theology and doctrine. But they must use all their skill and knowledge to aid the unlearned members of their congregations, who can at best read scripture in a vernacular translation, and who know at best the sum of doctrine in the catechism. This creates a bit of tension, as Calvin thinks that it takes quite a bit of learning to become a teacher of the unlearned, and you do then get a strong dichotomy between a very learned pastor and the rest of the congregation. But the pastor is to dedicate all his efforts towards eradicating that dichotomy as much as possible, and he must never forget that scripture is the book of the unlearned, and scripture therefore has the objective of reaching the lives of everyone, of every person.

The other thing to be said about scripture is that it is accommodated to the capacities of people as they develop over time. Calvin has a very interesting notion, which he gets from Irenaeus of Lyons and the apostle Paul, that the human race develops over time. We start out at the most rude, untaught, and infantile level, which is reflected in Genesis, and then the human race in general, and the Jews in particular, develops its capacities over time. God intentionally adjusts the teaching of scripture to the capacities of the human race as these develop over time. Unfortunately for us, we have only reached the level of adolescence now, even after Christ has come, and must wait for the Last Day to reach full adulthood. So the New Testament is adapted to the capacities of teenagers, whereas the Hebrew Scriptures are adapted to lesser capabilities. But the human race develops over time, and it does actually become more mature. So when one says that scripture is the book of the unlearned, this is not to say that everyone is at the same level of unlearnedness all the way through. There is an increase in our capacity to be taught, and God adjusts God's teaching in order to be able to reach people at the level at which they are found. This strikes me as a very clever way of answering the objection of Marcion and others, who point out that the way God is represented in Genesis and Exodus is really different than the way God is represented in the preaching of Jesus and Paul. Marcion explained these differences by saying that they were describing two different gods, one who delights in punishing, and the other who delights in showing mercy. Sadly, most Christians still say that there are two different gods. If you ask a Christian, 'Who is the God who will smite you in wrath or hurl you into the sea? Who is that God?' they will say, 'That is the Old Testament God'. And if you ask them, 'Who is the God who loves and forgives?' they will say, 'That is the New Testament God'. And they say this quite easily and calmly, without realizing that they have told you that there are two distinct gods! So our use of 'the Old Testament God' and 'the New Testament God' is a reflection of the point made by Marcion, to which Calvin strenuously objected. But he is trying to account for the evidence cited by Marcion that God really does seem to change the way he works with people over time.

For Calvin, such change reflects God's accommodation to the changing capacities of the people over time, and not a change in God. Since human capacities change over time, God's method of teaching has to change over time. This insight is absolutely central to Calvin's interpretation of scripture and the way he applies the meaning of scripture. God adjusts the teaching of scripture to the capacities of the people whom God is teaching. In particular, God accommodates the teaching to the capacity of the Jewish people throughout their history, primarily by teaching them in earthly, temporal, and visible symbols about spiritual, eternal, and invisible realities. On the one hand, God really does convey God's grace and blessing to the Israelites in these symbols, even as God also points the Israelites to the coming of Christ, in whom all of these symbols have their full meaning. All of the symbols of the Law are expressions of God's love in themselves, even as they also point to the coming reality of Christ. So the land of Israel that is promised to Abraham is a genuine blessing of God, even as it is also a shadow and type of the kingdom of

Christ. David really is a king in whom the salvation of the people is secured, even as he is also a shadow and type of Christ the King yet to come. All of these symbols reveal the blessing of God and the person of Christ in accommodation to the capacities of the Jewish people. This accommodated self-manifestation of God holds the whole story together for him, in a way that accounts for the discontinuities noted by Marcion. And so Calvin is very frustrated, on the one hand, with Christians who reduce the meaning of every symbol in Israel to Christ, with Origen being the worst in this regard. This reminds me of a joke about a children's sermon, in which the pastor asks the children seated in front of her, 'What is brown and furry and has a fluffy tail, and lives in trees, and gathers nuts?' Tommy eagerly raises his hand, and when she calls on him, he says, 'It sounds like a squirrel, but I know it is Jesus!' This is the problem Calvin has with Origen and those like him: it looks like the Temple, but it is really Jesus; it looks like David, but he is really Jesus. Calvin insists to the contrary that every symbol contains a blessing in its own right, even as it also points to the fullness of its meaning in Christ. This means that you have to take the history of Israel seriously in its own right, as having its own legitimate theological meaning, even as you also follow this history to the coming of Christ, in whom it is fulfilled. So he has an Origen-like moment when he ascends to Christ by analogy and anagoge, but he does not want us to ignore the ways that God taught the Israelites throughout their history. For instance, Calvin insists that the return of the Jews from Babylon is itself a symbol of God's grace and love, even as it is also joined to the advent of Christ. He disagreed with Christian interpreters who refer the return directly to Christ:

> For it is not necessary nor expedient to introduce an anagogical sense, as interpreters are wont to do, by representing the return of the people as symbolical of what was higher, even of the deliverance that was effected by Christ; for it ought to be considered as one and the same favor of God, that is, that he brought back his people from exile, that they might at length enjoy quiet and solid happiness when the kingdom of David should again be established.[12]

---

12. *Commentary on Jeremiah* 33:17–18, *Opera Calvini* 39:71B.

He says that David is begotten as the Son of God when God reveals his kingship to Israel and Judah, even though this declaration ultimately points to the revelation of Christ in his resurrection. The symbols have meaning in their own historical context, even as they also refer to the coming of Christ.

This also means that each epoch has its own unique form of teaching that cannot be repeated. For instance, Abraham could offer a sacrifice wherever he felt like it, as when he offers sacrifice under the oaks at Mamre out of gratitude to the Lord. However, when God reveals the Law to Moses, this kind of freedom comes to an end. Once the tabernacle is built, sacrifices can only be offered there, and once the priesthood is initiated, sacrifices can only be offered by them, according to the forms of instruction delivered to Moses on Sinai. If you violate these ordinances, you can wind up dying, as Eli and his sons discovered. Once the tabernacle and priesthood are instituted, you cannot go back and offer sacrifice the way Noah or Abraham did. Similarly, once the temple is built, the priests are not supposed to offer sacrifices at any site than in Jerusalem, even though previously the sites of Bethel and Shiloh had been considered holy in this regard. So all the holy sites of the Northern Kingdom are off limits now, as is reflected in the statement in Deuteronomy that sacrifice may only be offered in Jerusalem. Once Christ is crucified, the practice of sacrifice must come to an end, even though it was rightly being offered in the temple the day before he died. This is how Calvin interprets the saying of Jesus before he died, 'It is finished'. Calvin thinks Jesus is telling us that the symbols of the law have now come to an end, and there is no going back. So each epoch has its own form of practice and teaching that is unique to it, and you cannot go back and you cannot go forward. You cannot pretend that the temple is built when it is not, and once it is built you cannot act the way you did before it existed. Once Christ is crucified, you cannot pretend that did not happen either. Just because it is written in scripture does not mean that it applies to you. We of course do this all the time, often in the name of Calvin. 'I find this teaching in scripture, and scripture is the word of God, because God is the author of scripture. Therefore this teaching applies directly to me by divine authority.' Calvin would reply, 'No, this teaching applies to Jews before the time of the temple, and it does not apply directly to you, or even to the time of the temple itself'. This is one of his chief criticisms of the Roman Church, for they have a priesthood that offers a repeated sacrifice on an altar, and so try to go back to the time before the coming of Christ, thereby implicitly proclaiming that Christ has not yet come. Priesthood, altar, and sacrifice may be found throughout scripture, but only before Christ died. Once Christ died, he both fulfilled all sacrifices and brought them to an end, so we cannot continue these practices any more, even though they are clearly taught by God in scripture. I find this limitation of the scope of the application of scripture to be a very interesting theme in Calvin, and one that is not always appreciated by those who cite him in support of the divine authority of scripture. The teaching of scripture is accommodated to the capacities of a certain people at a certain time, and this context must always be kept in mind. The teaching of a given passage of scripture may be limited to the time in which it was taught and people to whom it was taught, and that applies even within the history of Israel. So the audience of scripture is the unlearned, but the unlearned develop their capacities over time, and you have to take that accommodation of teaching very seriously, with great sensitivity to historical context.

The third question is, '*Is scripture enough?*' One hears the phrase '*sola scriptura*', 'scripture alone', consistently applied to Calvin as though it is a first principle of his theology. Yet Calvin would never agree with that phrase, and never follows it in his own theological thinking. I have never seen that phrase in Calvin's writing, and it makes absolutely no sense to me. Calvin is adamant that you can never just have scripture, and the church can never have scripture alone, for we need guides and interpreters who will lead us into the right interpretation of scripture. Such guides and interpreters are essential to the life of the church. This is where Calvin acknowledges the legitimacy of the point many Roman opponents of Luther made against his appeal to scripture, claiming that God never wanted scripture to be transmitted without the teaching of the church clarifying its meaning. Calvin agrees. So his basic argument with Rome is not scripture alone versus scripture and interpreters; rather, it is a question of who the godly interpreters are and where they are to be found? Who are the reliable interpreters? With what other interpreters are they in continuity? In other words, Calvin insists that scripture is not enough. There is an episode in Acts 8 which nicely illustrates this point for Calvin. The Ethiopian eunuch is riding back from Jerusalem, and Phillip is sent by the Holy Spirit to him. As he comes up to the carriage, he hears the eunuch reading aloud. It was the practice back then that people would read aloud because to read privately was a very selfish thing to do. If you had a book, you read it for everyone so that they could hear what you were reading. So the eunuch is reading aloud from the prophet Isaiah. When Phillip approaches him, he asks him, 'Do you understand what you are reading?' The eunuch answers, 'How can I, unless somebody guides me?' So Phillip guides him in his reading of the prophet, and this leads the eunuch to ask Phillip to baptise him. In light of this event, Calvin points out that God not only gives us scripture, but also gives us interpreters to guide us. And so for Calvin that is a beautiful example of the life of the church. Even if you are reading scripture yourself, you will not understand what you are reading unless somebody guides you. 'And we must keep in mind here, that not only is scripture given to us, but interpreters and teachers are also added to help us.'[13] Hence his argument with Rome was, 'who are the guides?' and 'how do they guide people?' But they both agreed on the need for the church to offer interpreters to Christians to guide them in their reading of scripture. I think this is quite significant, as it avoids the false dichotomy created by the slogan '*sola scriptura*'.

Calvin claims that the rightly ordered church has two levels of guides: teachers and pastors. The teachers teach pastors, the pastors teach congregations. I think that Calvin is badly misunderstood when we read what he wrote for one audience as thought it were written for another audience. We can see Calvin's awareness of the different audiences in light of his desire to have some of his works published, and his reluctance to have other works published. Calvin wrote his *Institutes* and his commentaries on scripture in Latin as a teacher, and he wanted them published everywhere, because as a teacher he is teaching pastors throughout the Catholic Church (which he sharply distinguished from the Roman Church). So as a teacher, he teaches pastors and other teachers everywhere. Calvin wanted his works to be read in Italy, France, England, Scotland, Hungary, Poland, Germany, and the Netherlands, and he wrote them in Latin so that they could be. But his sermons were preached in his office as pastor, and were

---

13. *Commentary on Acts* 8:31, *Opera Calvini* 48:192B.

delivered only in French, and hence were for the congregation in Geneva on the day in which they were delivered, and he never wanted them published. He was initially opposed to the idea his friends had of developing shorthand to take down his sermons verbatim, so that they could be published as widely as his other writings. He eventually agreed to this plan, but over his own protest, because Calvin thought that the pastor only has a responsibility to teach his own congregation, and is not called to teach those outside his congregation. He is not preaching to England; he is preaching to Geneva on 10 April 1551. It is interesting that he was so clear in his own mind about the different audiences he had in his different offices. We need to keep this distinction in mind when we read him.

What I will consider now is what the teachers need to do as interpreters of scripture, but it is important to keep in mind that the unlearned are reached primarily by pastors, and so the formation that I am talking about will be the formation of pastors as teachers of the congregation. But the ultimate goal, as I said earlier, is the formation of the congregation of the unlearned by the pastors themselves. Calvin really did think about how to organise a church that would actually hit the target at which he aimed. Most of the attention will be on Calvin's work as a teacher of other pastors, but these other pastors are in fact to teach their own congregations. Moreover, Calvin thought that Paul's statement in Acts 20:20, that he taught both in public and from house to house, was a better description of the work of the pastor than that which focuses on public preaching alone. Calvin was quite critical of those pastors who thought that once they had preached a sermon they were done with their work. The interpretation of scripture is supposed to be applied to each individual in the congregation, and this can only be done by going house to house. Preaching a sermon in public worship is like throwing seed in the wind, you have no idea what the results might be in peoples' lives. The interpretation of scripture takes root when you go into their kitchen and talk to them about the way their life is relating to the message of scripture right now, 'for general teaching will often have a cold reception, unless it is helped by advice given in private'.[14] That is going to be different in this house than it will be next door. It will be different with the mother than with the father; it will be different with

---

14. *Ibid*, 20:20, *Opera* **Calvini** 48:462.

the children than with the parents. Calvin thinks pastors are kidding themselves when they think, 'I have just preached a great sermon! My job is now done, and I will go home now and leave everyone alone.' You have to visit, you have to know your people individually, and you have to apply scripture to the context of their lives, house to house. So that is an indication of how concretely he wanted the meaning of scripture to be applied to life. But Calvin's most interesting insights regarding the interpretation of scripture come when he is acting in the office of teacher.

The first thing that the teachers have to know is the writings of classical antiquity. They have to know the writings of pagans. We already alluded to this when we spoke of the oral tradition of the fathers. Now we have to consider scripture as the book of the unlearned in the context of the writings of the learned. Calvin knew the writings of Cicero, Plato, Aristotle, Pliny, Virgil, Ovid, Horace, and countless other classical authors, and committed much of what they wrote to memory, for these are the writings of the learned, and if you want to be a teacher you have to know this literature. A learned person was someone who could recognise an allusion to Plato without having to look it up in the footnotes. In fact, a learned person in Calvin's day would find our practice of footnoting to be insulting, as though they could not recognise Homer when you alluded to him. And so for Calvin in order to be a teacher, and in order to be a pastor, you have to know all of the literature of classical antiquity, which was all written by pagans, because these are the books of the learned, and to be a learned teacher, you have to know them. The fact that scripture is the book of the unlearned does not eliminate the need to know the books of the learned, and these are of great value, even when they teach things in a very different way than does scripture. Calvin's favourite example of this phenomenon is astronomy. Moses calls the moon the second great light, but Calvin knows from the writings of the learned astronomers that actually Saturn is much bigger than the moon. But Calvin sees no contradiction here, because Moses was writing in a homely style accommodated to the unlearned, whereas the astronomers are writing for the learned. 'Here lies the difference; Moses wrote in a popular style things which without instruction, all ordinary persons, endued with common sense, are able to understand; but astronomers investigate with great labour whatever the sagacity of the human mind can comprehend."[15] Far from condemning the latter, Calvin commends it for marvelously unfolding the wisdom of God, even though it describes the world very differently than scripture. In fact, Calvin is convinced that Moses and all the prophets, including David, were students of Babylonian and Egyptian astronomy, but they did not set forth this learning in scripture, because they are teaching the unlearned. So for Calvin, the books and writings of the learned are essential for teachers to know, and he insists that they ultimately come from the same Spirit from which scripture comes. I love that thought. To neglect this gift of antiquity, which we call the liberal arts, is to despise the Holy Spirit. So you cannot reject the writings of the learned pagans for the sake of the unlearned for whom scripture is written, which is a thought that lives on in our day. Calvin would disagree, insisting that even though scripture is for the unlearned, the teachers and guides need to know the writings of the learned. Therefore future pastors and teachers need to study rhetoric, history, astronomy, anatomy, zoology, medicine, agriculture, etc., in order to interpret scripture. Otherwise, when scripture will refer to constellations, or birds, or fish, you will have no idea how to interpret those passages, and will simply make something up that has no basis in the way things really are. Calvin has some very caustic, nasty things to say about the rabbis, because the rabbis demonstrate no familiarity with Xenophon, Pliny, Livy, and Aristotle! Isn't that stunning? But this is how important this knowledge is for him if you want to be a teacher. If you do not know Aristotle, then you cannot interpret Amos, because Amos speaks of the One who made the Pleiades and Orion. Calvin says that Amos does not speak as an astronomer, but according to the common notions of his age shared by the unlearned. Nonetheless, Calvin says,

> There is no need of labouring much about such names; for the Jews, ignorant of the liberal sciences, cannot at this day certainly determine what stars are meant; and they show also their complete ignorance as to herbs. They are indeed bold enough; they define what every word means; but yet they betray, as I have said, their own want of knowledge.[16]

---

15. *Commentary on Genesis* 1:16, *Opera Calvini* 23:23.
16. *Commentary on Amos* 5:8, *Opera Calvini* 43:77A.

Calvin is quite upset by how ignorant the rabbis are of birds. He thinks that the rabbis make up fables about partridges and eagles because they do not know the writings of Pliny and Aristotle. Thus, when Jeremiah speaks of a partridge which sits on eggs but does not hatch them, Calvin says,

> The Rabbis, according to their practice, have devised fables; for they imagine that the partridge steals all the eggs of other birds which she can find, and gathers them into one heap; and then that the pullets, when hatched, fly away, as by a certain hidden instinct, they understand that it is not their mother. But neither Aristotle nor Pliny say any such thing of partridges. They indeed say that the bird is full of cunning, and mention several instances; but they refer to no such thing as that the partridge collects thus stealthily its eggs. These things then are fables, which it would be very absurd to believe. But it is said of partridges with one consent, by Aristotle and Pliny, as well as by others, that it is a very lustful bird.[17]

So the liberal arts are essential for interpreting what scripture is saying, even in terms of its metaphors. But Calvin also wants teachers to know this literature for its own sake, for it tells us the way the world actually works much more accurately than does scripture. If you want to learn astronomy, do not read scripture, read the writings of the learned astronomers, for these writings strengthen piety, because they unfold the wisdom and power of God revealed in the universe. So you have to know the writings of classical antiquity in order to be a teacher. One reason he has no respect for the rabbis is that they lack this kind of training. As awful as his remarks about the Jews are to us, they certainly reveal the high value he ascribed to such knowledge. This would also include the histories and poems of classical antiquity, which we noted when we spoke of the oral tradition surrounding scripture.

The other thing you need to know to be a reliable interpreter is a summary of true and pious doctrine. Otherwise, you will not know what to look for when you read scripture, for you will be ignorant of

---

17. *Commentary on Jeremiah* 17:11, *Opera Calvini* 38:272B.

the major topics for which you should be looking. Once again we see that scripture is not enough—we need a guide to tell us what the major topics of scripture are that we should be seeking out in our reading. Unless a teacher tells you what to look for in the Bible, you will not know what to look for yourself, and will likely get lost soon after you begin reading. Calvin thought that Melanchthon had provided such guidance in his *Loci communes* of 1543, and even translated this volume into French in 1546. And Calvin offers his own guidance to the reading of scripture in the various editions of his *Institutes*. In this work, Calvin sets forth the major topics that are taught in scripture so that the reader might have access to the meaning of scripture. All of the major topics in the *Institutes* are to function in this way, such as the knowledge of God and the knowledge of ourselves, the knowledge of God the Creator and the knowledge of God the Redeemer, Christ first revealed to the fathers in the Law and then revealed to us in the Gospel, etc. Calvin contrasts the efforts of godly teachers with those works that led people away from the central topics of scripture, especially the *Sentences* of Peter the Lombard; and this problem is compounded by the scholastics who comment on Lombard. It is interesting to note, however, that ever since Alexander of Hales, the scholastics thought that you could not be an interpreter and teacher of scripture if you did not first comment on Lombard's *Sentences*, which set forth the major topics of church teaching such as the Trinity, Christology, the sacraments, and the last things. Calvin agrees with this idea in principle, but insists that Lombard and those who followed him did an inadequate job, whereas teachers like himself and Melanchthon have done a more reliable job. But Calvin agrees with the scholastic theologians that in order to interpret scripture you need a handbook, a summary of right teaching. The *Institutes* are offered to future pastors to meet this need.

The next thing you need is to read other interpreters of scripture, from the very beginning of the church to your own day. You need to know the history of the interpretation of scripture. We have noted how you already need to know Greek and Latin to read the classical authors such as Virgil and Homer, but now you need Latin and Greek to read the early interpreters of scripture such as Augustine and Chrysostom, Ambrose and Basil the Great. Calvin was especially impressed by the interpretation of John Chrysostom. He thought that

Chrysostom was the best of the interpreters from the period, especially in the interpretation of the Greek New Testament, because he sought above all else to unfold the simple, natural, and genuine meaning of scripture. Calvin thought that Augustine was the best teacher of the early church, but even when Augustine gets the right teaching out of scripture, Calvin thinks that he twists scripture to derive this meaning. Calvin frequently accuses Augustine of twisting scripture with refined philosophical speculations, so he prefers to follow the method of interpretation found in Chrysostom.

You also need to know Hebrew, not only to read the Hebrew Scriptures, but also in order to read the interpretations of the Rabbis. Calvin always lines up the interpretations of the Rabbis with those of the Greek and Latin fathers, and often sides with the Rabbis over against the fathers, especially when he thinks the latter force scripture too hard to derive a Christological reference or proof. This habit of Calvin's led a Lutheran named Hunnius to accuse Calvin after his death of being a 'Judaizer', and to make his case he showed where Calvin agreed with the Jews against the Christian interpreters with regard to the meaning of passages that had traditionally been interpreted as proving the Trinity and the divine and human natures of Christ. Hunnius rightly points out that Calvin will not only side with the Jews against the fathers, but will also claim that the uses of scripture in the New Testament are not interpretations, but are rather adaptations of the message in a loose way to the issue the apostles are addressing. Calvin's willingness to fault the fathers and correct the apostles led Hunnius and others to think that Calvin was undermining the Christian faith out of sympathy for the Jews.[18] This is how seriously Calvin was seen to take the tradition of Jewish interpretation. It is not clear whether Calvin read Rabbinic sources for himself, or whether he used Christian sources that engaged Rabbinic interpretations, but it is clear that he took this tradition of interpretation as seriously as he took the Greek and Latin fathers. So in addition to summaries of pious doctrine, you have to know Greek to read the Greek fathers as well as Greek classical literature; you have to read Latin to read the Latin fathers as well as Latin classical literature; and you have to know

---

18. G Sujin Pak, *The Judaizing Calvin: Sixteenth Century Debates over the Messianic Psalms* (Oxford: Oxford University Press, 2009).

Hebrew to read the Hebrew Bible as well as the Jewish interpreters of the Hebrew Bible. This is already quite a demanding list of skills.

This leads us to speak of the goal of interpretation, which Calvin conceives of as 'revealing the mind of the author'. The sound interpreter reveals to the reader what the author in question had in mind when he or she wrote, and what he intended to say. All of the issues about which we have spoken—the accommodation of scripture to the unlearned capacities of the audience, the different authors of scripture, the summary of doctrine in the *Institutes*, the engagement with the interpretations of others—are all meant to aim at the target of proper interpretation, which is to reveal the mind of the author. So the interpreter must ask himself, 'What did Moses have in mind when he wrote Genesis? What was he trying to do in this book?' The same question would be asked of the apostle Paul. 'What did Paul have in mind when he wrote his letter to the Galatians? What did he want to address? What did he hope to accomplish?' Calvin thinks that when you write something, you are trying to do something, you have something in mind that you are trying to teach your audience, and you are trying to affect something in the audience that is reading your work. In order to learn what the author had in mind, you need to know who the person was who wrote the text, where the person wrote it, what the circumstances were at the time at which they wrote, and what was going on with the intended audience at the time when they wrote. In other words, you have to know the context, and you have to know the situation; you have to know the circumstances. Calvin is convinced that the mind of the author is naturally and simply revealed by the context. So the goal of the interpreter is to reveal what the author had in mind, and in order to know what the author had in mind, the interpreter has to know the context in which the author wrote. So you have to know the historical context, you have to know the situation, you have to know the goal they where trying to reach and you hold that goal before the reader at the beginning of your interpretation.

Thus, at the beginning of every commentary, Calvin would provide the reader with what he called the '*argumentum*' of the book. This sets forth to the reader Calvin's understanding of the context of the work, as well as its goal and objective, so that the reader knows the target at which to aim before even beginning the commentary proper.

He tells the reader of his Genesis commentary that there are five major topics for which to look in reading the text, which Moses had in mind when he wrote the book. He even provides an '*argumentum*' for each of the one hundred and fifty psalms in his psalm commentary. Calvin is frustrated, as you can imagine, if he cannot figure out who the author was, when they were writing, or what the circumstances were. Psalm 79 is a great case in point. The lack of prophets points to a context during the second temple period, likely the persecutions under Antiochus IV Epiphanes. But the burning of the temple suggests the period of the Babylonian exile. The psalm could be interpreted in either context, even though Calvin thinks it is most probable that it was written in the second temple period. He also wants to know if David or someone else wrote the psalm, or if Solomon took something David said on his deathbed and rendered it into a poem, which is how he interprets Psalm 72. So even within each of the psalms, you have different objectives to hold before the reader.

You also need to know the linguistic milieu of the text. Hebrew works differently from Greek and Greek works differently from Latin. So if you are trained in Greek or Latin eloquence, you are going to think that certain Hebrew phrases are barbaric, with all its repetitions and parallelisms. Such devices sound very awkward and inappropriate to a Greek or Latin mind, but to the Hebrew mind they represent eloquence. For instance, he notes that the phrase, 'You have abhorred and rejected him',

> . . . if criticised according to the rules of the Greek and Latin language, will be pronounced inelegant; for the word which is most emphatic is put first, and then there is added another which is less emphatic. But as the Hebrews do not observe our manner of arrangement in this respect, the order here adopted is quite consistent with the idiom of the Hebrew language.[19]

So you have to immerse yourself in three ancient linguistic worlds, as well as a fourth, French, because you are going to be preaching to people in French. The teacher and pastor therefore needs the ability to take a statement from Hebrew to Latin to French, and in some

---

19. *Commentary on Psalms* 89:38, *Opera Calvini* 31:826C.

instances from Hebrew to Greek to Latin to French, because Calvin also uses the Septuagint as a way of trying to arrive at accurate translations of Hebrew words and phrases. So Calvin expects his readers to be immersed in several ways of thinking and speaking, Hebraic, Greek, and Latin, as well as their native French.

You also have to keep in mind the cultural context of the text. For instance Calvin is a Frenchman, and as such his sense of decorum requires that we express our emotions with considerable reserve. However, he knows that in scripture people are often represented as expressing their emotions in ways that the French would judge to be inappropriately excessive. He asks his readers to keep in mind that people in warmer climates are less moderate in their emotional expressions than are people from colder climates, 'for these nations, having much greater warmth of temperament than we have who inhabit cold countries, display a greater vehemence in gesture, deportment, dress, and other outward signs'.[20] We can still see something of what he means today. If somebody dies violently in South Bend, Indiana, we do not flood the streets with people chanting and carrying the casket through the street; but if somebody dies violently in the Middle East, the casket is carried through the street, and people show their grief by hitting themselves on the head and pulling their hair. Calvin reminds his readers not to judge such expressions of emotion by cultural standards that do not belong to the context, but rather to be sensitive to the way different cultures express themselves. What would be appropriate in France or Geneva would seem quite cold in the Middle East.

Finally, you have to be able to tell what forms of expression are being used. Is this hyperbole, or is this irony? Is this metaphorical, or is it symbolic? Is this personification, or is this anthropomorphism? The meaning of the statement will change depending on the decision you make, and the best interpretation will flow most smoothly with the context, both in terms of its immediate literary context, and in terms of the context of the whole document. Of course the most famous decision Calvin made in this regard was to view the statement of Christ, 'This is my body' as being metonymy, where the sign is given the name of the reality signified. This decision of interpretation led to one of the most tragic divisions in the evangelical movement,

---

20. *Commentary on Isaiah* 36:22, *Opera Calvini* 36:614–15.

because the Lutherans attacked this interpretation relentlessly in the latter part of Calvin's life. The Lutherans insisted that the words must be taken at face value, without any interpretation, but Calvin could not imagine this ever being the case. Every statement of scripture is interpreted, including this one. This is simply unavoidable.

The interpreter uses all of these skills—historical, linguistic, and cultural—to let the meaning of the author emerge simply, naturally, and genuinely from the context. Once you know how the Hebrew or Greek mind works, once you know the circumstances in which the author was working, once you know the audience he was trying to address, once you place the text in its proper context, the mind of the author will reveal itself to you, which is the ultimate goal of interpretation. We can see the kind of interpretation Calvin valued by means of the contrasts he draws between good and bad interpretation. Good interpretation flows from the context, whereas bad interpretation is forced. Good interpretation is simple, whereas bad interpretation is overly refined. Good interpretation is natural, whereas bad interpretation twists the text to derive its meaning. Good interpretation arrives at a meaning which is edifying, whereas bad interpretation derives a meaning which is frigid. Good interpretation reveals the genuine meaning, whereas bad interpretation sets forth fables and dreams. Good interpretation is solid, whereas bad interpretation offers baseless conjectures and speculations. All of these goals reinforce one another, so that one can have an interpretation that appears to be natural, simple, solid, and genuine, but if it is cold, then another meaning must be sought. The right interpretation hits your affections as well as your intellect, and is edifying, so a frigid interpretation must be incorrect. This shows the pastoral goal of all interpretation of scripture; for the teacher is teaching future pastors how to interpret scripture for their own congregations, so that every member of the congregation may learn how to read scripture responsibly for herself, so that she can apply the genuine meaning of scripture to her life.

Part II

The Legacy and the Caricature

7
Thomas Chalmers and Scottish Calvinism in the Nineteenth Century

John Roxborogh

Introduction

This paper discusses the contribution of the Evangelical leader Thomas Chalmers (1780–1847)[1] to the theological and social understanding of Calvinism in Scotland in the era prior to and following the Free Church Settlement in Otago, New Zealand in 1848. It also considers the congruence of his attitudes with general cultural factors contributing to the passing of the Declaratory Acts by the Uniting Presbyterians in 1879[2] and the Free Church of Scotland in 1892[3] which liberalised the terms of subscription to the 1646 Westminster Confession. The Synod of Otago and Southland in New Zealand passed similar legislation in 1893.[4]

It is a commonplace comment that Calvin and Calvinism should not be confused. By the early nineteenth century in Scotland the term 'Calvinism' referred less to the teaching of Calvin himself than to the doctrine of predestination in general and of the Westminster Confession of Faith in particular.[5] The central role of the Confession in the

---

1. John Roxborogh, *Thomas Chalmers Enthusiast for Mission: The Christian Good of Scotland and the Rise of the Missionary Movement* (Edinburgh: Rutherford House, 1999), 38–65, 228–42. See also Stewart Brown, *Thomas Chalmers and the Godly Commonwealth in Scotland* (Oxford, UK: Oxford University Press, 1982).
2. Ian Hamilton, *The Erosion of Calvinist Orthodoxy: Seceders and Subscription in Scottish Presbyterianism* (Edinburgh: Rutherford House, 1990).
3. James Lachlan MacLeod, *The Second Disruption: The Free Church in Victorian Scotland and the Origins of the Free Presbyterian Church* (East Linton, Scotland: Tuckwell Press, 2000).
4. In America some Presbyterians rewrote parts of the Confession, but in Scotland and New Zealand it was felt to be easier to change the relationship of ministers and elders to the Confession than to change the Confession itself.
5. Including in the writings of George Hill (1750–1819), Professor of Divinity at

polity and discipline of the Church of Scotland, as among the 'Seceders' who broke away from it in the eighteenth century, contributed to this association. Scottish historical interest focussed on their own religious heroes, John Knox, Andrew Melville and the Covenanters even if the substantial debt to John Calvin was acknowledged. Although Calvinism has continued to be used as an imprecise and frequently negative catch-all phrase for forms of Scottish theology presumed to be old and strict, if not tyrannical, inquisitorial and relentlessly deterministic, over time the assumption that Calvinism equated to predestination and that predestination was central to Scottish Presbyterian theology weakened. Although determinism was recognised as a philosophical issue, not just a theological one and later came to be also attached to the theories of Marx and of Darwin, the belief that the old 'Calvinism' was responsible for excessive individualism, rigid determinism, a *laissez-faire* attitude to the predicament of the poor and the excesses of capitalism has continued. If the Confession more than Calvin is central to the story of Calvinism in much of the nineteenth century in Scotland, the change in the status of the Confession was also part of a more historical interest in Calvin which in due course provided a broader base for the renewal of his heritage. Steps towards historical and theological engagement with Calvin only came later. After the Disruption of 1843, the Free Church was involved in the publication and distribution of Merle d'Aubigne's *History of the Reformation* and Calvin's works were freshly translated and republished in Edinburgh from 1843 to 1855,[6] seemingly without direct reference to the Disruption struggles but perhaps as a response to the perceived challenge of the Catholicism of the Oxford Movement.

When the Declaratory Acts finally put some distance between the church and double predestination and relativised the status of the Confession, Calvin and Calvinism proved not to be captive to those

---

St Andrews from 1788. His 'History of Calvinism' traces the doctrine of predestination back from the Confession to Dort, Knox, Calvin, Augustine and Paul. Alexander Hill, *Lectures in Divinity by the Late George Hill, DD Principal of St Mary's College, St Andrews*, 6th edition (Edinburgh: W Blackwood, 1854), 447–58.

6. One subscriber to the series was in New Zealand. John Calvin, *Commentaries on the Epistles of Paul to the Galatians and the Ephesians,* translated from the original Latin by the Rev. William Pringle (Edinburgh: Calvin Translation Society, 1854). The twelfth annual report for the year 1854. Accessed from http://oll.libertyfund.org/title/1793/99061 on 10 August 2009.

particular expressions of the tradition. As long as the problem was the Confession, there was a sense in which Calvin himself remained to be rediscovered. Interest in Calvin's own writing was revived by a fresh reading of the texts, which in turn began to generate a renewal of the Reformed tradition as a whole.

In these developments the role of John McLeod Campbell (1800-72) in the theological undermining of Calvinism is undisputed. Although Chalmers was the more central figure, his theology is regarded as of less significance. Chalmers' place has been primarily associated with social and political causes and the leadership of the Evangelical party and Free Church of Scotland. Nevertheless examination of Chalmers' theology indicates that, although a person of his era in many respects, including his conservative social attitudes, theologically he often stood apart from the polarisations of the era. He did not attack Calvinism directly as did Campbell, yet he also can be seen as contributing significantly to the loosening of ties to the Calvinism of the Westminster Confession.

Chalmers' rejection of state intervention in poor relief has been seen by Donald Smith as part and parcel of his presumed adherence to the old Calvinism.[7] Smith's now classic analysis is important, but Chalmers' theological values do not fit the stereotype. He was certainly a social conservative who feared the capacity of welfare schemes to exacerbate poverty more than relieve it, but the linkage to his theology is more complex. Conservatism can be general across theology and politics, but cross-overs are also common. Scottish evangelicals were often left of centre politically while on the right theologically, though their Whig sympathies were often mild and seldom extended as far as radical social criticism. They championed the rights of congregations, not egalitarian democracy. Chalmers was active in seeking voluntary personal and social, if not state, means for amelioration of poverty, but was a Tory politically while on the left theologically. Further contrasts in the theological and social dimensions of Calvinism, including of Chalmers' influence, can be traced through comparative studies between Scotland, Canada, and the United States.[8]

---

7. Donald C Smith, *Passive Obedience and Prophetic Protest: Social Criticism in the Scottish Church, 1830–1945* (New York: P Lang, 1987), 88–91, 108–18.
8. Mark A Noll, 'Revival, Enlightenment, Civic Humanism and the Evolution of Calvinism', in *Amazing Grace: Evangelicalism in Australia, Britain, Canada, and*

Chalmers and Calvin

Chalmers was educated at St Andrews University and experienced an evangelical conversion around 1810. He became famous for his parish ministry in Glasgow from 1815 to 1823 and was, for some time, the most celebrated preacher in Britain. He was a strong supporter of home and overseas missions and reinvigorated the ministry of elders, deacons and Sunday school teachers. He taught theology in Edinburgh from 1828 and was the first moderator of the Free Church of Scotland in 1843. His vision of a Godly commonwealth and of territorial urban mission inspired students who took his ideas around the world, including to New Zealand where Port Chalmers was named after him.

Despite their obvious differences of time, context and temperament, Chalmers and Calvin had some notable similarities. Both were converted after a period seeking fame through academic publication and both came to live by their preaching and their writings. Each of them summarised their theology in an 'Institutes of Christian Theology'. Commentaries, correspondence and pastoral concern were features of their ministries. They both got out of their studies and engaged with people. Both had a capacity for taking things personally and taking things too far, though Chalmers had a more obvious sense of humour. Both had critical attitudes to the biblical text which can surprise. Both enjoyed alcohol and thought banning it foolish. Both were concerned for practical social systems as well as theological ideas. Both were concerned with the salvation of cities and not just of souls. Both attracted international visitors and had international influence. Both were concerned with general, as well as with theological, education. They both gave lay people a greater role in the life of the church.

Calvin brought a background in law to his theology and his drafting of regulations for Geneva and the church. His teaching and the model of the Genevan church and society provided an attractive and cohesive package of theology, polity and worship. His ideas were embodied in his *Institutes* and commentaries, the Ecclesiastical Or-

---

the United States, edited by George A Rawlyk and Mark A Noll (Grand Rapids Mich.: Baker Books, 1993): 73–107; Barry Mack, 'Of Canadian Presbyterians and Guardian Angels', in Rawlyk and Noll, *Amazing Grace*: 269–92.

dinances of 1541 and successive editions of *La Forme des Prières et Chants Ecclésiastiques*.[9] A factor in his international influence was the flexibility of his polity, a less rigid system than often perceived.[10]

Chalmers brought a fascination with science and scientific method to his preaching and parish ministry. His work in St John's Glasgow was styled as 'an experiment' and like Calvin he placed polity at the service of mission. His sermons, especially on issues of science and faith, and his writings on parish organization and church establishments had a wide circulation in Britain and North America. His writings replicated his gifts as a preacher. He vividly illustrated key ideas and held audiences spell-bound, yet the edges of his arguments lacked the precision and clarity of Calvin. Chalmers certainly thought theologically, but he had no passion for academic theology. He distrusted theological systems; it had been Calvin's vision to create one.

Chalmers attracted interest by his leadership, his breadth of pastoral sympathy and his ability to relate personal faith to scientific ideas, the economic theories of the day and to the values and fears of rising literate and mercantile middle classes. From his youth, he manifested a strong sense of wonder at nature. His interest in natural theology led to successful publications[11] and he ensured that science was taught to Free Church divinity students. His significance for Scottish theology lay in his values and attitudes—including a sense of what was secondary rather than central—and in what he did not say as much as in what he did. He was a convert to Christ, rather than to evangelicalism and he never felt bound to follow some of its common markers, such as the use of pious language, hostility to Catholics, or the idea that those who had never heard were necessarily damned. He also did not believe that predestination was really all that important. He never believed that subscription to the Westminster Confession required him to believe it all. His attitude towards the Calvinist heritage in Scotland was selective. He avoided drawing attention to the ways in which he

---

9. Philip Benedict, *Christ's Churches Purely Reformed: A Social History of Calvinism* (New Haven: Yale University Press, 2002).
10. Andrew Pettegree, 'The Spread of Calvin's Thought', in *The Cambridge Companion to John Calvin*, edited by Donald McKim (Cambridge UK: Cambridge University Press, 2004): 217.
11. Thomas Chalmers, *On the Power, Wisdom and Goodness of God as Manifested in the Adaptation of External Nature to the Moral and Intellectual Constitution of Man* (London: William Pickering, 1833).

was in reality significantly different. This may have helped keep him out of serious theological difficulty, but it also contributed to a failure to recognise just what his contribution has been. An exception can be found in M'Crie's 1907 survey of the changing place of confessions in the Church of Scotland,[12] but this is unusual.

Calvin in Scotland

The story of Calvin's influence[13] can be traced through the theology, values, polity, discipline and worship of the *Scots Confession* of 1560, the *Book of Discipline* of 1560 and of 1574 and through Knox's Genevan liturgy. The National Covenant and the Solemn League and Covenant and the Westminster documents including the Confession of Faith (1646), the Shorter and Longer Catechisms, and the Directory for Public Worship (1645) developed and, in some ways altered, the tradition in a more legalistic direction. Calvin's teaching and example was seen in a moral vision for a society under Christian discipline[14] and in expectations for the theological education of ministers.

Developments in international Calvinism also affected Scotland. French polity and Dutch theology were augmented by Puritanism, firstly English and then North American. French Huguenots and Scottish Covenanters alike had to adjust their ideal of a Christian society being a new Israel to the realities of being persecuted minorities.

When Presbyterianism was restored to Scotland in 1689 as a reward for its allegiance to William of Orange, this validated Westminster Calvinism politically and gave it a position beyond serious theological scrutiny. The flowering of a 'democratic intellect' in eighteenth century Scotland's transition from bankruptcy to an educational powerhouse owed something to Calvin and Knox's valuing of education and the middle-class experiences of governance provided by kirk-session, presbytery, synod and general assembly, but it was less reflected in theological creativity. Broad markers of Calvinist culture could be seen in concern for order and discipline in church and

---

12. CG M'Crie, *The Confessions of the Church of Scotland: Their Evolution in History*, Chalmers Lectures 7th Series (Edinburgh: Macniven & Wallace, 1907), 126–32.
13. James Kirk, *Patterns of Reform: Continuity and Change in the Reformation Kirk* (Edinburgh: T&T Clark, 1989).
14. Margo Todd, *The Culture of Protestantism in Early Modern Scotland* (New Haven: Yale University Press, 2002).

society. Calvin's influence can be traced in the social and psychological commentaries provided by literature, including by the evidence of hostile reactions to it. Abuses of piety were tellingly ridiculed by Burns and the temptations of the elect cuttingly depicted by James Hogg,[15] but how much these and the evocative narratives of Walter Scott were criticisms of theology and how much explorations of the ironies of humanity and the Scottish persona is perhaps moot.

In the eighteenth century, academic theology was more concerned with the philosophical dimensions of evidences and determinism and the threats of English Deists than with internal tensions in the Calvinist tradition. Calvinism was undiminished among Presbyterian seceders, though their debates about 'new light' laid the groundwork for challenging its accepted interpretations. If Methodism had been more successful in Scotland, it might have provided evidence of a willingness to move away from Calvinism, but Wesley's Arminianism was instead a factor in the weakness of Scottish Methodism.[16]

By the early nineteenth century interest in science, economics and how society functioned created a climate in which commitment to mission became informed by a social curiosity and a willingness to experiment. Signs of greater theological engagement are found in the pages of the *Edinburgh Christian Instructor*. Started by young Evangelicals in 1810, it displayed a developing concern for mission and for the independence of the church as base lines of Christian commitment. However it still remained difficult to raise questions about the integrity of the tradition. Fresh interest in Reformation history focused on Knox and Melville more than on Calvin and a romantic interest in the Covenanters was helped by Walter Scott.

John McLeod Campbell

Signs of tension between Confessional Calvinism and the emerging Evangelical tradition were largely hidden, but more public evidence

---

15. James Hogg, *The Private Memoirs and Confessions of a Justified Sinner: Written by Himself: With a Detail of Curious Traditionary Facts, and Other Evidence* (London: Longmans, 1824).
16. It did not help that Wesley required his ministers to itinerate rather than be settled, that their appointment was determined in England and not by the congregation when that was a key element in Scottish Evangelical identity, or that those appointed to Scotland had English accents.

of challenges to the virtual conspiracy of silence supporting Westminster Calvinism began to emerge in the 1820s.

At the May 1831 General Assembly, John McLeod Campbell of Row (Rhu) and his assistant AJ Scott were accused of teaching contrary to the Confessions and Catechisms of the Church.[17] The situation had arisen following Campbell's response to a lack of a sense of assurance of salvation amongst his congregation. He saw the root of the problem in the teaching of the Confession. His proclamation of God's love for all gave occasion for him to be accused of universalism by those troubled by other aspects of his ministry—including his teaching that assurance was essential to faith and his support of people influenced by Edward Irving who reclaimed the gifts of Pentecost.[18]

In 1829 Campbell wrote that 'As to the extent to which there is anything new in my views . . . when I go back to the writings of Luther and Calvin I find it not great'.[19] That his ideas were argued theologically and historically later came to be appreciated, but it did not immediately help his cause when he appealed to Scripture over the Confession to argue that Jesus had died for all. In his trial before the Assembly, a measure of sympathy did not translate into real support amongst either Moderates or the Evangelicals who were then on the cusp of dominating the Assembly. Both parties were concerned less for his theology than for the need to silence his unruly friends who threatened the order and discipline of the Church.[20]

When the motion was finally put, 185 abstained and Campbell was deposed by 119 votes to six. Towards the end of the debate, the principal clerk, meaning to say 'the Church of Scotland will remain and flourish after these doctrines of Mr Campbell have perished and are forgotten', instead declared 'these doctrines of Mr Campbell will remain and flourish after the Church of Scotland has perished and

---

17. For Campbell's theology see James B Torrance, 'The contribution of McLeod Campbell to Scottish Theology', in *Scottish Journal of Theology*, 26/3 (1973): 295-311; *Scottish Theology: From John Knox to John McLeod Campbell*, edited by Thomas Torrance (Edinburgh: T&T Clark, 1996).
18. John Roxborogh, 'The Charismatic Movement of 1830: A Reassessment after 150 years', in *Paraclete*, 18 (1980): 11-12, 19; and 19 (1981): 10-11.
19. John McLeod Campbell to Jean Mary Macnab, 6 March 1829. (Macnab of Macnab papers, Killin, NRA (3) 1126; bundle 111.)
20. Brown, *Thomas Chalmers and the Godly Commonwealth*, 216.

is forgotten'. Seated in the gallery, Thomas Erskine of Linlathen was heard to retort: 'Thus spake he, not of himself, but being high priest, he prophesised'.[21] Later Scott asked Campbell, 'Could you sign the Confession now?' He replied, 'No. The Assembly was right: our doctrine and the Confession are incompatible.'[22]

It has been noted that this decision marked a hardening of orthodoxy which Evangelicals carried into the Free Church at the Disruption. This is supported by church statements, by the invocation of the symbolic power of the Reformation and the Confession to imply that these represented what the Free Church was defending, and by the scholarship of William Cunningham (1805-61). Yet by 1847, Campbell believed that there was 'a great breaking up of the Calvinism of this country, and not only a preaching of the universality of the atonement, but a reaction against Calvinism'.[23]

At a social level, the Calvinist vision was indeed damaged. The fracture of the Church of Scotland in 1843 weakened the ability of any group to maintain 'the historic Calvinist standpoint that the Christian Church . . . could so impress itself upon the surrounding community that the standards of the Gospel became the rule of life for society at large'.[24] Other factors suggested that the Calvinist renaissance had little to do with Calvin or predestination and was unrelated to the challenges and religious interests of the era other than as a byproduct of its ecclesiastical politics. Even Cunningham's impressive work did not convince all. The very romanticism which was easily attracted by symbols of orthodoxy also signalled a shift away from reason as a source of truth.

Campbell's work on the atonement appeared in 1856,[25] giving depth to his critique of predestination. In 1847, when the United Presbyterian Church was formed from the union of the United Secession and the Relief churches, the formula for subscription to the Westmin-

---

21. John 11:51.
22. Thomas Erskine, *Letters of Thomas Erskine of Linlathen: From 1840 till 1870*, edited by William Hanna (Edinburgh: David Douglas, 1877), 106.
23. John McLeod Campbell to Jean Mary Macnab, 17 April 1847. (Macnab of Macnab papers, Killin, NRA (3) 1126; bundle 117.)
24. Andrew L Drummond and James Bulloch, *The Church in Victorian Scotland, 1843-1874* (Edinburgh: Saint Andrew Press, 1975), 1.
25. *The Nature of the Atonement* was republished by Eerdmans in 1996 with an introduction by James Torrance.

ster Confession dropped an earlier requirement that ministers affirm the Confession as their own confession and not merely that of the church.[26] In 1866, some seventy ministers of the Church of Scotland asserted in a petition that 'the old relation of our Church to the Confession cannot continue'.[27] By 1872, a drift in opinion across the Scottish churches was becoming obvious[28] and the place of Campbell in the changing fortunes of Calvinism recognised. His award of a DD in 1868 by Glasgow University may be seen as a belated act of contrition by the establishment.

Chalmers and Westminster Calvinism

Given the rhetoric of the Free Church and Chalmers' role as an evangelical leader, it is not unreasonable to assume that Chalmers would have been central to reviving Confessional Calvinism. However Calvinism is not the only strand in evangelical theology and on closer examination the evidence about Chalmers points in a different direction. Although many of the details, including for the formative period from 1810 to 1815, derive from sources in the archives, there are hints in his publications and records from the memory of his students which support the view that his evangelicalism was little interested in either Calvin or predestination, and that his acceptance of the Westminster Confession was selective.

Chalmers' encounters with Calvinism began in his family and then as a student at St Andrews where George Hill taught a reasoned Calvinist theology and recommended Calvin to students. At the student Theological Society meeting in March 1796, Chalmers opened a debate on the question 'Can man be held accountable for wrong belief?' and in 1798 gave a paper on predestination.[29] He was critical of the looming requirement to sign the Confession:

> How inconsistent . . . with reason and conscience, after we have finished our course at the Divinity College, to

---

26. Hamilton, *The Erosion of Calvinist Orthodoxy*, 22f.
27. AC Cheyne, *The Transforming of the Kirk: Victorian Scotland's Religious Revolution* (Edinburgh: Saint Andrew Press, 1983), 68.
28. *Ibid*, 71.
29. St Andrews University Theological Society Minutes, 2, 1786–1823, St Andrews University Library [hereafter StAUL], UY911.

subscribe our assent to the Confession of Faith after a superficial examination of its tenets and doctrines.[30]

Chalmers learnt from Hill that predestination was not pastorally helpful from the pulpit. He developed an enthusiastic interest in science, which he studied further in Edinburgh. In Edinburgh he discovered Baconian induction which appeared as a universal means of exploring the world and how it worked.[31]

In 1803, he was appointed to the parish of Kilmany, about ten kilometres from St Andrews. For six years he neglected his ministry to pursue literary and scientific fame, but as his schemes—including the prospect of marriage—failed along with his health, he turned to address the needs of his parish and his own spiritual state. Despite not sharing either their theology or their politics, he became impressed by those involved in the *Edinburgh Christian Instructor*. He read Pascal and Wilberforce and began to devour writers he had once despised. Yet it quickly became clear that he would follow his own path.

On his thirtieth birthday, 17 March 1810, Chalmers began a diary.[32] His wide reading in the next few years in particular laid a foundation of interest in missions and familiarity with the lives of church leaders. He received the *Edinburgh Review*[33] and read Boswell, Walter Scott, Burns and Wordsworth. He received Bible Society reports and read Claudius Buchanan's *Christian Researches* and Thomas Clarkson on the *History of the abolition of the slave trade*. As well as Baptist and Moravian *Periodical accounts*, he also read William Brown, *History of the Propagation of Christianity*, and Jonathan Edwards' *Life of Brainerd*. Moravians were important for their piety, commitment and missionary methods.[34]

He found inspiration in English Evangelical and Puritan traditions, including Hannah More, Richard Cecil and John Newton.

---

30. Thomas Chalmers to John Chalmers, 24 November 1796, New College Library, Edinburgh [hereafter NCL] CHA 3.1.17.
31. Brown, *Thomas Chalmers and the Godly Commonwealth*, 14f.
32. There are fragments from earlier periods, but from 1810 onwards he regularly kept a journal diary except for the years 1817 to 1821 and 1834 to 1837.
33. In 1843, Chalmers' library contained '38 volumes and many numbers' of the *Edinburgh Review*. Catalogue of books, p.50, NCL CHA 6.3.12.
34. Chalmers, Journal, 16 May 1813; 3 September 1814, NCL.

Philip Doddridge and Richard Baxter[35] became lifelong influences, as also were Joseph Alleine, Matthew Henry and John Owen. Yet it was their lives, more than their theology, which moved him. He read Thomas M'Crie's *Life of John Knox* late in 1812 and the *Marrow of modern divinity* recalled a 1722 controversy in which evangelicals were censured. Chalmers believed he would have been among their supporters.[36]

What he did *not* read in this period is also striking. Thomas Boston's *Memoirs* and his *Fourfold state* are not mentioned in his journals or borrowing records until 1826 and 1828 respectively. The *Pilgrim's Progress* was not mentioned at this time, nor was Samuel Rutherford's *Letters*. There was little systematic theology available. The *Theological Institutes* of George Hill were first published in outline 1803 and George Campbell's *Lectures on systematic theology and pulpit eloquence* was borrowed from the St Andrews University library[37] but this only amounted to suggestions for sermons alongside slender advice about the construction of theological systems.[38] It was an issue that Chalmers remained suspicious of systems, including Calvin's. In a letter to a friend he wrote:

> My Christianity approaches nearer, I think, to Calvinism than to any of the *isms* of Church History: but . . . I feel the influence of these systems to be most unfortu-

---

35. Baxter was probably the single most important writer during this period (William Hanna, *Memoirs of the Life and Writings of Thomas Chalmers*, volume 1 (Edinburgh: Thomas Constable, 1852), 282). Chalmers read Baxter's *Body of Practical Divinity, Call to the Unconverted*, and *Life* at this time though it appears he did not read the *Reformed Pastor* before the late 1820s. Chalmers used the *Call* as a tract, and gave copies to a painter working on the manse (Chalmers, Journal, 9 May 1812, NCL) and to several parishioners. Baxter's *Call* provided the structure for his sermon on Isaiah 27:3-5, 'Fury not in God'. Preached on seven occasions during 1814-15, it was rediscovered twenty years later and become one of his favourites. Thomas Chalmers, *Sermons by the Late Thomas Chalmers Illustrative of Different Stages in his Ministry 1798-1847*, in volume 6, *Posthumous Works of Thomas Chalmers*, edited by William Hanna (Edinburgh: Published for Thomas Constable by Sutherland and Knox, 1849): 422-40.
36. Chalmers, Journal, 23 August 1812, NCL.
37. St Andrews University Library borrowing record, 28 June 1815, in St Andrews University Library receipt book 1795-1828, StAUL.
38. George Campbell, *Lectures on Systematic Theology and Pulpit Eloquence* (London: Cadell, 1807).

nate in the pulpit . . . Is not this scrupulous orthodoxy of Calvin a principle altogether foreign and subsequent to the native influence of divine truth on the heart?[39]

In March 1812, he began Calvin's *Institutes* in Latin and then in English.[40] A year later, he finished Book Three, but found Book Four on the church 'heavy and uninteresting' and gave up.[41] When an independent minister[42] visited and preached, Chalmers hoped that 'his free, and unshackled, and scriptural divinity' would help to 'overthrow the spiritual tyranny of systems over me'.[43] Ironically it was a Moderate, Samuel Charters, who felt he had to tell Chalmers he was going too far in his distrust of systematic theologies.[44]

In 1814,[45] he revisited Jonathan Edwards[46] and worked through the major writings.[47] Although later warm in his praise, this should not be taken for total agreement. He noted at this time that Edwards impaired 'the freeness of the gospel offer and may embarrass and restrain a young convert in the outset of the work of seeking after God'.[48] In his view, Edwards' view on religious affections also had 'a tendency in it to unsettle gospel faith'.[49]

The lives of Arminian Methodists were more attractive than the theology of Calvinists. Chalmers was 'edified and impressed' by the life of the Methodist John Fletcher (1729–85)[50] and later developed a warm relationship with the Methodist leader Jabez Bunting. Like

---

39. Thomas Chalmers to J Anderson, 2 November 1811, NCL; Hanna, *Memoirs of the Life and Writings of Thomas Chalmers*, 1:241f.
40. Chalmers, Journal, 24 March, 10 November 1812, NCL.
41. Chalmers, Journal, 22 March 1813, NCL; Hanna, *Memoirs of the Life and Writings of Thomas Chalmers*, 1:327.
42. Thomas Snell Jones, minister of Lady Glenorchy's Chapel in Edinburgh from 1779.
43. Chalmers, Journal, 23 August 1813, NCL.
44. S Charters to Thomas Chalmers, 16 February 1814, NCL CHA 4.3.24.
45. C Stuart to Thomas Chalmers, 29 April 1813, NCL CHA 4.2.41; Thomas Chalmers to C Stuart, 24 May 1813, NCL CHA 3.5.79; Thomas Chalmers to C Stuart, 18 May 1815, NCL CHA 3.7.23.
46. Chalmers, Journal, 15 March 1814, NCL.
47. Chalmers, Journal, 27–9 June 1814, NCL.
48. Chalmers, Journal, 29 July 1814, NCL.
49. Chalmers, Journal, 14 August 1814, NCL.
50. Chalmers, Journal, 7 October, 15 December 1814; 17 March 1815, NCL.

the evangelical Anglican Charles Simeon, Chalmers came to believe it was more important to go with whatever the biblical text presented rather than with one or the other competing system of theology. In March 1813, he copied out an extract from Richard Cecil's *Remains*:

> The right way of interpreting Scripture is to take it as we find it without any attempt to force it into any particular system . . . Many passages speak the language of what is called Calvinism and that in almost the strongest terms. I would not have a man clip and curtail these passages to bring them down to some system . . . but let him look out as many more . . . which speak the language of Arminianism, and let him go all the way with these also.[51]

In 1828, Chalmers applied for the chair of divinity at Edinburgh and the question of his distaste for systematic theology was raised by opponents. Although his answers were evasive, he gained the chair but a student recorded him saying that,

> Calvinism is not to influence you . . . you have nothing to do except with what is revealed. Repent else you perish, believe in the Lord Jesus—Seek the Lord while he may be found. Cease to do evil.[52]

Another marker of evangelical and Calvinist identity lay in sensitivity to the dangers of 'good works' as vain efforts to impress God. Although in his own experience he knew the limits of self-reformation, he was unworried theologically by the risk of 'good works' and was in fact happy to encourage them for their value to the person and to society. His 1815 'Address to the people of Kilmany'[53] offended Calvinist sensibilities by advocating that people put themselves in a position of openness to the Gospel by how they ordered their life.

---

51. Thomas Chalmers, Commonplace book, 1813, NCL CHA 6.2.5; Hanna, *Memoirs of the Life and Writings of Thomas Chalmers*, 1:322.
52. Notes from Dr Chalmers' lectures on theology, no date (c.1831), University of Edinburgh Library Archives, Edinburgh, Dc.7.115, 23.
53. Thomas Chalmers, *The Duty of Giving an Immediate Diligence to the Business of the Christian Life: Being an Address to the Inhabitants of the Parish of Kilmany* (Edinburgh: William Whyte, 1815).

While there was sin and evil in the world, Chalmers observed that there was also virtue which a preacher was bound to acknowledge. He noted that Paul asked the Philippians to think on 'whatsoever things are true, whatsoever things are honest, whatsoever things are just'[54] without regard to whether these qualities were found before or after the exercise of saving faith. He expressed his dislike of 'injudicious defenders of orthodoxy' who proclaimed,

> The utter depravity of our nature . . . in such a style of sweeping and vehement asseveration as to render it not merely obnoxious to the taste but obnoxious to the understanding. Let the nature of man be a ruin, as it certainly is; it is obvious to the most common discernment that it does not offer one unvaried and unalleviated mass of deformity.[55]

The character of men in classical antiquity or in the contemporary commercial world could be perfectly moral, and should be applauded. Depravity did not lie 'in the utter destitution of all that is amiable in feeling . . . It may be expressed in one word. It lies in ungodliness.'[56]

Among those who took exception to Chalmers' praise of natural virtue was William Cunningham. In his view, 'works done before justification . . . are truly sins and deserve the displeasure and condemnation of God.'[57] Referring to Chalmers, he disputed the 'propriety of calling anything in the character of unrenewed men *good*, absolutely or without explanation.'[58]

AntiCatholicism ran deep in the Scottish religious identity, was expressed fiercely in the Covenants and was affirmed in the Confes-

---

54. Philippians 4:8.
55. Thomas Chalmers, 'On the Mercantile Virtues which may Exist without the Influence of Christianity', in *Discourses on the Application of Christianity to the Commercial and Ordinary Affairs of Life*, volume 6, Dr Chalmers' Works, 25 volumes (Glasgow: William Collins, 1836): 15f.
56. Thomas Chalmers, 'On the Paternal Character of God', in *Congregational Sermons*, Dr Chalmers' Works, 8:174.
57. William Cunningham, *Historical Theology: A Review of the Principal Doctrinal Discussions in the Christian Church since the Apostolic Age*, 4th edition (London: Banner of Truth Trust, 1960), 553.
58. *Ibid*, 554.

sion. Nevertheless, Chalmers told Protestant hearers in 1817 that they were guilty of the sins they attributed to Catholics. He refused to hold the Catholics of his own time responsible for sixteenth century abuses.[59] His support in the campaign for Catholic emancipation produced one of his most outstanding public addresses[60] and he is still favourably remembered among Scottish Catholics.

His attitudes were in fact quite contrary to those of the Confession at a number of points. In July 1811, he resolved to 'give it an attentive perusal' and he later extolled it whilst avoiding mentioning what he disagreed with. His summary is revealing:

> The natural depravity of man; his need both of regeneration and of an atonement; the accomplishment of the one by the efficacy of a divine sacrifice, and of the other by the operation of a sanctifying Spirit; the doctrine that a sinner is justified by faith, followed up . . . by the doctrine that he is judged by works; the righteousness of Christ as the alone foundation of his meritorious claim to heaven, but this followed up by his own personal righteousness as the indispensable preparation for heaven's exercises and heaven's joys; the free offer of pardon even to the chief of sinners, but this followed up by the practical calls of repentance, without which no orthodoxy can save him; the amplitude of the gospel invitations, and, in despite of all that has been unintelligently said about our gloomy and relentless Calvinism, the wide and unexpected amnesty that is held forth to every creature under heaven.[61]

Chalmers noted English critiques of Scotland's 'gloomy Calvinism' but argued from the evidence of Scottish experience, rather than

---

59. Thomas Chalmers, 'The Doctrine of Christian Charity Applied to the Case of Religious Differences: A Sermon Preached before the Auxiliary Society Glasgow to the Hibernian Society for Establishing Schools and Circulating the Holy Scriptures in Ireland', in *Sermons Preached on Public Occasions*, Dr Chalmers' Works, 11:87–122.
60. Brown, *Thomas Chalmers and the Godly Commonwealth*, 112-14, 183-9.
61. Thomas Chalmers, 'On the Respect Due to Antiquity: A Sermon Preached on Friday May 11, 1827, at the Opening of the Scotch National Church, London', in *Sermons Preached on Public Occasions*, Dr Chalmers' Works, 11:155.

from the theology itself, that the charges that it was antinomian and antimissionary did not hold.[62] He saw the Confession as an historical and not as a timeless document. Creeds and confessions were 'out of their place . . . as magazines of truth'. They had generally come into existence as 'mere landmarks against heresy'[63] and he lamented their use as 'insignia' for different denominations.[64] Even theology itself was subject to change:

> Although the subject-matter of theology is unalterably fixed . . . is there not a constant necessity for accommodating both the vindication of this authority and the illustration of this subject-matter to the ever-varying spirit and philosophy of the times? . . . In theology, as well as in all the other sciences, there is indefinite room for novelties both of thought and of illustration.[65]

The Bible was the all-important source book of Christian belief. Although he believed in its 'plenary' inspiration, that was 'responsible not for the thing recorded, but the truth of it'.[66] The problem with predestination was not the philosophical and theological difficulties of the doctrine—which he ignored—but with keeping it out of the way of 'the universality of the Gospel offer',[67] a message which had worked in his own experience. If Paul found no difficulty preaching the gospel and believing in election, then Chalmers saw no reason to quibble with apostolic precedent.[68] Predestination was irrelevant to practical

---

62. Thomas Chalmers, *Institutes of Theology*, in Hanna, *Posthumous Works of Thomas Chalmers*, 8:364–8.
63. Hanna, *Memoirs of the Life and Writings of Thomas Chalmers*, 4:456.
64. Thomas Chalmers, *On the Evangelical Alliance, its Design, its Difficulties, its Proceedings, and its Prospects with Practical Suggestions* (Edinburgh: Oliver & Boyd, 1846), 9–17.
65. Thomas Chalmers, *Institutes of Theology*, in Hanna, *Posthumous Works of Thomas Chalmers*, 9:xv.
66. Thomas Chalmers to AJ Scott, 22 March 1845, NCL; Erskine, *Letters of Thomas Erskine of Linlathen*, 569f.
67. Thomas Chalmers, 'On the Universality of the Gospel Offer', in *Congregational Sermons, Dr Chalmers' Works*, 10:380–99.
68. Thomas Chalmers to E Morgan, 1 March 1827, NCL; Hanna, *Memoirs of the Life and Writings of Thomas Chalmers*, 3:528f.; Thomas Chalmers, 'On the Doctrine of Predestination', in *Congregational Sermons, Dr Chalmers' Works*, 9:151–75.

Christian life[69] and he told his students that the subject could only be 'cautiously introduced into the pulpit'.[70] In a conversation he was reported as saying, 'I believe the doctrine to be true; nevertheless, the Christian's course of duty is precisely the same as it would be if the doctrine was not true.'[71]

By the time the issues being raised by John McLeod Campbell came before the General Assembly in 1831 there was some awareness that Chalmers was less than committed to some of the traditional evangelical benchmarks. Nevertheless, following the death of Andrew Thomson (1799–1831) he was effectively leader of the Evangelical party itself and about to become moderator of the Assembly in 1832. Chalmers may have been sympathetic to Campbell and friendly with Erskine of Linlathen, but it was prudent to say nothing on the issue.[72]

By the 1840s, many more—including his students—would have been aware that Chalmers' theology was out of alignment with other voices in the Evangelical party, but there were more pressing issues and, again, it was not politic to draw attention to internal differences in the party. After his death, it was also clear that his more liberal sentiments were shared by his biographer and son-in-law, William Hanna. His national prestige, business acumen and practical vision had been essential to the Free Church movement and it remained in the interests of its leaders not to draw attention to the latitude in the theology of their most senior and respected figure.

Chalmers was never an uncritical supporter of the Evangelical party, or of traditional evangelical shibboleths. He illustrates how it could be the gospel impulse, as much as the offence of double pre-

---

69. Thomas Chalmers, 'On Predestination', in *Institutes of Theology*, in Hanna, *Posthumous Works of Thomas Chalmers*, 8:345–413; Thomas Chalmers, *Five Lectures on Predestination. Delivered before the University of Edinburgh*, 2nd edition (London: Sherwood Gilbert and Piper, 1837).
70. Notes from Dr Chalmers' lectures on theology, no date (c.1831), University of Edinburgh Library Archives, Edinburgh, Dc.7. 115, 23.
71. Adam Philip, *Thomas Chalmers: Apostle of Union* (London: J Clarke, 1929), 223; Thomas Chalmers to Mrs Glasgow, 12 October 1825, NCL; Thomas Chalmers, *A Selection from the Correspondence of the Late Thomas Chalmers*, edited by William Hanna (Edinburgh: Thomas Constable and Co., 1853), 126.
72. Thomas F Torrance, 'From John Knox to John McLeod Campbell: A Reading of Scottish Theology', in *Disruption to Diversity: Edinburgh Divinity, 1846–1996*, edited by David F Wright and Gary D Badcock (Edinburgh: T&T Clark, 1996): 22.

destination to the Victorian mind, which corroded confidence in the Confession and the form of Calvinism it represented.

It is interesting to compare Chalmers' values and attitudes with the 'pervasive influences'[73] that Alec Cheyne has discerned as contributing to the passing of the Declaratory Acts. Cheyne noted a new sense of history and of moral sensitivity, a new picture of the natural world, a different estimate of human nature, a sense of tolerance and tentativeness, a preference for the apologetic as opposed to the dogmatic spirit, an awareness of other religions and of the problems posed by them, and also 'a new approach to evangelism (and possibly, in consequence, a new understanding of the Evangel)'.[74]

Although these trends developed through the course of the century and each had their particular exemplars, it is striking how consistent they are with the teaching, correspondence and informal comments of Thomas Chalmers that we have noted. Another influence—although it may be included in Cheyne's final factor—has to be the commitment to mission which marked Chalmers' career from the time of his conversion.

People recognised Chalmers as 'large hearted', if at times—as in the trial of Campbell—they were disappointed it did not extend to all the causes they hoped it might. His apologetic theology led him to avoid problematic doctrines. Through his interest in overseas missions, he was aware of issues arising with other religions and he contradicted the Confession in allowing that ignorance might indeed be an excuse in the eyes of God.

Summary and conclusion

While this evidence may not be enough to make Chalmers responsible for the changes which came later in the century, it appears sufficient to claim that Chalmers' voice was consistent with the themes identified by Cheyne. It suggests that, given Chalmers' profile in church and society and awareness among his students and others that he was not a supporter of uncritical attitudes towards predestination and the Confession, he needs to be acknowledged as a representative and formative figure contributing to the climate that eventually led to change.

---

73. Cheyne, *The Transforming of the Kirk* 73.
74. *Ibid*, 82.

Chalmers illustrates one of what may be seen as the three major approaches to a Calvinist heritage in the nineteenth century: firstly, avoiding confrontation with the issue in the face of other mission priorities; secondly, political ecclesiastical decisions that embody theological avoidance (as in the Declaratory Acts) in order to get seemingly insoluble problems off the church's agenda; and, thirdly, the longer task of theological engagement which can be represented by McLeod Campbell. Each of these has their time. That represented by Campbell may appear the most attractive in retrospect, yet no one approach was sufficient in itself to deal with the problems of continuity and change in a confessional Christian tradition.

Chalmers' commitment to mission and to an ideal of a Godly Commonwealth both drew on Calvin and required changes to Calvinism. The judgement Chalmers exercised in avoiding controversial theology because of the needs of mission is one that this avoidance is often appropriate for some aspects of the faith, even if delay in relation to enforced theological commitments may also be a sign of failure and even of corporate theological laziness.

The sort of political settlement represented by the Declaratory Acts may have had its season, though it, too, can be a form of theological escapism. If this particular arrangement has now run its course, this is not to say that it was without value. It may well have been all that was possible at the time.

In due course the theological renewal of the Reformed tradition following the enactment of the Declaratory acts was massive. A positive response to neo-orthodoxy from the 1920s was not just a reaction to some forms of nineteenth century theological liberalism; it was also made possible by the desire for an orthodox Christian faith which was not captive to the Confessional stream of Calvinism yet was still connected to it, a situation not dissimilar to Chalmers', if less pragmatic.

The story of Chalmers and Calvinism in the nineteenth century may be an indication that Reformed identity demands attention to theology, to mission and to the politics of participatory decision-making. Perhaps Calvin himself pointed in this direction, but Chalmers is also an authentic representative of what it means both to be true to a tradition and to address the needs of an age.

8
Calvin's Own Country? Calvinists, anti-Calvinists and the Making of New Zealand Culture

John Stenhouse

In 1967 Dunedin-born poet James K Baxter, Robert Burns Fellow at the University of Otago, claimed that New Zealand's seemingly secular society, like modern Western civilization, 'carries like strychnine in its bones a strong unconscious residue of the doctrines and ethics of Calvinism'. Baxter quoted a long section on human depravity from Calvin's *Institutes* which included these lines: 'For our nature is not only utterly devoid of goodness, but so prolific in all kinds of evil, that it can never be idle ... everything which is in man, from the intellect to the will, from the soul even to the flesh, is defiled and pervaded with this concupiscence.' Descended from Scottish Presbyterians on both sides, Baxter told readers that he used Calvin's 'heavy volumes' mainly as 'paperweights' and 'to give the impression I am a learned man'. He then extolled the 'superb energy, precision and humour' with which Scottish poet Robert Burns carried out 'the struggle of the natural man against [Calvin's] inhuman crystalline vision of the total depravity of the flesh and the rigid holiness of the elect'.[1] In almost apocalyptic language, the country's leading poet, a Roman Catholic convert, set out to deliver us from Calvinism.

Contests between Calvinists and their critics have profoundly shaped New Zealand society and culture. That is the central contention of this chapter. Focusing on the years between 1840 and 1970, I argue that Baxter rightly identified Calvinism as a potent culture-shaper. To Baxter, no academic historian, the term Calvinism served less as a precise historical description than as a label for a set of beliefs and behaviours which many other cultural critics would call puritan-

---

1. James K Baxter, *The Man on the Horse* (Dunedin: University of Otago Press, 1967), 91–2.

ism. In New Zealand, as elsewhere, critics often used Calvinism and puritanism interchangeably, without making much distinction between the two. Such lumping may annoy professional historians more inclined to splitting—drawing precise distinctions between different historical phenomena. Yet the tendency to conflate Calvinism and puritanism makes some sense because the two movements emerged as close kin in sixteenth-century Europe. Calvinism, inspired by the clear, powerful and this-worldly theology of French lawyer Jean Calvin, soon spread from Geneva across Europe to become strong in the Netherlands, Scotland and, later, the United States. 'puritan' originated as a term of abuse used against hot Calvinistic Protestants determined to reform the Elizabethan Church of England. The dominant variety of Calvinism in early modern England, puritanism travelled to Britain's North American colonies and, later, to Australasia. Although modern Calvinists and puritans evolved in ways with which their sixteenth-century originators would not necessarily have agreed, they continued to display a strong family resemblance.

Recognizing these traditions' culture-shaping power illuminates otherwise puzzling features of New Zealand historiography. On one hand, influential historians have sometimes claimed that religion never much mattered in what was an essentially secular society from almost the beginning of European settlement. Yet, on the other hand, many historians, including some who embraced this 'secular New Zealand' thesis, argued that the churches and their 'puritan legions' exercised great public influence well into the twentieth century, though often in unfortunate ways. My point, elaborated below, is simple. 'Secular New Zealand' and 'puritan New Zealand' cannot both be true. Christianity cannot have been a marginal and steadily declining force from early in our history and also a powerful, pervasive and mostly pernicious one several decades into the twentieth century. These contradictions in our historiography, explored below, make better sense once we recognise that the God-and-culture wars between Calvinists, puritans and their critics long bubbling in New Zealand popular culture and literary circles have also simmered, largely unrecognised, in our history-writing.

In criticizing hypercritical depictions of Calvinists and puritans, I do not intend to whitewash the latter. It was, after all, the great English Puritan Oliver Cromwell who insisted on having his portrait painted 'warts and all'. Yet, like the stereotypical Calvinist of legend, historians have tended to magnify the vices of Calvinists and puritans and minimise their virtues. AntiCalvinist and antipuritan traditions were understandable, and probably necessary, when the Protestant churches and their supporters were socially and politically influential, as they were until the 1970s. Today, however, shallow, ignorant, complacent and sometimes unctuous varieties of antiCalvinism and antipuritanism dominate the academy, politics, and the media. In a culture dominated by a dogmatic antipuritan orthodoxy, a better historical understanding of Calvinists and puritans, and a more critical perspective on their critics, may be timely.

Puritan New Zealand?

I begin with a classic text. R.M Chapman's influential and often-quoted essay, 'Fiction and the Social Pattern', appeared in the leading New Zealand literary journal *Landfall* in 1953. In it, the Auckland historian turned political scientist and cultural critic identified what he saw as New Zealand's dominant social pattern by weaving together evidence from British and New Zealand historical writing with insights gleaned from fiction writers. According to Chapman, puritanism dominated New Zealand society.[2]

What Chapman meant by puritanism corresponded closely to what Baxter meant by Calvinism. Many other New Zealand critics conflated these terms and used them less as careful, value-neutral historical descriptions than as pejorative labels designed to criticise or condemn movements, institutions, beliefs and practices they disliked. This chapter takes as one of its main foci, then, the ways in which cultural critics—poets, novelists, journalists and cartoonists—represented Calvinists and puritans. Readers interested in a careful and theologically-informed history of Calvin and Calvinisms in Australia and New Zealand can do no better than to consult Ian Breward's masterly chapter in this volume. Here, I take a different, but complementary, approach by exploring the language and images in which critics depicted Calvinists and puritans. I also ask why such representations emerged when and where they did and how far

---

2. Robert Chapman, 'Fiction and the Social Pattern: some implications of recent N.Z. writing', in *Landfall* 7/1 (1953): 26–58.

they reflected local historical realities. The Calvinists and puritans targeted by critics were mainly Presbyterians, Baptists, Methodists, Congregationalists and low church or Evangelical Anglicans. Their critics tended to come from the episcopal churches (Roman Catholic or Anglican) or to be atheists, rationalists or agnostics.

According to Chapman, the historical origins of New Zealand Puritanism lay in the evangelical Protestant revivals that swept across the English-speaking world from the mid-eighteenth century. In England, Anglican Evangelicals such as William Wilberforce and Hannah More 'coerced the English poor' into 'coercing themselves' by embracing a 'repressive, superstitious' and 'morose religion'. North of the border, the 'Calvinist enthusiasm' of the Scottish Free Church that emerged out of the 1843 Disruption sent its 'strong if dour message with the crofter and the mill-operative to New Zealand'. Although smaller minorities of nonCalvinists, mainly Methodists and Catholics, settled here too, these groups, Chapman argued, reinforced the dominant puritanical pattern established by Scottish Presbyterians and English low church Anglicans. Scottish Calvinism and English Puritanism, then, were New Zealand's most important ancestral religious traditions.[3]

Census data support Chapman's analysis. Anglicans, mostly English by background, were easily the largest denomination, around two-fifths of the population in 1900. Many clustered at the Protestant end of the Anglican theological spectrum, their faith centred on Bible and Prayer Book, suspicious of ritualism and Romanism, and low church or Evangelical in outlook. Hostile to fanaticism, whether political or religious, many Anglicans remained sufficiently attached to the Calvinism embedded in Anglican tradition to be described as mild or moderate puritans. Presbyterians, mostly Scottish by birth or background but including a significant minority of Northern Irish, comprised the second largest denomination, slightly less than a quarter of the population. They were particularly numerous and influential in Otago and Southland, especially in country areas. Added together, Anglicans and Presbyterians comprised around two-thirds of all settlers.

Most of these transplanted Anglicans and Presbyterians, argued Chapman, hailed from the working and lower middle classes of the

---

3. Ibid, 34–5.

Old World. Dominating the great immigration waves of the 1860s and '70s, these stolid, practical members of Britain's subordinated classes gave New Zealand its 'grey lower middle class' ideas and tone.[4] Recent research has tended to confirm Chapman's contention that working and middling class folk, especially females, numerically dominated most church congregations, here as in the United Kingdom.[5]

Yet the churches that spawned all these puritans, claimed Chapman, were soon 'left on one side' in New Zealand.[6] Puritan beliefs and behaviours, once internalised by the middling and working classes, no longer depended on the churches. In the new land, the churches dwindled into insignificance around 1900, as the failure of the prohibition crusade showed. Here Chapman expressed the 'secular New Zealand' thesis, depicting the churches as drifting into marginality by the end of the nineteenth century. Soon the old 'puritan virtues of work, thrift, abstinence ... and duty' themselves degenerated, leading, in a land of plenty, to 'a simple materialism' and 'self-complacency'.[7]

Chapman used value-laden and often pejorative language when writing about Calvinists and puritans. Anglican Evangelicalism was 'superstitious', 'repressive' and 'morose'. When describing Scottish Presbyterianism, he wrote of 'Calvinist rigours' and of the 'strong but dour message' of the Free Church. The male student hero of Dan Davin's novel *Cliffs of Fall*, he noted approvingly, found in university ideas, sexual experimentation and Bohemian party-going liberation from 'the manners and morals' his 'grandparents had brought with them from Scotland'.[8]

Calvinists and puritans gave New Zealand most of its problems. Chapman's long list included patriarchy (father-rule), a 'sexually polarized society', 'latent homosexuality' caused by 'intensive and lifelong separation of the sexes', adolescent rebellion, family conflict, the 'dominant mother', female 'frigidity', 'marital defeat', 'powerful frustration, loneliness, and lack of love' producing 'bitterness and hatred' in a 'conservative arid country' whose 'solid pressure' upon individu-

---

4. *Ibid*, 30 and 33–4.
5. John Stenhouse, 'Christianity, Gender and the Working Class in Southern Dunedin, 1880–1940', in *Journal of Religious History*, 30/1 (2006): 18–44.
6. Chapman, 'Fiction and the Social Pattern', 36.
7. *Ibid*, 36 and 39–40.
8. *Ibid*, 34–5 and 44–5.

als regularly caused homicidal or suicidal 'violence'. Puritanism, it seemed, was the root of almost all evil.⁹

Chapman's account of puritanism's impact on gender roles and family relations displayed intriguing contradictions. The 'central figure of the father' and 'a male figure of command' dominated discussion of 'the institutions of patriarchy' which identified male domination as a serious problem. Yet later, discussing 'the dominant mother', Chapman could not 'recall one New Zealand novel where the European father is treated as the dominating figure in the home'. Many writers, he noted, depicted women, especially wives and mothers, as wielding great religious, moral and emotional power over men and children, especially to grant or withhold sex and/or affection.¹⁰ I will return to the figure of the formidable female Puritan below.

Chapman concluded by urging the 'New Zealand writer' to 'attack' the 'distortions produced by an irrelevant puritanism of misplaced demands and guilts. The artist must sound his trumpet of insight until the walls of Jericho—the pattern as it is—falls down.' Chapman had pounded Puritanism and all its wicked works by preaching a neopuritan jeremiad. As historian WH Oliver observed of Chapman's essay, the 'scholar's gown' barely obscured 'the preacher's bands'.¹¹ Like Calvin in unreformed Geneva, Chapman felt alienated by and at odds with the kind of self, society and spirituality surrounding him. Most New Zealanders, he wrote, were 'driven and socially damned' souls trapped in puritanism. In Chapman's worldview, puritanism played a role analogous to original sin in Calvinist theology, dragging humans down into alienation, blindness, conflict and violence. Hope for this vast mass of lost souls, wrote Chapman, lay with an elect minority of writers and artists, whose insight and 'unjudging pity' might yet restore 'things of the spirit such as charity, humanity and joy'.¹² As Oliver noted, Chapman assigned the arts a 'reformist and almost redemptive role' in society.¹³ Artists and writers were supplanting clergy

---

9. *Ibid*, 36–55.
10. *Ibid*, 36, 38–9 and 42.
11. WH Oliver, 'The Awakening Imagination', in *The Oxford History of New Zealand*, second edition, edited by Geoffrey W Rice (Auckland: Oxford University Press, 1992), 539–70, quotation on 556–7.
12. Chapman, 'Fiction and the Social Pattern', 57–8.
13. Oliver, 'The Awakening Imagination', 556.

and theologians, yesterday's men, as the country's moral and spiritual guides. Moral and spiritual authority lay with the former.

This *Landfall* article first appeared in shorter form as an address to a New Zealand University Students' Association Congress in January 1952. A year earlier, at a Writers' Conference in Christchurch, most prose writers under the age of fifty had agreed about 'the formative, constricting and distorting effect of the mores and values of New Zealand puritanism on our human scene'.[14] Baxter, speaking on recent trends in New Zealand poetry, hailed the poet as 'a cell of good living in a corrupt society' who should 'by writing and example attempt to change it'.[15] In a comprehensive analysis of New Zealand novels appearing between 1935 and 1964, literary critic Lawrence Jones, writing in 1991, identified 'antipuritan humanism' as their dominant common theme.[16] Insofar as Chapman and Baxter were appealing to New Zealand writers and artists, then, they were preaching mainly to the choir.

Moreover, as Kirstine Moffat has shown, literary antipuritanism was flourishing decades earlier. Antipuritan novelists and poets, inverting Christian conversion narratives, had been depicting the Outsider/Rebel as saving lost souls from religion, repression and respectability since the 1880s, if not earlier. Seeing the light, in such narratives, generally entailed abandoning Christianity for atheism, socialism, and/or feminism. By the 1950s, as Robin Hyde, Frank Sargeson, Dan Davin, Denis Glover, James K Baxter and WH Pearson swelled the chorus, antipuritanism became orthodoxy in New Zealand literary circles.

Calvinists and their critics in the Old World

Antipathy toward Calvinists and Puritans, of course, long predated the British colonization of New Zealand. Theologians, historians, playwrights and poets had been attacking Calvin, Knox and the 'godly' since the sixteenth century. As noted above, 'puritan' began as a

---

14. Lawrence Jones, 'The Novel', in *The Oxford History of New Zealand Literature in English*, edited by Terry Sturm (Auckland: Oxford University Press, 1991), 105–202, at 146.
15. James K Baxter, *Recent Trends in New Zealand Poetry* (Christchurch: Caxton Press, 1951), 16.
16. Jones, 'The Novel', 170.

term of abuse coined by critics of the 'hot Protestants' trying to reform the Tudor-Stuart Church of England in more Calvinistic directions. In early seventeenth-century England, Thomas Manningham, a young man about town, defined a Puritan as 'one as loves God with all his soul, but hates his neighbour with all his heart'.[17] In eighteenth-century Scotland, Robert Burns took aim at Old Light Calvinists. Holy Willie's Prayer satirised the bigotry and hypocrisy of a Calvinist elder, a compulsive fornicator who remained confident that he would go to heaven 'a chosen sample, To shew thy grace is great and ample'. The God of Old Light Calvinism, wrote Burns,

> Sends ane to heaven and ten to hell,
> A' for thy glory,
> And no for any guid or ill
> They've done afore thee!

Yet, as Liam McIlvanney reminds us, the popular modern 'image of Burns as the scourge of Presbyterianism, attacking "the kirk itself and all that it stood for", is a poor caricature of his position'. Burns' kirk satires, though often anticlerical and antiformalist, had their roots 'in specific elements of the Reformed tradition: the competence of the layman; the primacy of scripture; the right of private judgement'.[18]

During the nineteenth century, Romantic historians such as Thomas Carlyle rescued the Puritans from Enlightenment condescension by depicting Oliver Cromwell, for example, as principled, courageous and heroic. Yet ambivalence characterised many of the Puritans' new defenders. 'My ancestors fought by Cromwell's side at Naseby and Marston Moor', enthused the Rev. Charles Kingsley, an Anglican socialist and historian. Although glorying 'in the God-fearing valour and earnestness of the old heroes', Kingsley insisted that 'I have utterly . . . thrown off their Calvinism'.[19] English writer Matthew

---

17. Patrick Collinson, 'Antipuritanism', in *The Cambridge Companion to Puritanism*, edited by John Coffey and Paul C Lim (Cambridge: Cambridge University Press, 2008), 28.
18. Liam McIlvanney, *Burns the radical: poetry and politics in late eighteenth-century Scotland* (East Linton: Tuckwell Press, 2002), 162.
19. John Nettleton, 'Of Philistines and Puritans', in *Puritanism and its Discontents*, edited by Laura Lunger Knoppers (Newark: University of Delaware Press, 2003), 67–84, on 68–9.

Arnold attacked the Dissenting and Evangelical descendents of the Calvinists and Puritans in *Culture and Anarchy* (1869) and *St. Paul and Protestantism* (1870). Convinced that modern science had made orthodox Christianity incredible, Arnold reinterpreted Christianity as a project of ethical and cultural formation led by a strong but post-theological national church. In describing Dissenters as Puritans and Philistines, Arnold chose for the latter epithet an Old Testament term that signified the enemies of God's People. 'Philistine gives the notion of something particularly stiff-necked and perverse in its resistance to light', wrote Arnold. It 'specially suits our middle class, who not only do not pursue sweetness and light, but who even prefer to them that sort of machinery of business, chapels, tea meetings, and addresses from Mr Murphy and the Rev. W Cattle, which makes up the dismal and illiberal life on which I have so often touched'.[20]

New Zealand's settlers, then, brought with them lively antiCalvinist and antipuritan traditions alongside Calvinist and Puritan ones. The former flourished amongst the rough as well as the respectable, particularly amongst men. Charles Darwin, visiting the Bay of Islands at Christmas 1835, noted that many local men, including the Beagle's artist Augustus Earle, 'abused or sneered at' the English missionaries who criticised their drinking, violence and sexual liaisons with Maori women.[21] From the beginning, Calvinists and their critics were battling it out.

AntiCalvinism and antipuritanism in New Zealand historical writing

Many historians of New Zealand, especially since the 1950s, have written present-centred histories depicting Calvinists and Puritans darkly, as obstacles to progress as the historian defined it. The larger metanarrative that framed these Whiggish mythistories was the skeptical Enlightenment story of modernity as progress from a dark Christian past to an enlightened secular future.[22]

---

20. *Ibid*, 74–5.
21. *Darwin and Henslow: The Growth of an Idea, Letters 1831–1860*, edited by Nora Barlow (Berkeley and Los Angeles: University of California Press, 1967), 114.
22. John Stenhouse, 'God's Own Silence: Secular Nationalism, Christianity and the Writing of New Zealand History', in *New Zealand Journal of History*, 38/1 (2004): 52–71.

In 1959, Chapman's friend and University of Auckland colleague Keith Sinclair, a published poet as well as a gifted historian, published *A History of New Zealand*. Still selling, it influenced many university-educated New Zealanders rising to power during the second half of the twentieth century. Characterizing the 'prevailing religion' as a 'simple materialism', Sinclair doubted whether the general population had been 'in any sense more religious' during the nineteenth century—a strong statement of the 'secular New Zealand' thesis. Like Chapman, Sinclair depicted Calvinists and Puritans darkly. Missionary ideas 'were as destructive' of Maori society 'as bullets', he wrote of the Anglican Evangelicals of the Church Missionary Society. The Rev. Thomas Burns, spiritual leader of Otago's Scottish Free Church settlers, was a 'censorious old bigot'. Many 'a "Kiwi" drinker must look into his nine-ounce glass', Sinclair wrote, 'only to discover there the disapproving face of his Primitive Methodist ancestor'. But the day of the wowser had gone, and now 'sunbathing and surfing, uninhibited striptease shows, the vast numbers of drinkers listening to singers or bands in suburban bars' illustrated the modern New Zealander's 'love of varied pleasures'. Sinclair's liberated modern kiwi, evidently a red-blooded secular bloke, defined his identity over against destructive missionaries, Calvinist bigots, and wowsers.[23]

That Sinclair secularised New Zealand's past seems intriguing when we consider the cultural context in which he wrote. During the 1950s, the Presbyterian church launched a New Life movement that sent Sunday School, Bible Class, and church attendance numbers soaring. The Student Christian Movement and Evangelical Unions flourished on university campuses, including Auckland's. The Public Questions Committee of the Presbyterian church lobbied often sympathetic politicians, many of whom had family church connections, on a wide range of issues. The Rev. Jack Somerville, chair of the Public Questions Committee of the Presbyterian Church, led a deputation criticizing the National government's harsh response to the 1951 Waterfront Strike. Prime Minister Holland raged, and then relented. The Billy Graham Crusade of 1959, supported by several government departments, attracted vast crowds; 110,000 people flocked to Auckland's Carlaw Park over two nights.[24]

---

23. K Sinclair, *A History of New Zealand*, revised edition (Auckland: Pelican, 1969), 42, 92, 105 and 287–8.
24. AK Davidson, '1931–1960: Depression, War, New Life', in *Presbyterians in*

God wars erupted amongst historians. In 1947, *Listener* editor Oliver Duff, a lapsed Presbyterian, savaged Dunedin Methodist and amateur historian AH Reed's popular *Story of Otago* as 'a swept and garnished Otago of his Puritan imagination'. Declaring it 'strange' that 'a good man can traffic in religion and a wise man confuse myths with history', Duff refused to publish reviews of Reed's histories in the *Listener*. Reed, whose publishing empire originated out of his determination to furnish Sunday School and Bible Class literature for the nation's young people, also clashed with academic historians such as AH McLintock, Keith Sinclair, and PS O'Connor, who criticised Reed's histories as amateurish, unreliable, pious and hagiographical. It probably annoyed the professionals that Reed refused to kowtow to their authority, sometimes criticised their work, pressed history into the service of Christianity, and sold thousands of books. His *Story of New Zealand*, a popular general history first published in 1945, reached a thirteenth revised edition by the early 1970s, outsold all other general histories, and was widely used as a textbook in New Zealand schools. During the 1960s and '70s, Reed campaigned courteously, often with Dunedin Presbyterians, against pornography, alcohol abuse, smoking, gambling and the permissive society, while continuing to visit and read to old people in residential care and children in hospitals and schools.[25]

As the universities expanded between the 1950s and the 1990s, Sinclair played a leading role in professionalizing as well as popularizing New Zealand history. He helped found the New Zealand Historical Association and the *New Zealand Journal of History*, which he edited for many years. From the 1960s, Whiggish, present-centred histories flourished, depicting Calvinists, Puritans and missionaries darkly, as enemies of the kind of past (and present) we ought to have.

Determined 'to save the souls of the heathen', wrote the biographer of CMS missionary Thomas Kendall in 1968, the Calvinistic evangelicals of the CMS aimed to 'destroy their culture, considered merely indicative of the degradation of its creators'. The missionaries were

---

Aotearoa, edited by D McEldowney (Wellington: Presbyterian Church, 1990), 103–43; AK Davidson, *Christianity in Aotearoa: A History of Church and Society in New Zealand* (Wellington: Education for Ministry, 1991), 156–66.

25. Ian Dougherty, *Books and Boots: The Story of New Zealand Publisher, Writer and Long Distance Walker Alfred Hamish Reed* (Dunedin: Otago University Press, 2005), 155 and 180–92.

'certain that the values they would preach were the absolute values of Christianity—when in fact they were the values of English middle class life'.[26] Such arguments were not baseless; evangelical missionaries sometimes criticised 'heathen' Maori in sweeping, indiscriminate and arrogant ways. Yet few saw nothing but depravity and degradation in Maori culture. Most missionaries learned to speak Maori, and many became notorious amongst settlers during the 1840s and '50s as deranged defenders of Maori land and political rights. The claim that missionary values reflected their class and culture, not Christianity, probably tells us more about 1960s academic culture than about early nineteenth-century evangelicals.

During the 1970s, as second wave feminism reached New Zealand, sympathetic historians sometimes depicted the churches as bastions of patriarchy. According to two historians writing on the European family, the churches provided 'the principal justification for the patriarchal family', with Otago's clergy serving as 'eyes and agents of community control'. During the 1920s, 'God's Police', the 'puritan legions', elaborated an 'ideal of sexual purity and temperance' and a 'cult of domesticity' and 'imposed these upon New Zealand society'.[27] According to another historian, the government Committee of Inquiry into abortion of 1936–7 'turned to the church' in order to 'counter the views of the feminists and political radicals' trying to liberalise access to contraception and abortion. This scholar depicted 'the church' as a monolithic institution largely out of touch with women's lives and hostile to 'individual autonomy' and women's 'right to freely elect, or deny, motherhood'.[28]

Here too, something may be said for such views. Male church leaders often took conservative positions on sexuality, reproduction and gender roles, and sometimes showed little sympathy for women. My main point, though, is that these arguments attributed major social and political influence to the churches and their 'puritan legions'

---

26. J Binney, *A Legacy of Guilt: A Life of Thomas Kendall* (Auckland: Oxford University Press, 1968), 1, 6 and 13–14.
27. E Olssen and A Levesque, 'Towards a History of the European Family in New Zealand', in *Families in New Zealand Society*, edited by PE Koopman-Boyden (Methuen, Wellington, 1978), 1–25, quotation on 3.
28. B Brookes, '"Housewives' Depression": The Debate Over Abortion and Birth Control in the 1930s', in *New Zealand Journal of History*, 15/2 (1981): 127 and 131–4.

several decades into the twentieth century. Such claims, if true, undermined 'secular New Zealand'. The churches could not have been both marginal and declining by about 1900 yet still politically powerful several decades later.

Did the tendency to make sweeping and critical generalizations about the churches and their 'puritan legions' reflect a particular cultural moment that soon passed? It seems not. James Belich's *Paradise Reforged* claimed that Presbyterian Lloyd Geering's heresy trial of 1967 split Christianity into conservative and liberal wings. The conservatives tried to reassert 'traditional values' while liberals 'tried to reform the church and make it relevant in the new world'. But 'the efforts of both parties', Belich tells us, were 'doomed'. This strong statement, consigning Christianity to oblivion, was not just a careless slip of the pen. It played a key structural role in the narrative. Belich depicted New Zealanders as finding themselves during the 1970s by abandoning both Britishness and Christianity. The 'moral evangelists' who had tightened up society 'like a giant spanner' between the 1880s and 1920s were left behind. This mythistory—by which I mean not a fairy story but an historical narrative shaped and coloured by secular nationalism—reflected the ambivalence or hostility toward Calvinists and Puritans pervasive amongst literary and academic elites since the nineteenth century. By such standards, Belich's account was impeccably orthodox.[29]

What happens if we return Calvinists, Puritans, and their critics to New Zealand's past? How does our history look if we refuse to secularise it? In the rest of this chapter, focusing mainly but not exclusively on transplanted Presbyterians and their critics, I argue that both church history and general New Zealand history appear more lively, contentious, colourful, and complex when Calvinists, Puritans and their critics are given their appropriate place. That requires writing what Oliver Cromwell called 'warts and all' portraits of all parties. Such a framework raises larger questions about New Zealand history and identity. Have New Zealanders coped particularly well—better than most other societies—with their differences? Did this society develop an unusual capacity for fair-mindedness, social inclusion and tolerance, particularly of religious Others? Or have we struggled

---

29. James Belich, *Paradise Reforged: A History of the New Zealanders from the 1880s to the Year 2000* (Auckland: Penguin, 2001), 514–15.

with our deepest differences about as successfully—or unsuccessfully—as most other cultures?

Presbyterianism and its critics in Dunedin 1848–1900

Early Otago illustrates the religio-political tensions that transplanted Calvinists generated in the new land. Scottish Free Church Presbyterians, led by Captain William Cargill and the Rev. Thomas Burns, arrived in 1848, determined to build a godly commonwealth. Thomas Chalmers, leader of the Evangelical party, had led the Free Church out of the established Church of Scotland five years before. The issue that sparked the Disruption, the most significant event in nineteenth-century Scottish history, was a congregation's right to reject a minister nominated by a wealthy and powerful lay patron. Its origins lay deeper, however, in what Evangelicals perceived as the dominant Moderate party's apathy about the Church of Scotland's declining hold on the people, especially in booming industrial cities such as Edinburgh and Glasgow. Free Church ministers and people left parish churches, manses and stipends in 1843 not because they rejected the idea of an established church but because they wanted to retain and extend the Kirk's place in the minds and hearts of the people. The Free Church retained much of the public, communal and world-transforming ethos of its Calvinist heritage.

Few Otago Presbyterians were content to confine religion to the private and personal realm. On the new settlement's first anniversary in 1849, Burns called the community together for a solemn day of thanksgiving, prayer and humiliation. The English Anglican 'Little Enemy', refusing to bow the knee, celebrated instead with water sports, horse races and a ball.[30] The gold rushes of the 1860s drew thousands of miners into Otago. This 'New Iniquity' included English Dissenters, Irish Catholics and Protestants, freethinkers and, after 1865, 'heathen' Chinese from Victoria. Dunedin boomed, overnight, to become the largest and richest city in the country.

Reflecting the Scottish tradition of the democratic intellect—that access to education should be as open as possible—Presbyterians

---

30. AH McLintock, *The History of Otago: The Origins and Growth of a Wakefield Class Settlement* (Dunedin: Otago Centennial Historical Publications, 1949), 276–9.

took the lead in establishing the Girls and Boys High Schools and the University of Otago in 1869, and helped to endow its first professorial chairs. The University chose as its motto the phrase *sapere aude* (dare to be wise), from the German philosopher Immanuel Kant's essay *Was ist Aufklärung?* (What is Enlightenment?). In Scotland and New Zealand, as throughout the English-speaking world, the Enlightenment developed largely within a Protestant framework. At the University's official opening in 1871, however, one of the new professors expressed in his inaugural lecture theological and philosophical views that annoyed some conservative Calvinists.

Duncan MacGregor, the tall, dark, and charismatic professor of Mental and Moral Philosophy, had been a brilliant student at the University of Aberdeen, before studying medicine under Joseph Lister at the University of Edinburgh. Following the Scottish philosopher Sir William Hamilton, who mediated Kantian philosophy to Scotland, the United States and Australasia, MacGregor argued that science explained phenomena, things as they appear to us, not things as they are in themselves. Theology's domain, by contrast, was the realm of the Absolute. Quoting Herbert Spencer, MacGregor called the Absolute a 'mysterious Power', a 'Great First Cause' or a 'Central Unity'. Since it was Absolute and Unconditioned, nothing could really be said or known about it. To some Presbyterians in the audience, MacGregor seemed to be saying that God was unknowable, and that theology—understood as the knowledge of God, humanity and the world as revealed in nature and supremely in Scripture—was a dubious if not mistaken enterprise. The Professor of Philosophy, taking up a chair endowed by the Synod, would seem to have been telling Dunedin Presbyterians that they could not know God.[31]

Early in 1876 MacGregor published a series of articles entitled 'The Problem of Poverty in New Zealand'. Having 'run the gauntlet' of 'natural selection' to get here, New Zealand colonists enjoyed an 'unparalleled chance' to solve a social problem that stumped the Old World. Darwin had scotched utopian socialist dreams of 'amiable

---

31. *Opening of Otago University: Addresses by Hon. Major Richardson, The Chancellor; G.S. Sale, M.A., Professor of Classics and English Language and Literature; John Shand, M.A., Professor of Mathematics and Natural Philosophy; D. M'Gregor, M.A., M.B., Professor of Mental and Moral Science* (Dunedin: Daily Times Office, 1871), 54–68, quotations on 57, 60 and 61.

philanthropists', MacGregor argued, by showing that society obeyed nature's universal law of competitive struggle. Success in the modern economic struggle for existence depended upon moral and mental superiority more than physical strength. 'Thriftless' and 'stupid' people, lacking 'intellectual ability' and moral discipline, passed their 'unspeakable curse' to their offspring, 'the common sewer of society'. MacGregor outlined his solution. Habitual drunkards, criminals and paupers should be deprived of liberty, isolated from society, made to work for their own support, and prevented from breeding in order to stop them passing on their 'curse' to their children. In the Old World, said MacGregor, the churches had become paid servants of the state, cared only for the comfortable, and left the poor to the police. He did not regret that they had become even more marginal in Australasia.[32]

MacGregor's outspoken agnosticism, anticlericalism and social evolutionism sparked controversy. As soon as the first part of his 'Problem of Poverty' series appeared, rumours swirled that the Synod was about to rebuke or dismiss him. The Rev. James Copland, Calvinist minister of North East Valley Presbyterian church, led the charge. Born and raised in Scotland, Copland studied arts and theology in Edinburgh and Berlin, obtained a PhD from Heidelberg University in 1858, and an MD from the University of Aberdeen in 1864. Copland suggested that Presbyterian theological students training for the ministry should be withdrawn from MacGregor's lectures. Moderates and liberals in Synod, including the Rev. DM Stuart of Knox Church, refused to do so. The *Otago Daily Times* congratulated them on their 'good sense and breadth of view' in distancing themselves from the 'Torquemada' within their midst.[33]

Freethinkers joined the fray. In 1878 Robert Stout, a lapsed Presbyterian turned freethinker who had been a student of MacGregor, introduced into the House of Representatives the University of Otago Amendment Act, which proposed giving the University Council the sole right to appoint and dismiss professors. Stout, a lawyer, aimed to 'relieve the university of the intolerable incubus of ecclesiastical

---

32. D MacGregor, 'The Problem of Poverty in New Zealand', in *New Zealand Magazine*, 1/1–3 (1876): 60–75, 207–16 and 310–21, quotations on 57, 60, 75 and 316–21.
33. J Stenhouse, 'The Rev. Dr James Copland and the Mind of New Zealand Fundamentalism', in *Journal of Religious History*, 17/4 (1993): 475–97.

censorship'. Yet fiery freethinkers alienated the moderate majority as surely as crusading Calvinists. Stout's bill failed.[34]

This secularist attack spurred Copland to suggest that the Synod divert its endowment to a new chair in the Presbyterian Theological Hall at Knox College. Once again, moderates in the synod opposed this suggestion as sectarian and illegal. MacGregor stayed put until he left Dunedin for Wellington in 1885. Copland applied for the vacant chair. But his impassioned defence of a deeply conservative, biblicist, and rationalistic variety of Calvinism had alienated too many, within and beyond Presbyterian circles. MacGregor's chair went to a more liberal rival, the Rev. Professor William Salmond, who had been Professor of Divinity at the Theological Hall. In 1888 conservative Calvinists attached to the Westminster Confession accused Salmond himself of heresy. Two years later, they levelled the same charge at the Rev. James Gibb, the popular minister of Dunedin's First Church.[35]

Conservative, moderate and liberal Presbyterians were playing important and often controversial roles not just in churches and parachurch organizations but also in universities, schools, scientific and literary societies and voluntary associations. They profoundly shaped New Zealand's theological, philosophical, scientific, intellectual, educational and civic life, as well as farming, business, and politics. They could generally be found on both sides of the controversial questions of the day. If some Presbyterian clergy supported the campaign to ban the 'demon drink', Salmond dismissed prohibition as a blunder.[36] Whereas conservative Calvinists such as Copland expressed scepticism about biological evolution, Salmond became such an enthusiastic convert that by the early twentieth century he was denouncing antievolutionist Christians as 'crass supernaturalists'.[37] George Malcolm Thomson, science master at Otago Boys High, botanist, leading light of the Otago Institute and an elder at Knox Presbyterian Church, did not hesitate to correct Presbyterian clergy who got their science wrong.[38] The lively and fruitful debates and divisions that Presbyte-

---

34. *Otago Daily Times*, 3 October 1878, 2.
35. Laurie Barber, 'James Gibb's Heresy Trial, 1890', in *New Zealand Journal of History* 12/2 (1978): 146–57.
36. William Salmond, *Prohibition: a blunder* (Dunedin: Jolly and Braik, 1911).
37. *The Outlook* 8/28 (1901): 5.
38. *New Zealand Presbyterian*, 1 November 1888, 96.

rians sparked within and beyond the churches may be unsettling to modern ecumenical Christians and secular nationalists but we distort our past if we forget them.

Culture wars 1880–1930

While the previous section focused on debates amongst educated middle class people, similar conflicts erupted amongst the working classes, to which church and labour historians have as yet paid little attention. Before zooming in on a working class Presbyterian family in southern Dunedin, some context is required. According to James Belich, a Great Tightening transformed New Zealand between 1880 and 1920. Economic, political, military and cultural ties to the Mother Country tightened as Britain recolonised these islands. Simultaneously, an army of moral evangelists—doctors, nurses, feminists, government bureaucrats, and clergy—tamed and tightened a loose, boozy, bloke-dominated frontier society. New Zealand was 'the very opposite of irreligious' during this period, claimed Belich, as lively prohibition, sabbatarian, Bible-in-Schools, antigambling and revivalist movements burgeoned. Yet, undermining this perceptive insight, he depicted the Great Tightening as 'a mainly secular crusade' in which 'religion', isolated as a separate variable, operated as just one of its five main drivers. The other four—the state, feminism, the medical profession, and race and patriotism—Belich depicted as secular phenomena.[39] This interpretation illustrates the problems induced by social scientific approaches that isolate religion as a separate category sealed off from the rest of culture. Such an approach is particularly likely to distort world-transforming Calvinist traditions such as Presbyterianism that, even in liberal form, did not comprehensively retreat into the private sphere of heart, home and house of worship. In what follows, I will argue that neither first wave feminism nor the workings of the state during this period can be understood without reference to evangelical religion in general, and Presbyterianism in particular.

Thanks to the 1860s goldrushes, Dunedin's southern suburbs mushroomed. Industries—government railway workshops, breweries, gasworks, and brickworks—arrived from the 1870s. Soon

---

39. Belich, *Paradise Reforged*, 122, 157 and 184.

churches, hotels, sports clubs and lodges sprouted. By 1900 southern Dunedin had become the most densely populated, highly industrialised and working-class urban area in the country.[40]

For much of the twentieth century, many historians assumed that urbanization and industrialization spelled doom for religion. As societies modernised, they secularised. According to one historian, for example, secularization advanced rapidly in southern Dunedin, where working class radical Samuel Lister's *Otago Workman* newspaper, launched in 1887, fired 'atheism, anticlericalism, republicanism and the values of brotherhood and democracy' into the public square, helping turn 'Dunedin's working men into a self-conscious class'. Attacking cutthroat capitalists, parasitic politicians and even Queen Victoria, Lister reserved his 'most savage blows' for 'the churches and the clergy'.[41] In southern Dunedin, then, we might expect to find working-class irreligion burgeoning; dwindling congregations of middle-class folk; and Christianity ceasing to have much public, political significance.

Recent research paints a different picture. Protestant Christianity remained pervasive among working as well as middle class occupational groups, especially amongst women. Working-class people, and skilled workers in particular, dominated most southern Dunedin congregations, especially in the evangelical churches (Presbyterian, Baptist, Congregationalist, Methodist, Brethren and Salvation Army). In terms of their active membership, most churches were inclusive, cross-class institutions more than exclusively middle class ones. Women outnumbered men amongst the actively religious, constituting the backbone of the churches and of household and community religion.[42] A larger proportion of southern Dunedin women signed the 1893 suffrage petition, calling for votes for women, than anywhere else in the country. Transplanted Scottish Presbyterians and

---

40. A Cooper, E Olssen, K Thomlinson and R Law, 'The Landscape of Gender Politics: Place, People and Two Mobilisations', in *Sites of Gender: Women, Men and Modernity in Southern Dunedin, 1890–1940*, edited by B Brookes, A Cooper and R Law (Auckland: Auckland University Press, 2003), 15–49.
41. Erik Olssen, *A History of Otago* (Dunedin: John McIndoe, 1984), 107–9; E Olssen, *Building the New World: Work, Politics and Society in Caversham 1880s–1920s* (Auckland: Auckland University Press, 1995), 61–2 and 171–7.
42. C Daley, *Girls & Women, Men & Boys: Gender in Taradale, 1886–1930* (Auckland: Auckland University Press, 1999), 10–11.

English Baptists, many from skilled working class families, signed in particularly high proportions. Hailing from historically Calvinist denominations, these women, sometimes supported by their menfolk, wanted the vote to build a safe, sober, family-friendly God's Own Country.[43] The hostility such women (and their male supporters) aroused, especially from working class men, illustrates the moral and political power the former wielded.

Samuel and Jane Lister illuminate the conflicts simmering within one working class Presbyterian family. Born in Edinburgh in 1832 or '33 to Isabella Inglis and William Lister, a house-factor, Sam served an apprenticeship as a printer before marrying Jane Miller, a dressmaker, in 1862. In 1865, they sailed with two children to Auckland. Sam served as precentor to the Presbyterian congregation aboard the *Resolute*. Arriving in Dunedin in the mid-1860s, the Listers settled in Roslyn before buying a comfortable villa in South Dunedin. Sam mastered the engraving and printing trades, and formed several business partnerships, hoping to make his fortune. All failed. According to Erik Olssen, the death of their eldest son in 1875, and money worries caused by a growing family—the Listers eventually had eight children—may have turned Sam to heavy drinking. Reproved at church, probably by a minister or male elder, possibly at his wife's request, Sam left, and declared war.[44] In the *Otago Workman*, founded in 1887, Lister attacked the 'church of the present day' as a 'gigantic fraud'. Ministers, 'in it for gold and not for souls', do 'not believe what they teach'.[45] Lister ridiculed local clergy for 'wearing slippers' and 'gossiping' with the women of their congregations, and derided 'goody goody' male prohibitionists as a 'miserable lot of weaklings' attacking the innocent pleasures of the working man.

In July of 1892, as the prohibition and female franchise campaigns heated up, Lister warned *Workman* readers that an unholy alliance between female franchise campaigners—'male women'—and their male supporters—'female men'—threatened the country. The 'tab-

---

43. See J Stenhouse, 'Christianity, Gender and the Working Class in Southern Dunedin, 1880–1940', in *Journal of Religious History*, 30/1 (2006): 18–44.
44. Olssen, *A History of Otago*, 107–9; Olssen, *Building the New World*, 61–2 and 171–7; K O'Connell, '"Be Strong and Show Thyself a Man": Christian Masculinities in Southern Dunedin, 1885–1925' (BA Hons Dissertation in History, University of Otago, 2001), 40–56.
45. *Otago Workman*, 28 June 1889, 5; 5 December 1896, 11.

bies' leading the franchise campaign had joined forces with their 'favourite parson' to lobby for prohibition, religion in schools and votes for women, all causes he detested. 'The greatest danger of the Female Franchise', said Lister, 'is that for many years the votes of the unattached females will be at the command of every sky pilot'. He warned the 'working man' that this parson-feminist alliance might undermine the country's free secular primary school system, 'the dearest privilege the children enjoy'.[46]

Lister's own wife Jane, he told readers, had joined forces with the 'parson' of the 'gospel shop' she 'assiduously attends'. If Jane went to Kensington Presbyterian, her 'parson' was probably Rutherford Waddell, the Irish Presbyterian minister of St Andrew's Church in Walker (now Carroll) Street, whose parish included Kensington Presbyterian. Waddell supported votes for women, socialism and unions. Jane, a committed and active Presbyterian, went to a Bible Women's Association on Wednesday evenings, a prayer meeting on Thursdays, and a Bible study at the minister's home on Friday evenings. She did home missionary work three afternoons a week and campaigned for prohibition and the vote. All this religious activity outside the home was turning his world upside down, complained Sam. He now had to 'dress and scrub' his 'little flock' of children, mend their clothes 'without a murmur', and 'love, honour and obey' his often absent wife. 'I intend to set out tomorrow with a fencing stake, and inform that parson that he is duly warned off the premises', he thundered in August of 1892.[47] Lister's determination to drive a wedge, if not a stake, between parsons and churchgoing feminists suggests that he saw their alliance as a threat to his vision of New Zealand as a white workingman's paradise. To him, southern Dunedin had too much religion of the wrong, all too public and political kind. The *Workman* would hardly have attacked the 'tabbies' so often if Lister had not considered them a threat.

Refusing to return to the kitchen, Jane continued to go to church and to campaign for prohibition, Bible in schools and the vote. 'She always slings the Bible at me because she thinks it does me good', chaffed Sam. 'And so it does, when it misses me.' In December of 1892 she dragged Sam along to a temperance meeting at the Town Hall

---

46. *Ibid*, 9 July 1892, 4.
47. *Ibid*, 13 August 1892, 4.

where the audience, he noted sourly, consisted 'as usual' of 'four-fifths bonnets'.[48]

As Jane Lister illustrates, churchgoing Presbyterian women did not necessarily kowtow to male authority. Like generations of Protestants before them, such women read and interpreted the Bible for themselves, sometimes in ways that annoyed or alarmed their menfolk. Rachel Reynolds provides a second example of a Presbyterian feminist. Largely self-educated, she grew up in Australia, arriving with her family in Caversham in 1855. A year later, she married William Reynolds, a leading Dunedin merchant who became a local and national politician. Rachel and William helped found St Andrews Presbyterian church, and became friends and supporters of its minister, Rutherford Waddell. Rachel joined women's committees that established Otago Girl's High School and, in 1871, admitted women to the University of Otago. Convinced that 'no one can be living a truly Christian life who does not mingle frequently with the poor', Rachel joined Waddell in ministering in nearby Walker (now Carroll) Street, popularly known as the Devil's Half Acre because of its brothels and slums. She forged a strong friendship with working class Mary Lee, mother of John A Lee, helping her find work, and supporting Lee against snobbish female critics. As president of the Dunedin Free Kindergarten Association Reynolds worked tirelessly to establish the Walker Street Kindergarten and eight others, convinced that early training 'with tenderness, sympathy and pity' could develop the 'all round possibilities lurking in every child'. At St Andrews, she organised the making and distribution of clothes for the poor, gave away fresh fruit and vegetables from her home, and every Sunday walked to the Otago Benevolent Institution to read to the elderly.[49]

When Waddell's 1889 sermon, 'The Sin of Cheapness', exposed the fact that respectable Dunedin businessmen were forcing women and girls to work long hours for low wages in poor conditions, Reynolds joined Waddell and Robert Stout on the government Sweating Commission to investigate and fix the scandal. A leader in the Dunedin WCTU, Reynolds interpreted the Genesis account of the creation

---

48. *Ibid*, 10 December 1892, 5.
49. Dorothy Page, 'Reynolds, Rachel Selina, 1838–1928', in *Dictionary of New Zealand Biography: Volume Two: 1870–1900*, edited by WH Oliver (Wellington: Dept of Internal Affairs, 1993), 419–20.

of Adam and Eve to support votes for women at a crowded public meeting in 1891. 'Women had a right to equality with man in the very nature of things', said Reynolds. The unjust and mistaken idea of female inferiority and subordination arose out of 'a misunderstanding and misinterpretation of the fall of man'. After Adam ate the forbidden fruit, 'it was man alone who was turned out of the garden'. Women, she concluded, 'had a right not only to be regarded as man's equal but even as his superior'.[50] Roars of laughter and applause, as well as mutters of dissent, greeted Reynolds' feminist liberation theology. Opponents and supporters filled the correspondence columns of Dunedin newspapers for over a week, many discussing Scripture. Reynolds' champions often quoted Galatians 3:28 ('There is neither Jew nor Greek, there is neither bond nor free, there is neither male nor female: for ye are all one in Christ Jesus') against those who cited more restrictive texts.[51] Working class feminist Harriet Morrison, vice-president of the Tailoresses Union, the first female union in the country, also quoted Galatians 3:28 in a WCTU address that attacked the drink trade and called for the vote. Morrison told a Dunedin audience that Jesus, 'the first founder and head of the women's franchise movement', considered 'both sexes equal'. Women, 'the first and warmest friends Christ had on earth', stood 'by Him to the last at the cross'.[52]

Whereas Morrison came from an Irish and Bible Christian background, many of the Dunedin leaders of the WCTU and the Women's Franchise League were Presbyterian. As well as Reynolds, these included Helen Nicol, Mrs Kirkland, and Catherine Fulton, who grew up in an Evangelical Anglican family, attended West Taieri Presbyterian church, and forged strong links with Hanover Street Baptists. Baptist women such as Annie Hinton and Mrs ER Dick were also prominent.[53] Despite—or more likely because of—public hostility from Sam Lister and Dunedin mayor Henry Smith Fish, a leading parliamentary supporter of the liquor trade, such women succeeded

---

50. *Otago Daily Times*, 11 July 1891, 4.
51. *Evening Star*, 15 July 1891, n.p.
52. *Ibid*, 13 April 1892, n.p.
53. See further, Paulette Wallace, 'The Faithful for Franchise: Religion and First-Wave Feminism, with special reference to Dunedin, 1885–1895' (BA Hons Dissertation in History, University of Otago, 2005).

in making Dunedin the liveliest feminist bastion in the country. According to Reynolds, women needed the vote not 'merely because man had it, but in order to help the world to higher and nobler things'.[54] With all due respect to Belich, I cannot see first wave feminism as an essentially secular movement that can adequately be understood without reference to religion.

The populist newspaper *Truth* certainly didn't. Close study of *Truth* articles and cartoons suggests that male hostility toward the parson-churchwoman alliance remained strong during the opening decades of the twentieth century. Founded in Wellington by the Australian Anglican press baron John Norton early in the century, *Truth* set out to appeal to the white working man. By setting a low subscription rate of thirteen shillings a year, and printing racy and sensational stories, it soon became the best-selling newspaper in the country. New Zealand historians have sometimes described *Truth's* constituency, white working-men, as largely secular in the sense of religiously indifferent or antireligious. Close study of *Truth* between 1900 and 1930 suggests a different picture.

A 1910 article warned readers that our promising 'young new world' faced danger from 'the cruellest of old world inheritances': the 'cursed Presbyterian domination of Scotland'. *Truth's* black picture of Scottish history relied on the English rationalist historian HT Buckle, who, according to his biographer, 'denounced all forms of religion, at all times and in all places, with equal contempt'.[55] The moral code the Kirk imposed on the Scottish people, wrote Buckle, condemned 'all the natural affections, all social pleasures, all amusements, and all the joyous instincts of the human heart' as 'sinful' and 'sure to displease God'. Today, *Truth* warned, 'savage Puritans' such as the Rev. James Gibb were 'foistering on New Zealand the yoke of Presbyterianism' by lobbying the Wellington City Council against allowing trams, trains, steamers and evening concerts on Sundays. Gibb had forged an unholy alliance, *Truth* warned, not only with 'black-hearted' Baptists such as the Rev. JJ North but also with an army of female Puritans.[56]

---

54. *Evening Star*, 29 April 1892.
55. John Kenyon, *The History Men: The Historical Profession in England since the Renaissance*, second edition (London: Weidenfeld and Nicholson, 1993), 116.
56. *New Zealand Truth*, 30 April 1910, 1.

In Christchurch, a bastion of female 'sin-snifting' even worse than Dunedin, a vast network of twenty-three women's organizations blanketed the city. Church and parachurch organizations such as the YWCA and WCTU established 'hen conventions, catmittees [sic]', and 'female holiness guilds' to fight poverty, alcohol abuse, 'cuss words and cruelty to children' and women. Although the city 'squirms again under the restlessness of their effort', *Truth* admitted, grudgingly, that the poor stood 'a better chance of escaping starvation in Christchurch than in any other New Zealand city'.[57] This faint praise was unusual. More often, *Truth* demonised such women as 'Puritan plotters' and 'Pharisees' in league with the parsons to 'establish an odious tyranny such as distinguished the rule of the Presbyterian Calvin in Geneva'.[58] *Truth* had no doubt about the key role that evangelical women played in the Puritan legions, nor about the power of their vote to influence politicians. In its view, the parsons and tabbies had far too much influence on the state.

Everything we know about the great religio-political movements of the period 1880–1930—temperance and prohibition, first wave feminism, Bible in Schools, Sabbatarianism, antigambling and censorship—suggests that the hostility expressed in the *Otago Workman* and *Truth*, however colourful, went beyond sheer paranoia. Evangelical Protestants dominated all these movements, with clergy from historically Calvinist denominations—Presbyterians, Baptists and Congregationalists—particularly prominent. Presbyterian, Baptist and Congregationalist women, supported by their Methodist and Salvation Army sisters, dominated the leadership and the rank-and-file of first wave feminism. As historian Dorothy Page has noted, both the WCTU and prohibition flourished where Presbyterianism was strong. No wonder *Truth* complained in July 1918 that evangelical women 'are the chief supporters of the wowsers'.[59]

Anglicans and Catholics, by contrast, were much less likely to support these movements (with evangelical Anglicans partly excepted). Yet few historians have paid much attention to the significance of this evangelical-episcopal divide, or to the religiosity expressed on

---

57. *Ibid*, 3 August 1912, 4.
58. For these and similar views see *ibid*, 30 April 1910, 1; 26 February 1910, 4; and 2 April 1910, 4.
59. *Ibid*, 20 July 1918, 1.

all sides. Far from eschewing Christian language, imagery and rhetoric, Lister's *Workman* and Norton's *Truth* generally attacked their religious enemies from within Christian tradition, not outside and against it. They, too, seized the high religious and moral ground.

Although he went to church only occasionally, Lister retained much of his Presbyterian heritage. Like Robert Burns, whom he often quoted, Lister believed in the competency of the layman, the primacy of Scripture, and the right of private of judgement. A genuine Christian, he declared in June 1891, 'is a follower and imitator of Christ as he is exhibited in the Bible'. Judge the behaviour of churchgoers by 'the text itself', he urged *Workman* readers. The ordinary man should 'trust in the mercy and charity of his Maker', instead of joining 'sects' that 'arrogantly interpret' the Bible.[60]

Although Lister often criticised clergy, sometimes scathingly, he had no qualms about praising the 'right sort' of minister, such as the Rev. Bates of Trinity Church in Devonport, who 'did not regard staying away from Church as any sign of a man not being a Christian'.[61] Modestly ecumenical, Lister praised Pope Leo XIII, whose 1891 encyclical *Rerum Novarum*, supporting the worker's right to a wage sufficient to support his family, should be emulated by all Protestant churches.[62] Calvin's vision of a godly commonwealth that looked after the poor and vulnerable still glowed. Lister insisted that Christ's command to 'love our neighbour' required at the very least 'feeding him'. In 1890, as the trans-Tasman waterfront strike polarised the country, he hailed unionism as a necessary step 'before the Nazarene's kingdom can be established on earth'.[63]

The old Calvinist hostility toward idolatry and blasphemy sometimes flared. In May of 1890 Lister denounced the 'brazen candlesticks' and 'voluptuous incense' that Anglo-Catholic 'perverts and renegades' such as Bishop Nevill were introducing into Otago's 'Episcopalian Church'.[64] Appalled that so many people 'bandied about' the 'eternal name of God', he urged the Trades and Labour Councils to

---

60. *Otago Workman*, 13 June 1891, 4; 21 November 1891, 4; see also O'Connell, '"Be Strong and Show Thyself a Man"', 40–56.
61. *Otago Workman*, 24 January 1890, 4.
62. *Ibid*, 13 February 1892, 1.
63. *Ibid*, 9 August 1889, 1; 13 September 1890, 1.
64. *Ibid*, 31 May 1890, 2.

lead an 'anti-blasphemy campaign' to suppress this 'terrible national affliction'.[65]

Similarly, *Truth* pressed Christ and the Bible into its blokish brand of Christian socialism. The 'Merciful One' of Nazareth 'was hunted and persecuted by the Puritan sects of His time', wrote *Truth* in January 1909, because he 'went about "doing good" and preaching a Gospel of the Poor'. Modern Presbyterians, Congregationalists, Baptists and Wesleyans, 'Puritanical Pharisees', displayed all the fanaticism of Christ's persecutors. New Zealand had 'plenty of Puritan plotters of this type' in 'Public Morals Associations' and 'Women's Christian Temperance Unions'. But their 'gloomy predominance' here, as in Calvin's Geneva, 'is not in harmony with the teachings of Jesus', who would 'as vigorously denounce the Wowsers as He did the Pharisees'.[66] Like the *Workman*, *Truth* writers and cartoonists attacked God's religious enemies with puritanical zeal.

Conclusion

New Zealand's antipuritans often depicted Puritans as selfish, loveless, harsh, and divisive—enemies of the ideal society. The country's Puritans have often depicted antipuritans as selfish, loveless, harsh and divisive—enemies of the ideal society. The two groups have had more in common than meets the eye.

---

65. *Ibid*, 26 April 1890, 4.
66. *New Zealand Truth*, 9 January 1910, 4.

9
The Reception of Calvin and Calvinism in New Zealand: A Preliminary Trawl

Peter Matheson

Calvinism has enjoyed, for almost a hundred years, a poor press in New Zealand. In church circles, too, even within Presbyterianism, there has been remarkably little interest in Calvin and his thought, and in the influence of Calvinism on our culture. From an early period, such comment as it attracted tended to be negative. For nineteenth-century Anglicans in New Zealand Calvinism tended to be characterised as 'dour'. Dean Stanley's preference for Rabbie Burns over the pharisaical tendencies of Calvinism was approvingly noted in the *Otago Witness* of 1 December 1877. Bishop Neville in Dunedin blamed Calvinism for people resorting to Freethinking, quite a widespread *topos*.[1] In the popular mind, as early as the Victorian period, Calvinism stood for something we had outlived, part of a confessional era marred by religious wars and rigid dogmatism. A favourite focus for criticism was the 'medieval' doctrine of predestination; the restrictive nature of Sabbatarianism, although hardly to be credited to John Calvin, was another cause for complaint.

More damningly, Calvinism was associated with spiritual arrogance, the pretensions of the elect. The much quoted poet of Empire, Rudyard Kipling, for example, saw an analogy between Calvinist doctrines of election and the British government's reluctance to assist poorer immigrants to the colonies.[2] Calvinism was regarded by others as fatalistic, in a not dissimilar way to eugenic theories. And of course it was morally censorious and puritanical. Dr Findlay, addressing the Kent Terrace Presbyterian Young Men's Association in 1899, suggested that reforming parsons, in the wake of Calvin and

---

1. *Otago Witness*, 14 October 1882.
2. As quoted in *ibid*, 17 March 1909.

Knox, found compensation for their own sad lives in inhibiting the legitimate pleasures of others.[3]

These days, in popular and journalistic parlance, Calvinism is largely deployed as a term of abuse. Jim Gorman's illustration for James K Baxter's 1967 poem, *A Small Ode on Mixed Flatting* sums up this misanthropic reading. A sombre Calvin, with one enormous finger pointing to heaven, is confronted by a grinning Rabbie Burns, who gives him two fingers![4] Calvinism, in a nutshell, was identified with some of the least unattractive features of nineteenth-century evangelicalism.

Yet a new consensus is emerging about the heritage of Calvinism, and New Zealand is an interesting test case. This is due in part to a good-natured debate about the nature of Evangelicalism: its relationship to the Reformation, to Puritanism, and in particular Bebbington's thesis about its debt to the Enlightenment, Pietism and Methodism. This is accompanied by a rather less good-natured debate about the origins and essence of Anglicanism. In Sydney, in September 2009, two parallel conferences were devoted to the theme of Calvinist influence, one in Moore College, the engine-room of Anglican Evangelicalism there, one in Parramatta, the Uniting Church's theological centre, noted for its emphasis on public and contextual theology. As so often in historical theology the issues are not purely academic, but about myths of origin, and the validation for present stances. We have to be aware of the danger that Calvinism can be instrumentalised for contemporary agendas.

To return, though, to the nineteenth century. Like other pakeha New Zealanders, Presbyterians saw themselves as a people in exile. Home was infinitely far away, back in Northern Ireland or North Britain, as Scotland was sometimes called, occasionally in England. In his own day Calvin had been a radical theologian of exile. Many of his followers were either in flight from their home country, or at odds with the authorities there. A mark of sixteenth-century Calvinists had been their broad internationalist networks, their openness to hu-

---

3. *The Evening Post*, 22 July 1899.
4. Reproduced in WH Oliver, *James K Baxter: A Portrait* (Wellington: Port Nicholson Press, 1983), 106; note two lines in the poem: 'King Calvin in his grave will smile / To know we know that man is vile;' *Collected Poems: James K. Baxter*, edited by JE Weir (Wellington: Oxford University Press, 1979), 397.

manist scholarship and their adaptability to new situations. It raises the interesting question: Were the settlers in New Zealand aware of this shared diasporic situation? What manner of Calvinism came out in the emigrant ships?

On the one hand, it is true, Calvinist orthodoxy had tended since the Enlightenment to attract to itself the more conservative or even reactionary circles within the Churches. There seems some mirroring of this in the New Zealand Presbyterian world. An 'iron creed for iron men', was how Calvinism was commended to some.[5] Yet, as the Bebbington thesis suggests, there were positive relations to the Enlightenment in that transmogrification of Calvinism we call Evangelicalism. We are perhaps still too slow to recognise the tough, disciplined determination of New Zealand Presbyterians to build a better, fairer society in the new colony, their commitment to schools, universities, education and sound scholarship, the emphasis on the dignity of work and the active involvement of lay people in the outward looking, and often rapidly expanding, networks of the presbyteries; nor can one overlook the rather remarkable missionary élan, the commitment to a moral critique of society, and for a minority, to a social critique. Here we catch a different aspect of the inheritance.

New Zealand Presbyterianism, in other words, was a multifaceted phenomenon. Probably no nineteenth- or early twentieth-century minister, elder, lay person, parent, young Presbyterian, male or woman saw themselves primarily as Calvinists. They saw themselves, rather, as Scots, or Northern Irish, as we know from everything from place names to pipe bands; they also saw themselves also as 'liberals' in a perplexingly varied sense of that word, to be sharply differentiated from later theological liberalism. It suggested support for free enterprise, and a robust individualism, critical of privilege and hierarchy. They felt themselves to be progressive, unlike the obscurantist Papists. They were proud children of the British Empire, their optimism and activism perhaps reflecting the religious assurance and postmillennialism which marked their reading of Scripture. Most would have thought of themselves as Evangelicals.

Above all, the emerging breed of New Zealanders was a practical people, little interested in abstract speculation and flights of mysti-

---

5. Thus the Congregational leader, the Rev. JW Jones of Bournemouth, as reported in *The Evening Post*, 15 June 1914.

cism. It seems clear that aspects of the Reformed heritage cohered with that. New Zealand Presbyterianism's priorities, as one distils them from Presbytery and Synod and Assembly reports, lay with pastoral oversight and Christian education. One can argue, I think, that there was a considerable overlap here between Calvinist, or should we say evangelical, values and the needs of the young colony. On the other hand, we would do well not to measure the influence of Calvin simply by adherence to, or alienation from, the Westminster Standards, which would, indeed, be rather similar to equating Catholic theology in New Zealand with the decrees of the Council of Trent, or Anglicanism with Richard Hooker's *Ecclesiastical Polity*!

We face, however, considerable difficulties in assessing the influence of Calvin and Calvinism in this country. Tracing the impact of a set of ideas or values such as Calvinism on something as complex and changeable as a society and culture always has something of the will-o'-the-wisp about it. Moreover, very little of the basic research has been done.[6] The question we are addressing is a largely unexplored one. We have no published monographs at all, though there are some unpublished theses and biographies, including an extensive biography by John Keddie on one of the most prominent advocates of Calvinism in this country, the redoubtable James MacGregor (1829–94), one time Professor at New College Edinburgh, who was a distinguished Presbyterian minister in Oamaru from 1882.[7] He must hold the record for the lengthiest and most recondite letters to the paper in nineteenth-century New Zealand. He was able to demonstrate that many of the crude accusations thrown at Calvinism (for example, that the Westminster Confession necessarily excluded un-

---

6. A modest exception is the attention that has been paid to the contribution of JM Bates, who was frozen out of the professorial chair he richly deserved in Knox Theological Hall, but who led a considerable resurgence of interest in Calvin in the middle decades of the twentieth century; Clive Pearson, 'JM Bates. Presbyterian Theology in New Zealand from 1930–1980; A Personal Retrospect, 1995', Unpublished Papers from the Archives. [Typescript]. Hewitson Library, Knox College, Dunedin.
7. John W Keddie, 'James MacGregor: A Life in Old Scotland and New Zealand', 2010; compare also Ian Breward, 'James MacGregor 1829–1894', in *Dictionary of New Zealand Biography*. Volume 2, 1870–1900 (Wellington: Bridget Williams Books, 1993), 286–7. A general introduction to some of the issues relating to Calvinism can be found in *Presbyterians in Aotearoa 1840–1990*, edited by Dennis McEldowney (Wellington: Presbyterian Church of New Zealand, 1990).

baptised children or indeed all nonChristians, the heathen, from salvation) were incorrect. This would be to limit God's grace in a way which leading exponents of Calvinism down the ages such as Richard Baxter had rejected.[8]

Given the paucity of previous scholarship any conclusions about the impact of Calvinism on this society and its churches must obviously be very tentative. It does seem clear, however, that from the later decades of the nineteenth century its advocates felt themselves very much on the defensive. Take, for example, the letter by 'Presbyter', responding to a report from the *London Quarterly Review* that the retreat from Calvinism there has become a stampede; Calvinism, the writer retorted angrily, will last as long as Paul's epistles because it is the logical exponent of their contents.[9]

Clearly, we need to define our terms. A distinction is often drawn between the theology of Calvin himself, and later orthodox or classical Calvinism, which moved in a more contractual and rationalist direction; by the beginning of the twentieth century there was already some awareness of this in New Zealand Presbyterianism.[10] Probably most Presbyterians in the nineteenth century favoured an eclectic approach: they generally favoured Evangelicalism, but took from Calvin what appealed to them, while repudiating the rest, rather like HW Beecher, the prominent Congregationalist preacher and social reformer (1813–87), who had a considerable reputation in New Zealand:

> I consider myself Calvinistic, you know, and in this way: I believe what John Calvin would have believed if he had lived in my time and seen things as I see them: My first desire is to know what is true, and I am glad if John Calvin agrees with me; if not, so much the worse for him.[11]

---

8. *The Southland Times*, 5 March 1890; similarly note the long article by 'Presbyterian' in the 29 July 1889 issue of *ibid*, containing ample quotations from the Reformers and pointing out that Calvinism is not fatalistic. Spiritually we may be fallen; metaphysically man is a free and responsible agent. One notes the perhaps surprising mention of Baxter.
9. *North Otago Times*, 25 March 1881.
10. Compare the Rev. J Chisholm's address to the 1909 celebrations in First Church. *Otago Witness*, 14 July 1909.
11. *The Nelson Examiner and New Zealand Chronicle*, 27 November 1872.

Sources

What are the sources for the study of Calvinism's impact on New Zealand? The Rare Books Collection in the Hewitson Library in Knox College offers us a glimpse of the heavy artillery available in the middle decades of the nineteenth century to a handful of scholars at least. Here are lined up the (literally) weighty sixteenth- and seventeenth-century folio tomes of Calvin's commentaries on the Bible, together with editions of his *Institutes of the Christian Religion*, all in Latin of course. Many of these volumes will have belonged to James MacGregor, or to William Salmond, the first Professor at the Theological Hall, and to his successors such as John Dunlop, William Hewitson and John Dickie. Alongside Calvin's own works are arrayed the big leather-bound volumes of seventeenth-century classical Calvinists such as Turretin, who was greatly admired by MacGregor. It seems highly improbable, though, that much of this percolated down even to the ablest of the parish ministers and elders of the time. There will have been exceptions. The Rev. Gillies of Oamaru proudly reported to all and sundry that he had fifty-three volumes of Calvin on his shelves.[12] The hectographed student notes on Dickie's rambling lectures on the Westminster Confession give us some indication of what information was available to the average minister.

More indicative of lay interest is the very substantial collection of pamphlets, some seven hundred in number, relating to the 1843 Free Church Disruption in the Hewitson Library, many of our copies again stemming from James MacGregor. Their theological content and relevance to an assessment of Calvinism's influence, however, are very limited, though they do raise interesting issues about the relationship between Church and State.

Puritan theology is another area well represented in the Hewitson Rare Books collection and, of course, its debt to Calvinism was considerable. Puritanism, too, has remained a strong focus of interest to New Zealand historians such as Ian Breward, Tim Cooper and others. Another well-documented source of influence on New Zealand Presbyterianism were the writings of nineteenth-century Free Churchmen such as William Cunningham of New College, Edinburgh, and then, towards the end of the century, of the outstanding Edinburgh

---

12. *The Tablet*, 4 September 1896, 28.

preacher and Principal of New College, Alexander Whyte. Principal Rainy's visit to New Zealand should also be mentioned. Another crucial source of influence was the Princeton School in the United States, whose leading proponents such as Charles Hodge mounted a trenchant defence of Biblical infallibility. James MacGregor's correspondence showed that he kept in close touch with both New College and Princeton.[13]

An unexpectedly rich resource, however, are New Zealand newspapers, up and down the length and breadth of the country. They testify to a lively public interest in certain aspects of the Calvinist tradition, for example its cultural and moral role, and, especially around 1889–90, in controversies about the Westminster Confession.[14]

Religious polemic

One reason why interest in Calvin remained lively was the sniping between denominations. Books, addresses and sermons attacking the Pope, the alleged indiscretions of priests, and the devious ways of the Jesuits were not uncommon in Presbyterianism and were repeatedly countered by the Catholic publication, *The Tablet*. Ultimately it blamed the 'bloodthirsty bulldogs', Calvin and Knox, for the scandalous attacks on the Jesuits and the Papacy.[15] Calvin's persecution of the antitrinitarian Servetus, who had been burnt to death in Geneva in 1553, was lovingly depicted. It was even alleged that the autocratic Calvin lived a life of luxury and introduced the indiscriminate torture of offenders![16]

Father Le Menant des Chesnais SM, who was knowledgeable about Calvin's life and the doctrine of the *Institutions*, emphasises his hatred of the Papists in a series of lengthy rebuttals of the Presbyterian, John Dickson.[17] Throughout the 1890s these polemical exchanges contin-

---

13. There is a wealth of material relating both to his time in Scotland and New Zealand in the Archives Research Centre of the Presbyterian Church of Aotearoa New Zealand, Knox College, Dunedin [hereafter PCANZ-ARC]; Rev. James MacGregor, NZPC 3/60; PCANZ-ARC; the advice of the Archivist, Ms Yvonne Wilkie, was invaluable for the writing of this paper.
14. The National Library's website, 'Papers Past' provides superb, indexed access to newspapers from 1840 to 1915: http://paperspast.natlib.govt.nz.
15. *The Tablet*, 2 May 1879; 1881.
16. *Ibid*, 15 January 1892.
17. For example, *ibid*, 1 May 1896, 6; 15 May 1896.

ued. *The Tablet* chortled at the decision of Presbyterians in the United States of America to modify their adherence to the Westminster Confession in 1902,[18] and commented on the 1909 celebrations of Calvin that Calvinism has now fallen into total disrepute, and though a section of Protestantism celebrated his personal achievements, there was a careful avoidance of his doctrines. Calvinism was a 'spent star'.[19]

As the chief scholarly defender of Calvinism, James MacGregor was a conservative, but in no way a bigot. He had defended Professor W Robertson Smith's right to argue in 1875 for a historical-critical approach to the Old Testament in the *Encyclopaedia Britannica*, though personally disagreeing with his conclusions. He was formidably learned, had an international reputation, and enjoyed telling a joke against himself. His main apologetic work, however, followed a rationalistic bent which was a far cry from Calvin's Scriptural approach.[20] He found the most elegant and recondite reasons for opposing innovation of any kind, whether the introduction of hymns, or amendment to the Westminster Confession. He bitterly opposed church union proposals with the Methodists and Congregationalists on doctrinal grounds: their Arminianism, or advocacy of free will, detracted from God's sovereign grace. For him the Westminster Confession was, as Professor Massam had said, the Euclid of Calvinism. The Churches in New Zealand, by comparison, he feared were effectively creedless.[21]

Emergence of the Liberal alternative

A succession of well-documented and fierce theological controversies, particularly in Dunedin, throws considerable light, however, on the waning strength of this brand of traditional Calvinism. William Salmond had been something of a banner-carrier for Presbyterianism in Dunedin, having had considerable success with a series of public lectures on biblical inspiration and Christology in what was an intellectually lively civic community. The challenge of historical-

---

18. *Ibid*, 26 June 1902.
19. *Ibid*, 23 September 1909.
20. James MacGregor, *The Apology of the Christian Religion Historically Regarded, with Reference to Supernatural Revelation and Redemption* (Edinburgh: T&T Clark, 1891).
21. *Otago Witness*, 14 September 1904.

critical approaches to the Bible, and of the scientific discoveries and theories of Darwin and others, were discussed with remarkable openness in Dunedin and Salmond was in the midst of this. After, however, he had moved from the Theological Hall to a chair of philosophy at the young University of Otago, Salmond launched in 1886 an electrifying attack on what he termed the 'intellectual terrorism' of Calvinism. His racily written pamphlet, *The Reign of Grace,* proved a best-seller, swiftly going through five editions. It was highly critical of traditional understandings of predestination, and clearly touched a sensitive nerve, though it lacked the Christological and biblical depth of McLeod Campbell's similar critique in Scotland. The heart of his message was that Christ had died for all. Calvinism had become too closely associated with the Westminster Confession and the latter with dogmatic rigidity. Likewise, the Rev. R Somerville spoke for many, especially in the North, when he argued for more 'liberty' in regard to the Confession, for prudence and care on issues such as predestination and the rejection of the idea of eternal punishment in Hell.[22]

Predictably, no doubt, James MacGregor led the attack on Salmond in his pamphlet *The Day of Salvation.*[23] Very similar views were expressed, in less academic language, by the Rev. J Treadwell who argued that since Calvinism was about the sovereignty of God, all true Christians were Calvinist. There had never been a better confession than the Westminster Confession.[24] The support of Dunedin's most prominent preachers at the time, such as Rutherford Waddell and James Gibb in First Church, prevented the charge of heresy against Salmond being pursued.[25] Newspapers throughout New Zealand, from *The Grey River Argus* to *The Evening Post*, were fascinated by this

---

22. *Te Aroha and Ohinemuri News*, 26 October 1889; compare *ibid*, 20 February 1889 for Somerville's address to the Presbytery of Auckland suggesting that it take the issue to Assembly, since the Westminster Confession causes conscientious problems to young ordinands. Note the fuller statement of views in *The Poverty Bay Herald*, 26 March 1889.
23. James MacGregor, *The Day of Salvation Obscured in a Recent Pamphlet on the Reign of Grace* (Dunedin: New Zealand Bible Tract and Book Depot, 1888).
24. *The Wanganui Herald,* 16 June 1890; reproduced in the *Marlborough Express,* 30 October 1890; also in *The Southland Times, The Timaru Herald, The Evening Post* and *The Wanganui Herald.*
25. Peter Matheson, 'William Salmond 1835–1917', in *Dictionary of New Zealand Biography.* Volume 2, 440.

controversy and took it as evidence of a dislike of the Westminster Confession, which was 'more Calvinistic than Calvin', was unknown in England, and was driving young ordinands who have to sign it into despair.[26] Feelings ran high, as did public interest. The audience at the protracted Otago and Southland Synod meeting in 1890 hissed the supporters of the 'unimpaired' Westminster Confession, who did, however, narrowly carry the day on that occasion.[27] By 1901 the Declaratory Act, permitting liberty of opinion on nonessential matters, reflected the majority opinion within a now-united New Zealand Presbyterianism. Rigid adherence to the Westminster Confession was no longer required.

The theological tide was changing. There was much loose talk about the 'mind-fettering creeds' of the Scot.[28] The steady move towards a more liberal brand of Presbyterianism paralleled similar transformations in Scotland and Australia.[29] Liberals such as the Congregationalist Dr RF Horton, who rejected what he called an absolutist view of Scripture and dismissed Calvinism as 'an idle dream', were quoted approvingly.[30] In his irenic survey of Presbyterian theology in New Zealand, JM Bates describes the emergence of a liberal witness characterised by 'evangelical warmth, religious seriousness and a respect for knowledge and truth' which from the late nineteenth century accompanied the main current of orthodoxy.[31] Thus when the Quatercentenary celebrations of Calvin were held in 1909, at the high tide of Liberalism, the fulsome recognition of the greatness of the reformer was qualified by concern at his rigorism. Calvin was regarded as having been rather severe on Predestination, a hard man for hard times. 'A colder thinker never existed.' The tenets of Calvinism were rigid but produced pure lives.[32] Calvinism, it was acknowledged, provoked a 'moral shiver'.[33]

---

26. *The Grey River Argus*, 17 September 1889.
27. *Marlborough Express*, 30 October 1890; the report on this Synod meeting was carried not only in *The Southland Times*, but in many other papers, including *The Timaru Herald*, *The Evening Post* and *The Wanganui Herald*.
28. *Otago Witness*, 1900.
29. AC Cheyne, *The Transforming of the Kirk: Victorian Scotland's Religious Revolution* (Edinburgh: St Andrew Press, 1983).
30. *The Bush Advocate*, 16 June 1909.
31. Pearson, Unpublished Papers, 2.
32. Compare the celebrations of Auckland Presbytery, reported in the *The Outlook*, 4 September 1909; *The Colonist*, 28 August 1909.
33. Thus John Chisholm: *Otago Witness*, 14 July 1909; a review of an adulatory

Side by side with an increasingly formal adherence to the Westminster Standards went a growing openness among ministers and laity to biblical criticism, to evolutionary ideas, to German theologians such as Ritschl and Schleiermacher, and to the Romantic poetry of Wordsworth and Coleridge. 'Liberty of opinion' on many issues became more prevalent. A sermon by James Chisholm at the opening of Maori Hill Church, Dunedin, in 1905, for example, cites George Adam Smith on the prescriptural origins of the Biblical text, and offers quotations from Matthew Arnold, Emerson, JM Barrie, and Tennyson, as well as evoking the heroic martyrs of the Presbyterian tradition, the Covenanters, and the baptism of fire in the Disruption. The warm, personal piety of this sermon, without much theological rigour or social critique, is probably typical of this time.[34]

Folk Calvinism

The real strength of the Calvinist tradition now lay at a more popular level, especially, one suspects, in the rural districts, though this would have to be documented by further research. I suspect that it was the populist variant, which we may perhaps characterise as 'folk Calvinism' which had the most direct impact on New Zealand. In its Free Church form, for example, which had considerable early influence on the Otago settlement, Calvinism was filtered through the experience of the seventeenth-century Scottish Covenanters and the 1843 Disruption. The Covenanters, who preached illegally and sometimes took paramilitary measures for their defence, were regarded as traitors by the Stuarts and ruthlessly suppressed. Under Thomas Chalmers, the Disruption had led to the formation of the Free Church of Scotland, and the 'Crown Rights of the Redeemer' were championed against the legal rights of aristocratic and patrician patrons to nominate the minister for a congregation. In the young colony of New Zealand, Presbyterians felt they were in a sort of apostolic succession with these heroic figures from the past. It was 'Oor Calvinism'! John Knox, Covenanters such as Samuel Rutherford and the iconic figure of Thomas Chalmers himself tended to figure as prominently as Calvin himself in the imaginations of New Zealand Presbyterians,

---

biography of Calvin by CH Irwin described Calvin as someone 'whose personality was as repellant [sic] as his genius was commanding'. *Ibid*, 16 June 1909.
34. In Memoriam Rev. James Chisholm. John Chisholm. Dn 1917, PCANZ-ARC, DA 2/4.

as stained glass windows such as those of Knox Church, Dunedin testify. Bookshelves of lay people and ministers, as well as countless little congregational libraries, would often contain books with dramatic illustrations of Covenanting martyrs, male and female, or depicting the hardships of the Disruption, as the parishioners trooped out of their beloved church into the snow. There was an abundance of popularly written books about the Covenanters, and the 'Worthies', or outstanding personalities, of the Disruption.[35] Romantic reproductions of Sir George Harvey's paintings such as 'Quitting the Manse' or preaching in the open air mediated, so to speak, a coffee-table view of Calvinism. Idealised depictions of ministers, elders, precentors jostled with a flow of improving and humorous anecdotes. These books were destined for Sabbath reading, and went into many editions.

The iconography of the Disruption testifies to the imaginative appeal of the sacrifices made at the time. The DO Hill calotype of the first Disruption assembly was to be found in many church halls and indeed in private homes throughout New Zealand, together with its explanatory pamphlet. At least one copy of a rather wonderful Disruption Brooch also found its way to New Zealand. A fine horsehair couch, presented to Mrs John McKinlay in recognition of her hospitality to those ejected from their homes, churches (and graveyards) in the wake of the Disruption, also found its way to Otago.[36] In the young colony, however, the distinctions between the various brands of Presbyterianism in Scotland: the Established Church, the Free Church, the United Presbyterians and even a few Reformed Presbyterians, proved irrelevant and unsustainable, and rapidly eroded, though those in the South opposed to union with Northern Presbyterianism drew on Free Church traditions. Even the Disruption controversies had a diminishing hold on the pious imagination. The covenanting tradition rapidly died out. Yet Presbyterians in New Zea-

---

35. For example, *Disruption Worthies: a memorial of 1843*, edited by Hugh Miller (Edinburgh: John Greig, 1876); Nicholas Dickson, *The Kirk and its Worthies* (Edinburgh: TN Foulis, 1914); A Smellie, *The Men of the Covenant* (London: A Melrose, 1908); John H Thomson, *A Cloud of Witnesses for the Royal Prerogatives of Jesus Christ: Being the Last Speeches and Testimonies of Those who have Suffered for the Truth in Scotland since the Year 1680*, reprint edition (1714; Edinburgh: Johnstone Hunter, 1871).
36. Details in Peter Matheson, *The Finger of God in the Disruption: Scottish Principles and New Zealand Realities* (Alexandra: Synod of Otago and Southland, 1993).

land long continued to identify with this tradition of hardship and exile. Calvinism, an oft repeated theme, had made Scotland what it was, and Presbyterians in New Zealand, presumably, the fine tough people they were.

When the four hundredth anniversary of Calvin's birth was celebrated in 1909 it was an exclusively Presbyterian affair, organised by the Dunedin Presbytery. Calvin had been decked out, so to speak, in kilt and sporran. Calvin was now seen above all as the founding father of Presbyterianism, and of its allegedly biblical patterns of church life.[37] There was a notable absence of any reference to Calvin within New Zealand Anglicanism, despite the influence of Calvin on Anglicanism's foundational Thirty-Nine Articles and of course the long evangelical tradition within Anglicanism. This is worth noting, because in 1936 the four hundredth anniversary of the first appearance of Calvin's *Institutes of the Christian Religion* was characterised by a more scholarly and inclusive approach.

Calvinism, then, was hailed in 1909 as the mother of heroes and martyrs, and inflated claims were made for Calvinism as the basis of most of today's modern liberties.[38] It was argued in a public meeting at First Church, Dunedin, that (unlike Luther) Calvin had successfully reformed the Church. He had overturned Rome's errors from the foundation. Calvinism had paved the way to democracy, liberty, social progress, political freedom. Conscious of the sovereignty of God and the primacy of grace, an earnest and self-disciplined people had been reared who were prepared to challenge monarchs and privilege.[39]

At the General Assembly in Christchurch on 21 October, a gathering of the Assembly augmented by members of the public heard Gray Dixon on Calvin and Modern Life, James Gibb on the church and Social Protest, and AE Axelsen on the Presbyterian Church and Social Service. Calvin's theology was scarcely mentioned.[40]

---

37. *The Feilding Star*, 10 July 1909, offered an unsigned tribute to Calvin and Calvinism as the basis of modern liberties and stressed that Calvinism constituted a world-wide movement today
38. As in James Gibb's long rambling speech to the General Assembly, hailing Calvin as the originator of modern democracy.
39. *Otago Witness*, 14 July 1909.
40. Alexander Whyte's accurate, if rather adulatory summary of the main doctrines of Calvin's *Institutes* in his chapter, 'The Calvin Centenary', in Alexander Whyte,

Such sentimental evocations of the past hardly encouraged any real wrestling with Calvinist thought. In the wider community, Calvinism, when seen positively, was valued for its character-building qualities and resistance to tyranny. Its doctrine, polity and discipline had created in Scotland and the Netherlands people of strong character.[41] The *North Otago Times* of 26 April 1872 featured a long quotation from a speech of Froude defending the moral strength of Calvinism. Grapes cannot grow on bramble bushes; likewise the moral grandeur of the followers of Calvin cannot be explained except in terms of the heritage of their founder. In not dissimilar vein, John Morley's views that Calvinist discipline had provided a new moral direction and created a revolutionary movement which saved Europe were given extensive coverage in *The Evening Post*.[42]

The Westminster Confession and the Shorter Catechism did remain important for Presbyterian preaching and teaching until well into the twentieth century, though often little more than a formal nod of deference to them was offered. In some congregations, however, the Shorter Catechism was still being taught to Sunday School students in the early 1950s. In a world of bewildering change, the Westminster documents appeared to a substantial minority to be the most comprehensive framework within which the world and its history could be understood, with a particular emphasis on the key doctrines of the sovereignty of God, the atonement, and the divine inspiration and authority of Scripture.

Fundamentalism and revivalism

By the beginning of the twentieth century, the evangelical tradition had split between those of a liberal and a more fundamentalist persuasion, and adherence to what was perceived as classical Calvinism was increasingly the preserve of the latter. From the 1870s and 1880s, however, the revivalist ethos and techniques of Moody and Sankey, among others, had put down deep roots in evangelical religious cir-

---

The Doctrines of Grace and their Application: Some Studies of a Colonial Ministry (Dunedin: New Zealand Bible, Tract and Book Society, 1909), 55–67 is an exception.
41. An article from the *Contemporary Review* to that effect was cited in the *Otago Witness*, 7 February 1889.
42. *The Evening Post*, 4 September 1909.

cles offering a more mellow, less intellectually rigorous form of evangelical piety, and although fundamentalism and revivalism represent distinct alternatives in principle, both were culturally conservative and many individuals and congregations combined elements of both approaches. Keswick revivalism could be seen as Calvinist, in modified form.[43]

The Australasian monthly, *The Biblical Recorder*, edited for decades by the fiery New Zealand Presbyterian minister, PB Fraser, is a rich source for what it describes as evangelical Calvinism in the early decades of the twentieth century. It covered a considerable range of international publications and events. Charles Hodge and his successor at Princeton, Benjamin Warfield, were among the authorities most frequently cited. Its large circulation extended well beyond the Presbyterian camp, and its contributors often conducted a polemic against what it regarded as 'German infidels', including 'superficial' New Zealand scholars such as Professor John Dickie, who was accused of abandoning supernatural revelation.[44] PB Fraser's *Brief Statement of the Reformed Faith* boasted sales of fifteen thousand copies. Yet in its negativity towards contemporary thought and critical biblical scholarship and its emphasis on revivalism and personal conversion, the *Biblical Recorder* represented a rather bizarre form of Calvinism. Fraser himself, for example, preferred Zwingli's more symbolist view of the sacraments to Calvin's.

New Calvinism

On the other hand what can be seen as a genuine renascence of Calvinist scholarship did emerge briefly in New Zealand in the 1930s as part of a fascination with the theology of Karl Barth and Emil Brunner, and flowing from disenchantment with Liberalism. There was excitement about a 'New Calvinism' and an awareness that this was

---

43. Report in the *Boston Watchman*, reprinted in *The Evening Post*, 17 November 1906.
44. On Dickie, compare W John Roxborogh, 'John Dickie 1875–1942', in *Dictionary of National Biography*. Volume 3, 1900–1920 (Auckland: Auckland University Press, 1996), 134–5; and Geoff King, '"Organising Christian Truth": an investigation of the life and work of John Dickie' (PhD thesis, University of Otago, 1998).

a world-wide phenomenon.[45] Leading Presbyterians such as James Gibb, now at St John's, Wellington, who had begun as a strong evangelical Calvinist, and then moved on to champion Liberalism and Christian Socialism, now showed considerable interest in Barth and, though him, in Calvin. Prominent Anglicans, Baptists, and in particular a group of very able young Presbyterian ministers, JM Bates, IW Fraser, JTV Steele and James Baird, were involved in launching, in the Depression years, the short lived *New Zealand Journal of Theology* in 1932. The same group raised awareness of the struggles of the Confessing Church in Germany against National Socialist totalitarianism. To foster the Reformed heritage theological refresher courses were conducted; Bates believed, looking back, that 'there has not been any other period in the history of the Presbyterian Church when theology was so alive'.[46] Worship, too, was deepened within Presbyterianism by a focus on Calvin's and Knox's Eucharistic thought. The unstructured forms of Puritan and Evangelical piety which had pervaded many quarters of the Church were criticised, and the Church Service Society, which still exists, was formed.

At the General Assembly of November 1935, JD Salmond, one of the more internationally minded Presbyterians, successfully moved that the Life and Work committee commemorate in fitting form the 'call of John Calvin', one of the outcomes being special sessions at the 1936 Assembly.[47] The special issue of *The Outlook* to commemorate Calvin's 1536 *Institutes* exemplifies the aims of Steele, Bates and their colleagues: not to recover, as they put it, the antiquarian bones of Calvin, but through this 'greatest man in the history of the Reformed Catholic Church' to rediscover the Bible as the Word of God.[48] Their enthusiasm ran away with them somewhat. Acres of closely written print imposed considerable demands on the reader. The *Institutes* were paraphrased, their historical background traced, and in the biographical material the humanity of Calvin is rightly emphasised. Yet the apologetic tone was evident in the comments on the burn-

---

45. *The Outlook*, for example, carried reports from the *British Weekly* about the shifts in theological outlook, partly as result of the challenges from National Socialism. *The Outlook*, 22 June 1936.
46. Pearson, Unpublished Papers, 19.
47. Presbyterian Church of New Zealand: General Assembly, *Proceedings of the General Assembly of the Presbyterian Church of New Zealand*, 1935, 258.
48. *The Outlook*, 27 July 1936, 3–6.

ing of Servetus for his views on the Trinity.[49] Professor John Dickie commented in one of his letters to James Gibb that Steele had swallowed Calvin *'holus bolus'*.[50] Nevertheless, there are useful sections on Calvin's ethical thought, and on his churchmanship, emphasizing his catholicity of outlook.

The vigour of the 1930s revival concealed weaknesses. It was marred by hagiographical tendencies, and was blind to the hermeneutical challenge of reading Calvin in a very different cultural context and time. There was little awareness of New Zealand's or indeed Australasia's particular history and place in the world. Yet we have to remember that it did not have the benefit of the scholarly work on Calvin's pastoral, exegetical and linguistic achievements available to us today. As the work of a few enthusiastic ministers, working in their spare time, it deserves respect.

Nothing quite comparable to this enthusiasm for Calvin was to be witnessed after World War 2, although interest in him and the Reformed heritage never died away. New Zealand theologians regularly contributed to the *Reformed Theological Review*, for example. Yet Bates himself concluded towards the end of his life that the main theological influences on the churches in the postwar period had been those of Barth, Brunner, Bultmann, and perhaps above all Tillich.[51] Bonhoeffer was also important. Attitudes to Calvinism in New Zealand mirrored those in Australia, the United Kingdom, and the United States of America. The Calvin renaissance, it would seem, had been short-lived. There have been, apart from due references to his historical importance, less obvious traces of interest in Calvin in church life and thought in recent years.

As the twentieth century neared its end an interest in Calvin tended, therefore, to be a minority concern. Those within Presbyterianism who were critical of what they saw as liberal or postmodernist tendencies in theology sometimes turned to a form of Westminster orthodoxy, but there was little creative encounter with Calvin him-

---

49. *Ibid*, 25.
50. 'Steele has been reading Calvin and has found a number of things in him that he did not expect to find and has swallowed them holus-bolus.' John Dickie/James Gibb; 19/7/35. GIBB Correspondence (inward) 1934-5; 391/3, DB13/1, PCANZ-ARC.
51. Pearson, Unpublished Papers, 31.

self. Neither the Modernism of Lloyd Geering nor the Evangelicalism of his opponents really engaged with Calvin's theology. Perhaps the emergent concern for public theology, contextual theology, and for a theology of exile, reflective of the diaspora situation of the churches in New Zealand, will lead to a renewed interest in the exegetical, socio-political and ecclesiological initiatives of Calvin and his immediate followers. It will also be interesting to see whether the new resources we now possess will enable Calvin to be read again today as the scholar and provocateur he was in his own time.

10
Popular Piety, the Sacraments and Calvinism in Colonial New Zealand

Alison Clarke

On an autumn day in 1891, James Baird, Presbyterian minister at Winton, set off early for the tiny settlement of Benmore, twenty kilometres north. His wife Elizabeth and her sister Mary accompanied him. There was nothing unusual in any of this; Baird rode or drove many miles in caring for his large, scattered parish, and the women sometimes kept him company, especially when he was to conduct a baptism. This was, however, no ordinary day, for Baird had been called to baptise a set of triplets, born just five days earlier to Henrietta Matthews, wife of rabbiter Edward Matthews.[1] The Matthews boys were one of just two sets of triplets born alive to New Zealand parents in 1891.[2] Henrietta and Edward Matthews were experienced parents who had nine older children; they held serious concerns for the fate of these new babies, who were frail, and probably premature as well as tiny. These concerns led them to request a visit from James Baird, the closest resident minister of any denomination.

It was rare for Presbyterian baptisms to take place in 'emergency' situations like this; most babies in colonial baptismal registers were at least a month old. By contrast, Catholic and Anglican sources reveal some urgency to baptise sickly babies before they died, with laymen and women delivering the sacrament in emergency cases when there was no priest at hand. This urgency arose from the fear that a baby who died unbaptised bore the taint of original sin, and was bound for damnation. The difference in Presbyterian baptismal custom was the

---

1. Jessie Baird diary, 11 March 1891, cited in Elizabeth Waddington and Susan Maclean, *The Bairds of Winton: The Children of James and Elizabeth* (Masterton: Greenlees Print, 2005), 41.
2. *Statistics of the Colony of New Zealand for the Year 1891* (Wellington: Government Printer, 1892), 27.

practical outcome of Calvin's teaching that baptism was not essential to salvation; an infant who died unbaptised could still be destined for eternal bliss.[3] This precept had the potential to relieve parents of a huge emotional burden, for infant death was all too common in the nineteenth century. In 1891, the year of the triplets' birth, there were just over thirty-two thousand non-Maori babies born in New Zealand. Of those, 332—about 1 per cent—died before they were a month old, and 5 per cent failed to reach their first birthday.[4] Though the Calvinist doctrine of double predestination seemed harsh, it was kinder with respect to infant death than other theologies.

It is unlikely, though, that Edward and Henrietta Matthews held strong Calvinist beliefs; they were not even committed Presbyterians, but English migrants from rural Gloucestershire.[5] James Baird had baptised one of their daughters, Lucy, the previous year, but I have been unable to trace the baptisms of the oldest Matthews children.[6] Henrietta bore five more children after the triplets and in 1896 two of these, along with a daughter whose baptism was evidently neglected earlier, were baptised by the Anglican vicar of Winton. Other than with the triplets, the Matthews showed no urgency about the baptism of their children—the four that I traced ranged from four months to eight years on receiving the sacrament.[7]

The Matthews's fears for the lives of their triplets proved well founded. Harry Matthews died three days after his baptism and his brothers Andrew and Thomas both succumbed two days later,

---

3. John Calvin, *The Institutes of the Christian Religion*, IV.xv.20, http://www.reformed.org/master/index.html?mainframe=/books/institutes/, accessed 11 August 2009. For local examples expounding Calvinist theology on infant salvation, see two responses to William Salmond's controversial *Reign of Grace*: Adam D Johnston, *The Two-Edged Sword* (Dunedin: Wise, Caffin and Company, 1888); and James MacGregor, *The Day of Salvation* (Dunedin: New Zealand Bible, Tract, and Book Depot, 1888).
4. *Statistics of the Colony of New Zealand for the Year 1891*, 27, 37. Statistics were not kept for Maori births and deaths.
5. *Otago/Southland (N.Z.) Assisted Passengers 1872–1888* (Dunedin: Early Settlers Museum, 1992).
6. Winton Presbyterian Church Baptismal Register 1879–1901, 22/49 2007/16/33. Archives Research Centre of the Presbyterian Church of Aotearoa New Zealand, Knox College, Dunedin [hereafter PCANZ-ARC].
7. Holy Trinity Anglican Church, Winton, Baptismal Register 1876–97, MS-2358/001. Hocken Collections, Dunedin.

aged just ten days. They were buried at the Dipton Cemetery; when their father died twenty-six years later he joined them in the same grave.⁸ The Matthews's anxiety to have the triplets baptised probably stemmed from concerns for their fate in the afterlife, but concerns about burial may have contributed also. In the England they had left just twelve years earlier, the unbaptised were forbidden burial in churchyards and condemned to lie in unconsecrated ground without Christian ceremony.⁹ This is not the sort of fate the Matthews can have desired for the first of their family to be buried in New Zealand soil. They perhaps did not realise that in this country the cultural and religious diversity of the colonists, and the lack of an established religion, meant that most could find a respectable burial place somewhere within a municipal cemetery. Many cemeteries, including Dipton, did, however, have sections consecrated by particular religious denominations and Anglican authorities did, on at least one occasion, bar the burial of the unbaptised in their cemeteries.¹⁰

We cannot know what advice or consolation James Baird offered to the Matthews family. He was certainly willing enough to carry out the urgent baptism of their babies. As the only resident minister in the district, it cannot have been unusual for him to provide pastoral services to people whose connection with Presbyterianism was at best tentative. An obituary later described him as 'tactful and conciliatory and wise'.¹¹ In catering for the needs of these English migrants did he, unwittingly or not, confirm the idea that baptism was necessary to salvation? Perhaps he also offered them a more conventionally Calvinist reassurance, that the children of professing Christians were church members by birth. As Otago Calvinist theologian James MacGregor wrote, 'If they die in infancy, we have the same warrant for cherishing a good hope of their eternal salvation as if they had been adults making credible profession of personal faith'.¹²

---

8. Dipton Cemetery records transcript. Hocken Collections.
9. Frances Knight, *The Nineteenth-Century Church and English Society* (Cambridge: Cambridge University Press, 1995), 86–7.
10. Frances Porter, *Born to New Zealand: A Biography of Jane Maria Atkinson* (Wellington: Allen and Unwin/Port Nicholson Press, 1989), 207–8.
11. 'Obituary', in Presbyterian Church of New Zealand: General Assembly, *Proceedings of the General Assembly of the Presbyterian Church of New Zealand*, 1931, 64.
12. James MacGregor, Christchurch, to 'My Dear Cha', 3 January 1882, outward

The tale of the Matthews family demonstrates some of the motivations leading parents to seek baptism; they wanted every possible reassurance that their baby would receive a Christian burial and have a safe passage in the afterlife. There were, of course, other motivations. In Scotland and Ireland, ancestral homes of most colonial Presbyterians, various folk beliefs supplemented more orthodox Calvinist ideas about baptism as a sign and seal of God's grace. Some believed an unbaptised baby was vulnerable to the evil eye, or to the fairies; if a child died unbaptised, it might come back and haunt the parents. Speaking the child's name before baptism was unlucky; numerous aspects of childbirth and baptism were labelled either lucky or unlucky.[13]

I have found little evidence of such folk beliefs in the colonial setting, though they are more likely to be passed on in oral tradition than in written records. One interesting example comes from outside the Calvinist or Celtic tradition. Johann Wohlers, from a north German peasant background, was Lutheran missionary on Ruapuke, in Foveaux Strait. He lived among Ngai Tahu, with only a few Europeans nearby, including his English wife and a Scottish neighbour, Christian Kelly. As Kelly prepared the robe the Wohlers's baby daughter was to wear for her baptism, an agitated Johann Wohlers begged her to stop. 'Don't iron the robe', he cried, 'that would bring bad luck'. Christian Kelly was greatly struck by the pastor's behaviour. She regularly recounted the story and it later appeared in a collection of tales of pioneer women.[14] Had Wohlers lived with other German migrants, this tradition may have continued unquestioned in his family. Few colonists were as isolated from their cultural upbringing; indeed the only reason the story of his daughter's christening gown survives is that other people found it peculiar. Though this story comes from

---

correspondence, James MacGregor papers. PCANZ-ARC. On MacGregor, see Ian Breward's biographical essay in the *Dictionary of New Zealand Biography [DNZB]*, updated 22 June 2007 http://www.dnzb.govt.nz/dnzb/, accessed 29 July 2009.

13. Margaret Bennett, *Scottish Customs from the Cradle to the Grave*, 2nd edition (Edinburgh: Birlinn, 2004), 48–71; Rosalind Mitchison and Leah Leneman, *Girls in Trouble: Sexuality and Social Control in Rural Scotland 1660–1780* (Edinburgh: Scottish Cultural Press, 1998), 71.
14. *Tales of Pioneer Women: Collected by the Women's Institutes of New Zealand*, edited by AE Woodhouse, 2nd edition (Christchurch: Whitcombe and Tombs, 1940), 316–17.

the margins it demonstrates how, in mixed communities, folk beliefs could quickly lose hold.

Whatever their motivations, most parents valued baptism and sought its benefits for their children, regardless of their level of commitment to the church. In 1896, more than half the infant baptisms carried out in the Presbyterian Church of New Zealand were for parents who were not communicant members.[15] In the same year the Synod of Otago and Southland reported that parents prized baptism, but,

> ... in not a few cases the readiness ... does not spring from any very intelligent apprehension of its meaning, but rather from a desire to comply with a seemly custom, or from some vague fear that the neglect of Baptism may in some way be a drawback to their children.[16]

Most ministers agreed willingly enough to baptise the children of anybody prepared to make the required promises concerning their Christian faith, provided they were not guilty of any obvious sin. They did sometimes deny baptism to those whose theology was questionable. In 1873 the kirk session at Tokomairiro (Milton) refused baptism for George Mackie's child because the father, although a church member, 'held views that were unscriptural as to the divinity of Christ and as to Miracles'. Three years later the session agreed to Anne Mackie's application 'to have her children baptised to herself (as her husband has been hindered on account of holding unsound views)'. George and Anne Mackie clearly valued baptism highly, despite any unorthodox views; they had previously submitted to discipline by the Tokomairiro church session for antenuptial fornication in order to obtain baptism for their first child.[17]

---

15. 'Report on the State of Religion and Morals', in Presbyterian Church of New Zealand: General Assembly, *Proceedings of the General Assembly of the Presbyterian Church of New Zealand. Held at Wellington, February, 1896* (1896), 59.
16. 'Report on the State of Religion', in Presbyterian Church of New Zealand: Synod of Otago and Southland, *Proceedings of the Synod of the Presbyterian Church of Otago and Southland, 1896* (1896), 58.
17. Tokomairiro Presbyterian Church, Session Minute Book, 15 May 1870, 28 July 1873, 28 September 1876. PCANZ-ARC.

Another who encountered problems was Andrew Wilson, a Port Chalmers blacksmith. In 1863 Wilson asked Presbyterian minister William Johnstone to baptise his baby. But Johnstone had heard that Wilson had on several occasions worked on a Sunday and the kirk session called Wilson, a church member, to appear before them. He admitted he had worked at his usual trade on the Lord's Day, but pleaded he had done so as a work of necessity. The session did not accept his excuse and delayed baptism until Johnstone could 'confer with him in order to bring him to a right state of mind about the matter'. Wilson was not prepared to compromise with the session, and neither was he willing to delay his child's baptism. Tragedy had already struck the Wilson family once, with a ten month old son dying just two weeks before the new baby arrived. At the next session meeting Johnstone reported that Wilson had obtained baptism for his child from the local Wesleyan minister.[18]

Their authority to withhold the sacraments of baptism and communion, often referred to in minutes as privileges, enabled church sessions to exercise some disciplinary control over their congregations. Presbyterians demonstrated their attachment to baptism by admitting their sins before the session in order to obtain the sacrament for their children. Church discipline was an important feature of Calvinism.[19] Though not peculiar to Calvinism, it had a more public face and retained its stricter elements longer among Presbyterians than in some other faith communities. Indeed, discipline was, in some respects at least, harsher in the Scottish variant than in other early Calvinist traditions: Karen Spierling notes that the sixteenth-century Genevan Consistory did not discipline the parents of illegitimate children until after those children had been baptised; meanwhile, in Scotland, parents had to repent of their sins before a minister would baptise their illegitimate child.[20] Calvin's doctrines were thus adapted—for better or worse—to fit local conditions and local traditions. It was the Scottish version of Calvinism which was brought to New Zealand by migrant Presbyterians, though by the middle decades of

---

18. Port Chalmers Presbyterian Church, Session Minute Book, 18 May 1863, 27 May 1863, and 22 June 1863. PCANZ-ARC; Ian Church, *Some Early People and Ships of Port Chalmers: c.1830-c.1990* (Dunedin: Ian Church, c.1990), 872.
19. For Calvin's system of church discipline, see Calvin, *Institutes*, IV.xii.3.
20. Karen E. Spierling, *Infant Baptism in Reformation Geneva: The Shaping of a Community, 1536-1564* (Aldershot: Ashgate Publishing, 2005), 166-7.

the nineteenth century the disciplinary role of Scottish kirk sessions was on the wane, and by the end of the century had largely disappeared.[21] This was, in part, symptomatic of a move from the Calvinist ideal of a Christian community to a society where religion was a more individual undertaking. It is intriguing to note what happened in the very different colonial context during this period.

I have examined the records of four New Zealand parishes in some detail; all had very different experiences of discipline. First Church of Otago was the first Presbyterian church in the Free Church colony of Otago; by the 1860s its membership was largely confined to the urban area of Dunedin. Port Chalmers centred on Otago's main port while Tokomairiro was a large rural parish. Lawrence, which neighboured Tokomairiro, was a goldfields town with an outlying farming district. Sex and alcohol accounted for almost all disciplinary cases in these four parishes, as in Britain in this period. At Port Chalmers, with hospitality on tap for visiting sailors, alcohol was a ready temptation and ministers reported sightings of drunken parishioners to the session on a regular basis. Sexual offences did not, however,

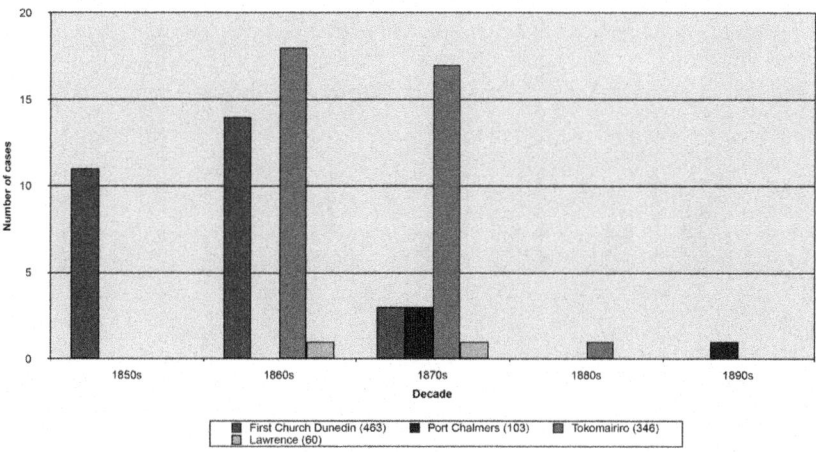

Figure 1: Disciplinary cases for sexual offences in four parishes (Source: Session Minute Books of First Church (Dunedin), Port Chalmers, Tokomairiro and Lawrence Presbyterian Churches. PCANZ-ARC).

---

21. Christine Lumsden, 'Church discipline in nineteenth-century Edinburgh: Contrasts and Comparisons', in *Records of the Scottish Church History Society*, 38 (2008): 83–101.

feature much on that session's radar. As a goldfields centre, Lawrence might be expected to feature numerous sexual and alcohol-fuelled offences, but its kirk session dealt with very few disciplinary cases of any kind. Alcohol-related cases appeared before the sessions of First Church and Tokomairiro from time to time, but their main concern lay with sexual offending.

As Figure 1 shows the differences between the four parishes with regard to sexual offending are startling; the other notable feature is the abrupt drop in cases later in the century. Two-thirds of the cases involved antenuptial fornication, where a couple now married had indulged in sex before their wedding. All other cases were simply labelled fornication: most often the parties were unmarried or widowed. Sessions did not take action concerning parishioners' sexual lives unless there was clear evidence of an offence; in other words, a pregnancy.

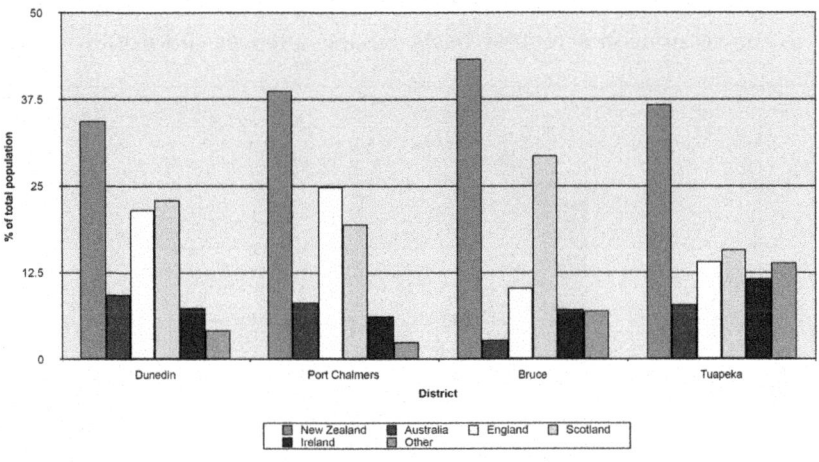

Figure 2: Birthplace: 1874 Census (Source: Registrar-General's Office, *Results of a Census of the Colony of New Zealand, taken for the Night of the 1st of March, 1874* (Wellington: Government Printer, 1874)).

These statistics prompt the question, were the ministers and elders of Tokomairiro obsessed with sex? And what about the good colonists of that parish: were they more sexually active than the citizens of Dunedin, Port Chalmers and Lawrence? This may seem a ridiculous proposition, but perhaps holds some explanatory power. 1874 census statistics (see Figures 2 and 3) reveal that Tokomairiro was quite different from the other three districts. A larger proportion of its residents were Scottish-born, and those born in New Zealand were likely to be the children of earlier colonists, who were often Scots. Residents from the other parishes were a more diverse group. The other districts also showed more diversity of religious affiliation, while in Bruce County, the district more or less equating to Tokomairiro parish, Presbyterians ruled supreme. Tokomairiro was, to a large extent, a community of rural Scots translated to the opposite side of the world: here they could continue their cultural practices with little interference from other traditions. Furthermore, the hegemony of Presbyterianism permitted the kirk session to exercise church discipline more thoroughly, and for longer, than other parishes.

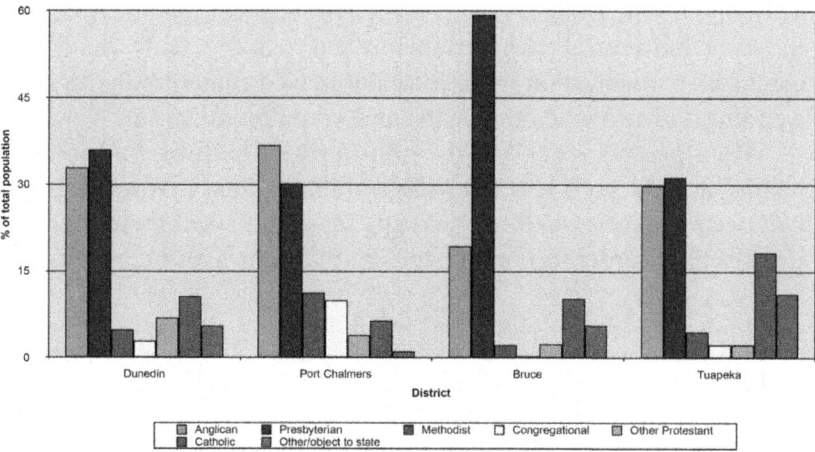

Figure 3: Religious Affiliation: 1874 Census (Source: *Results of a Census of the Colony of New Zealand,* 1874)).

Scotland was noted for its illegitimacy rate, higher than in England and many other European countries. Within Scotland, rates varied greatly: they were lower in the Highlands, and higher in the rural northeast and southwest. While the middle classes closely supervised their daughters, and urban employers monitored their servants' leisure activities, the living and working conditions of the rural working class promoted social and sexual interaction and many young women bore illegitimate children or were already pregnant when they married.[22] The cases which appeared before the Tokomairiro session suggest a continuance of this Scottish pattern in the district. In this environment even the supposedly respectable could fall prey to temptation, with one of the elders disciplined for fornication in 1874.

Sex does not always lead to pregnancy, and many couples must have indulged prior to marriage without being caught out; others claimed their firstborn was premature if anybody examined the dates too closely. Seven months gestation was considered the borderline of viability in the nineteenth century.[23] I was able to trace the dates of marriage and childbirth for twenty-one antenuptial fornication cases which appear in session minutes (see Figure 4 on the next page). Most of the women were well advanced in pregnancy by the time they married, and several gave birth before the wedding. Only one couple confessed to fornication when the baby arrived eight months after the wedding and two when the birth came seven months later.

When parents requested the minister who had married them to baptise a child born less than seven months later, it was obvious it had been conceived before marriage. Most confessed their sin readily enough in order to obtain baptism; they appeared before the ses-

---

22. Christopher Smout, 'Aspects of sexual behaviour in nineteenth-century Scotland', in *Bastardy and its Comparative History: Studies in the History of Illegitimacy and Marital Nonconformism in Britain, France, Germany, Sweden, North America, Jamaica and Japan*, edited by Peter Laslett, Karla Oosterveen and Richard M Smith (London: Edward Arnold, 1980), 192–216; Mitchison and Leneman, *Girls in Trouble*; Kenneth M Boyd, *Scottish Church Attitudes to Sex, Marriage and the Family 1850–1914* (Edinburgh: John Donald, 1980); Andrew Blaikie, 'Scottish Illegitimacy: Social Adjustment or Moral Economy?', in *Journal of Interdisciplinary History*, 29/2 (Autumn 1998): 221–41.

23. William Leishman, *A System of Midwifery, Including the Diseases of Pregnancy and the Puerperal State* (Glasgow: James MacLehose, publisher to the University, 1873), 614. This was the text recommended to students of the Otago Medical School.

sion, expressed remorse for their fault, were reprimanded and, as the formula went, were 'absolved from the scandal of their sin'. Thomas Barnett made a mistake when he asked James Copland, Presbyterian minister at Lawrence, to baptise his child in 1869. Copland discovered the baby had arrived six months after the parents' marriage, but Barnett claimed the child was conceived legitimately. Copland, who was also a trained doctor, knew this was very unlikely and consulted his session, which ruled that before it considered baptism Barnett 'must lay before it a medical certificate confirmatory of his statement'. There is no further mention of the case in the minutes; presumably Barnett instead sought baptism elsewhere.[24]

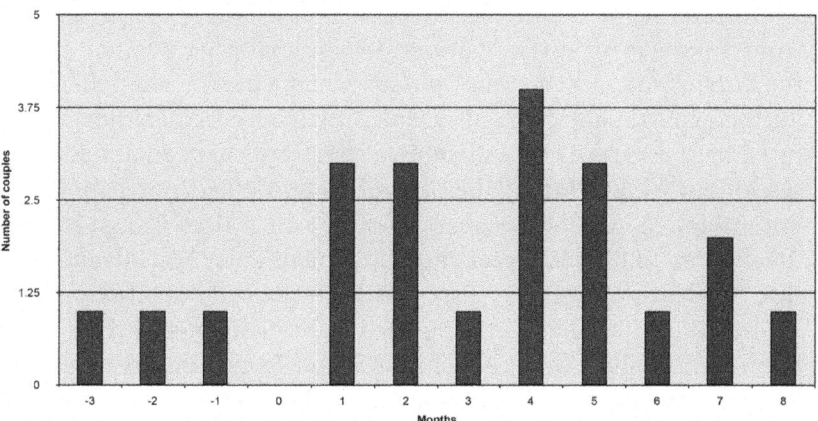

Figure 4: Gap between marriage and childbirth in antenuptial fornication cases (Source: Session Minute Books, Marriage Registers and Baptismal Registers of First Church (Dunedin), Port Chalmers, Tokomairiro and Lawrence Presbyterian Churches, New Zealand. PCANZ-ARC; Birth, Death and Marriage Historical Records, https://www.bdmhistoricalrecords.dia.govt.nz/Home/).

For single mothers the process of session discipline could be especially intimidating, particularly at First Church during the first decade of the Otago colony, when six unmarried women appeared for fornication. Some of these women appeared twice before the session. At the first meeting they confessed their sin and were interrogated about the circumstances, particularly the identity of the child's father.

---

24. Lawrence Presbyterian Church, Session Minute Book, 30 June 1869. PCANZ-ARC.

On the second appearance they received a reprimand and absolution. Of the six women, three had given birth on the voyage to Otago, and one other had also conceived before leaving Scotland. In the two cases where the children had been conceived in Otago, the session ensured the father did not escape discipline. Cornelius Todd, the father of Jessie Peterson's child, was disciplined by the East Taieri session. The First Church session wrote to the Free Church minister in Sydney so that William Elliot, who had fathered Jessie Robertson's child before departing the province, would be liable to discipline if he sought church privileges there.[25]

Some fathers of illegitimate children escaped discipline altogether, while others applied to the session some time later. Some 1860s cases from Tokomairiro reveal that sex outside marriage was not rare in the district and only became an issue when a parent sought baptism for their child. Church member Jane Brown bore an illegitimate child to Isaac Wyber in 1863 and shortly afterwards appeared before the session for fornication. Wyber, an adherent of the congregation, was not disciplined until three years later, by which time Brown had left the district. In the same year church member Peter McGill confessed that, while a widower, he, also, had been guilty of fornication with Brown. Both men had since married other women and their wives had recently given birth; their motivation in coming forward now was to obtain baptism for their new children.[26]

In 1862 Mary Ann Raitt was disciplined by the Tokomairiro session for fornication, having borne an illegitimate child three years earlier. Her son was baptised that same day, and Raitt admitted as a communicant member. A year later, Robert Lochore and his wife Isabella Wright appeared before the session. Lochore confessed two offences: he was the father of Mary Ann Raitt's illegitimate child and thus guilty of fornication; he had also indulged in antenuptial fornication with his wife. The Lochores were absolved from their sins and their daughter duly appeared in the baptismal register shortly afterwards.[27]

---

25. First Church of Otago, Session Minute Book, 13 August 1852, 22 October 1855, 29 October 1855. PCANZ-ARC.
26. Tokomairiro Presbyterian Church, Session Minute Book, 14 January 1866, 9 September 1866, 3 October 1866; Baptismal Register. PCANZ-ARC.
27. Tokomairiro Presbyterian Church, Session Minute Book, 12 October 1862, 25 August 1863, 30 August 1863; Baptismal Register; Communion Roll. PCANZ-ARC.

It cannot have been a pleasant experience to appear before the session and receive a severe reprimand. Offenders had to appear genuinely remorseful before they received absolution. No doubt many sincerely regretted their behaviour, but others perhaps put on an appearance in order to obtain what they really wanted: baptism for their children. Most offenders had already been interviewed in private by the minister prior to their appearance and few can have mourned when this became the sole step in discipline later in the century.

The question remains, why did the session of Tokomairiro, which had diligently disciplined its congregation in Calvinist style for two decades, suddenly drop the practice in the 1880s? It may be no coincidence that Milton's first resident Methodist minister arrived in 1878.[28] James Chisholm, who had been Presbyterian minister at Tokomairiro since 1870, was in 1895 convenor of the Synod of Otago and Southland's Committee on the State of Religion. In his report he noted 'a growing tendency to deal in private with cases that used formerly to be dealt with in open session . . . kindly yet faithful dealing in private is more likely to lead to repentance than the somewhat cold formalities of ecclesiastical discipline'. Significantly, he also noted that discipline could only be effective 'when there is little temptation to evade its salutary effects by the prospect of a ready welcome awaiting the offender in other denominations'.[29] The records of other denominations in New Zealand during this period reveal little evidence of disciplinary procedures. If these churches disciplined their members and potential members they did so much more discreetly than the Presbyterians, possibly through private counsel by a minister or elder. Furthermore, they appear to have baptised willingly any baby, regardless of the sins of its parents.

We have already seen an example of a Presbyterian evading discipline, where Port Chalmers blacksmith Andrew Wilson took his baby to the Methodist minister for baptism. Another member of the Port Chalmers Presbyterian Church avoided discipline for antenup-

---

28. DJ Sumpter and JJ Lewis, *Faith and Toil: The Story of Tokomairiro* (Dunedin: Otago Centennial Historical Publications, 1949), 58–9.
29. 'Report on the State of Religion', in Presbyterian Church of New Zealand: Synod of Otago and Southland, *Proceedings of the Synod of the Presbyterian Church of Otago and Southland October-November 1895* (1895), 42.

tial fornication by joining her husband with the Methodists.[30] Indeed, the negligible degree of session discipline for sexual behaviour at Port Chalmers and Lawrence may have been entirely due to the presence of other thriving Protestant churches in those districts. In the urban setting of Dunedin, there were numerous alternative options. Thomas Burns of First Church married Agnes Gray and David Blackie in 1864. Seven months later he recorded the birth of their daughter in the baptismal register, but noted that she had not actually been baptised, because the Blackies, guilty of antenuptial fornication, had 'gone to the Baptists fugitive from discipline'.[31] The fact that session discipline did survive through the 1860s at First Church probably had much to do with the commitment of Thomas Burns; it quickly fizzled out after his death in 1871.

The agency of parishioners, who could take their baby, and themselves, to another congregation, clearly played a part in the decline of traditional Calvinist church discipline in New Zealand, as it did elsewhere. Parishioners also exerted considerable control over the form that infant baptism took. Church authorities regularly asserted that baptism should take place in the church, in the face of the congregation; it was, after all, a sacrament which symbolised the integration of the infant into the Christian community. In practice, though, many Presbyterian baptisms took place in the parents' home.

George Brown, the pioneer Presbyterian minister at Onehunga, kept a careful record of the baptisms he performed there in the early 1860s. Of forty-nine baptisms, twenty-three—just under half—took place in the church, and the rest in homes. Most babies were between one and three months of age at their baptism, with six weeks the most popular age. Two baptisms were conducted urgently: one on the same day the child was born and another, which Brown annotated as 'sick', when the baby was just three days old.[32] Clearly parents had little difficulty convincing their ministers to conduct baptisms privately, and sometimes urgently, however much this contradicted the Calvinist

---

30. Port Chalmers Presbyterian Church, Session Minute Book, 10 December 1879, 5 April 1880. PCANZ-ARC. Jessie Moir's husband, F Lean, is listed as a regular attendant at Methodist quarterly meetings from 1877: Port Chalmers Methodist Church, Quarterly Meeting Minutes. Hocken Collections..
31. First Church of Otago, Baptismal Register, entry 1247. Copy of register at Hocken Collections.
32. Onehunga Presbyterian Church, Baptismal Register 1860–4. PCANZ-ARC.

ideal. As the century drew to a close, the Onehunga kirk session began a campaign against private baptism: the minister was to 'in all cases endeavour to get parents applying for Baptism to bring the children to the church'. Three consecutive annual reports expressed pleasure that 'parents are more and more conforming to the Rule of having Baptism celebrated before the assembled congregation', though clearly some still clung to private ceremonies.[33] At the other end of the country, in 1897 the Synod of Otago and Southland's Committee on the State of Religion reported that,

> private baptisms are greatly in excess of those which take place in church. Distance from church is often assigned as the reason for this arrangement; but as there are some town congregations that scarcely ever witness a public baptism, there is evident need for a change of procedure.[34]

Private baptism shifted the emphasis of the sacrament from the congregation to the family; christening, as it was more often called, was as much about the integration of a new baby into the family as it was a Christian ceremony. This is typified by the celebrations which took place at the Thomson home in Dunedin in 1887. George and Emma Thomson were devout Presbyterians; George, who was a high school science master, served over the years as precentor, deacon, elder and Bible class leader at Knox Church. When their fifth child was two months old, they arranged for their minister to come up to the house and baptise her, together with the fifth child of George's brother William and his wife, born just three weeks after theirs. Three generations of the extended Thomson family gathered to welcome the new babies into the family; three friends were also present. After DM Stuart baptised the cousins in the drawing room, all adjourned to the dining room for a party.[35]

---

33. Onehunga Presbyterian Church, Session Minute Book, 29 April 1892; annual reports for 1893–5, written into minute book. PCANZ-ARC.
34. 'Report on the State of Religion', in Presbyterian Church of New Zealand: Synod of Otago and Southland, *Proceedings of the Synod of the Presbyterian Church of Otago and Southland 1897* (1897), 66–7.
35. Emma Thomson diary, 2 November 1887, MS-1312/1. Hocken Collections; GM Thomson diary, 2 November 1887, AG-926/2. Hocken Collections. On GM Thomson, see his entry in the *DNZB*.

Baptism also held cultural significance for its association with the naming of the baby. Even for a devout, educated, middle-class Presbyterian like George Thomson this was perhaps the most significant aspect of the ceremony: he recorded in his diary 'Baby was christened today "Elizabeth Anna", and William and Sarah had theirs christened James Douglas, by Dr Stuart'. Many families recorded their details at the front of a Bible, and adding a new baby's name to the list was another act which conflated the integration of the child into the family with its welcome into the Christian community. No matter where the baptismal ceremony took place, many babies had special christening robes previously worn by siblings or earlier generations of their family; again, this symbolised their integration into that family at their baptism.

Though their motives may not have been all that John Calvin, or contemporary church authorities, preferred, most people with any sort of affiliation to Presbyterianism in colonial New Zealand participated willingly and in significant numbers in the sacrament of baptism. The same can not be said of the other sacrament, communion. Kirk sessions controlled access to communion and individuals had to become communicant members before they could participate; many avoided having their names added to the communion roll. Over a ten year period the Presbyterian Church of New Zealand—which included all parishes north of the Waitaki—asked kirk sessions to supply statistics on the number of church adherents as well as communicants.[36] Adherents were, by definition, people sixteen years of age and over who rented a pew or regularly attended services, but were not communicant members.[37] When first collected in 1874 (see Figure 5 at end of text), these statistics revealed that, of the twenty-nine parishes which returned the full information, only one, Leeston,

---

Thomson diary, 2 November 1887, AG-926/2. Hocken Collections. On GM Thomson, see his entry in the *DNZB*.

36. The results were printed every year from 1874 to 1883 in Presbyterian Church of New Zealand: General Assembly, *Proceedings of the General Assembly of the Presbyterian Church of New Zealand*.

37. *The Book of Order; or, Rules and Forms of Procedure of the Presbyterian Church of New Zealand* (Dunedin/Wellington: New Zealand Bible, Tract, and Book Society, 1887), 3. Prior to this date the Presbyterian Church of New Zealand used the Victorian *Book of Order* as its guide.

had more communicants than adherents. In most parishes, less than a third of regular adult churchgoers took communion. By 1883 (see Figure 6 at end of text), when the statistics on adherents were last collected, communicant numbers had increased and they outnumbered adherents in eleven of forty-four parishes but, overall, adherents remained more than half of the total.

There were still six parishes where fewer than one in five of the congregation took communion. Two of those parishes were districts well known as Highland Scottish settlements, Waipu and Turakina. Highlanders were notorious for their reluctance to take communion and Presbyterians in these parishes were simply continuing the accustomed practice of their homeland. Accounting for the other four parishes is more difficult. Two—Reefton and Kumara—were mining districts on the West Coast. Their residents were more mobile than those in other parts of the country, so perhaps less likely to commit to church membership. There were also more Highlanders there than in some parts of New Zealand, though, as elsewhere, Lowlanders provided the majority of Scottish migrants.[38] For the other parishes, Gisborne and Blenheim, I have no explanation. At the other end of the scale, the rural Canterbury parish of Leeston was exceptional, with 82 per cent of the adult congregation committed to communicant membership in 1883. The long-serving minister, James Warnock Cree, may have been responsible for these impressive figures. Cree, though originally from Ayrshire, had been ordained in England and served as minister at Shrewsbury before his migration to Canterbury. In England, where Presbyterianism was a gathered tradition, he may have been accustomed to placing more emphasis on commitment to full church membership; he was said to have a forceful personality.[39]

It is clear, though, that most ministers had limited success in convincing adherents to commit to full church membership. Mary Ramsay, a Scottish daughter of the manse, migrated to Dunedin in 1867. She wrote to her mother three months later,

---

38. Jock Phillips and Terry Hearn, *Settlers: New Zealand Immigrants from England, Ireland and Scotland 1800–1945* (Auckland: Auckland University Press, 2008), 108.
39. Register of Ministers; family history information at http://www.cree.ie/genealogies/frameset.htm?p=http://www.cree.ie/genealogies/cree-o/p46.htm, accessed 10 August 2009; personal communication with Yvonne Wilkie, Director of PCANZ-ARC.

> I am very much astonished that so many here attend Church regularly and yet have never communicated even Fathers and Mothers I know several, and have spoken to them, they don't seem to look upon it as a duty, far less as a most blessed privilege.[40]

In 1880 the Synod's Committee on the State of Religion took particular interest in attendance at communion, reporting that in about half of the parishes of Otago and Southland participation was not what it ought to be.

> This state of matters indicates, it is to be feared, a low state of personal religion, when the privilege of commemorating the dying love of the Saviour is neglected, and an opportunity of refreshing their souls and holding communion with God is disregarded. It is also to be regretted that some who might be expected to unite with the Church keep aloof, so far as the Sacrament of the Supper is concerned.[41]

Individual kirk sessions regularly expressed regret at the failure of some, especially young men, to join the ranks of communicant members.[42]

I suspect, though, that reluctance to participate in communion often arose not from 'a low state of personal religion', but from a sense of unworthiness. Many a scruple developed over Paul's warning in

---

40. Mary Stuart Ramsay, Dunedin, to her mother Mary Ramsay, 19 June 1867, Misc-MS-1800/002. Hocken Collections.
41. 'Report on the State of Religion and Sabbath Observance', in Presbyterian Church of New Zealand: Synod of Otago and Southland, *Proceedings of the Synod of the Presbyterian Church of Otago and Southland* (1880), appendix, 6.
42. For example, see 'Annual Report of the Session & Deacons' Court of Knox Church, Dunedin. For Year ending 31st December, 1878', 7. Knox Church Dunedin archives, Dunedin; St Paul's Presbyterian Church, Oamaru, Session Minute Book, 12 November 1889, 2619/27b. North Otago Museum; report on annual meeting of St James's Presbyterian Church, Auckland, *Daily Southern Cross*, 11 August 1865, 5; report on annual meeting of St Andrew's Presbyterian Church, Gisborne, *Poverty Bay Herald*, 1 February 1882, 2; report on annual meeting of St Peter's Presbyterian Church, Christchurch, *The Star*, 25 January 1889, 4.

scripture: 'For he that eateth and drinketh unworthily, eateth and drinketh damnation to himself . . .'[43] Agnes Macgregor, daughter of the Calvinist theologian James Macgregor, was just fifteen when she took communion for the first time in 1883. Her diary reveals her as very devout, yet she felt considerable hesitation about her readiness to join the church:

> . . . Nellie and I are to be communicants next Lord's day. I hope we are fit. I don't quite know about it, for at least am [sic] not living the sort of life I ought to be. But it is God's command, and must be obeyed, and we must not trust in our own righteousness.[44]

For many other young people, hesitation won out. Some, as in the Highlands, would not join communion until they were much older, out of fear that they were vulnerable to falls from grace in their younger years.

Though church authorities regretted the failure of many Presbyterians to join communion, their own words and actions encouraged such behaviour. Most kirk sessions purged the communion roll every year or so and would not dispense the token required for admission to the Lord's Table to anyone of suspect behaviour. The services leading up to communion encouraged self-examination and in many southern districts the traditional fast day holiday, which focused the attention of churchgoers on preparation for communion, survived into the late nineteenth century. But it was the fencing of the table, where, immediately before the sacrament, the minister warned the congregation against taking communion unworthily, which probably had the most to answer for.

John Christie was the long-serving minister of the rural parish of Waikouaiti. In 1887 he addressed the communicants there: 'Let us pause as it were to think on what we are about to do, lest we put forth our unclean hands rashly to touch the holy things of God'. He then read, and briefly expounded, the Ten Commandments and a passage from Galatians 5 detailing the 'works of the flesh' and the 'fruits of

---

43. 1 Corinthians 11:29.
44. Agnes MacGregor diary, 15 March 1883, Misc-MS-1291 (photocopy of original). Hocken Collections. 'Nellie' was Agnes's sister Helen.

the spirit'.[45] The communion was no open invitation: 'There are no qualifications required to come to Christ, but just to flee to him as we are. We are to come to him in our sinful condition. But qualifications are required for the sacrament . . .'[46] This is typical of the traditional Presbyterian fencing address, except that in earlier periods the discussion of the Ten Commandments and sins of the flesh was unlikely to be brief.[47]

A more positive attitude towards communion developed in the later nineteenth century. Many sessions replaced communion tokens, which members came forward to obtain at fast day services, with communion cards, delivered by elders as an invitation: Presbyterians were increasingly invited to communion rather than having to prove themselves fit to attend. With this changing mood came the decline of fencing, which began its gradual demise in Scotland in the 1860s.[48] There is insufficient evidence to determine when fencing fell out of favour in New Zealand, but the conservative John Christie was using the traditional form in 1887, and he was unlikely to be the only one.

Calvin himself emphasised the grace of God in the sacrament of communion. He criticised those who demanded 'a perfection of faith to which nothing can be added' in those who partook of communion;

> it were too stupid, not to say idiotical, to require to the receiving of the sacrament a perfection which would render the sacrament vain and superfluous, because it was not instituted for the perfect, but for the infirm and weak, to stir up, excite, stimulate, exercise the feeling of faith and charity, and at the same time correct the deficiency of both.[49]

---

45. John Christie, 'October Sacrament 1887', John Christie papers, DA 12/1. PCANZ-ARC.
46. John Christie, sermon, October 1885, *ibid*.
47. On fencing the tables, see George B Burnet, *The Holy Communion in the Reformed Church of Scotland* (Edinburgh: Oliver and Boyd, 1960), 39–41, 262–3; Leigh Eric Schmidt, *Holy Fairs: Scottish Communions and American Revivals in the Early Modern Period* (Princeton: Princeton University Press, 1989), 109–13.
48. Burnet, *Holy Communion*, 278; Douglas M Murray, 'Continuity and Change in the Liturgical Revival in Scotland: John Macleod and the Duns Case, 1875–1876', in *Continuity and Change in Christian Worship: Papers Read at the 1997 Summer*

Although Calvin's followers in the Presbyterian Church valued the grace of God very highly, other elements of the reformer's theology, including the emphasis he placed upon church discipline, led them to develop a communion tradition which, however unintentionally, discouraged many of the faithful from participation.[50]

Practice is critical to religion. It also provides a convenient way into the religious world of the past. Some colonists left behind letters or diaries which reveal their religious beliefs, but for the majority of lay people we have no such sources. What, then, do the sacramental practices of Presbyterians in colonial New Zealand reveal? It is clear that most Presbyterians valued the sacraments highly. Indeed, they valued communion so highly that many felt unworthy to participate in it. Baptism was a different matter. With the interests of their children in mind, parents avidly sought the sacrament and, if deemed unworthy, many voluntarily appeared before the session in order to obtain the privilege. Those not prepared to undergo discipline expressed their commitment to baptism by obtaining it elsewhere.

The practices of baptism and communion had changed significantly since the days of John Calvin. His assurance that baptism was not essential to salvation meant that Presbyterians, on the whole, felt less urgency about the sacrament than some other denominations, but they still regarded it as an essential life ritual. Sacramental traditions evolved in response to popular belief and practice, and reveal that Presbyterian ministers had less influence than we may have realised. Against the teaching of church authorities, parishioners preferred baptism to be a family-centred private ritual. Many also resisted the urgings of their leaders to join the sacrament of communion.

Church records also reveal that nineteenth-century Presbyterians were not always as puritanical as we may have imagined. Sex before marriage was clearly fairly common among the rural working classes of Tokomairiro. Their church leaders did not approve such behaviour,

---

Meeting and the 1998 Winter Meeting of the Ecclesiastical History Society, edited by RN Swanson (Woodbridge (Suffolk): Ecclesiastical History Society/Boydell Press, 1999), 396–407.

49. Calvin, *Institutes*, IV.xvii.41–2.
50. For further discussion of the rituals of the Presbyterian communion season, see Alison Clarke, "'Days of Heaven on Earth': Presbyterian Communion Seasons in Nineteenth-Century Otago', in *Journal of Religious History*, 26/3 (2002): 274–97.

but this did not discourage parishioners from their accustomed social patterns; it simply meant that, when caught out by pregnancy, they had to appear before the session and appear remorseful, or leave the church for another. Later the session disciplinary requirement was dropped and any moral lapses dealt with by a personal visit from the minister. Church discipline evolved, not because of theological disapproval of the Calvinist ideal, but because it had to fit the realities of a more heterogeneous society; once again, the people in the pews were largely in control.

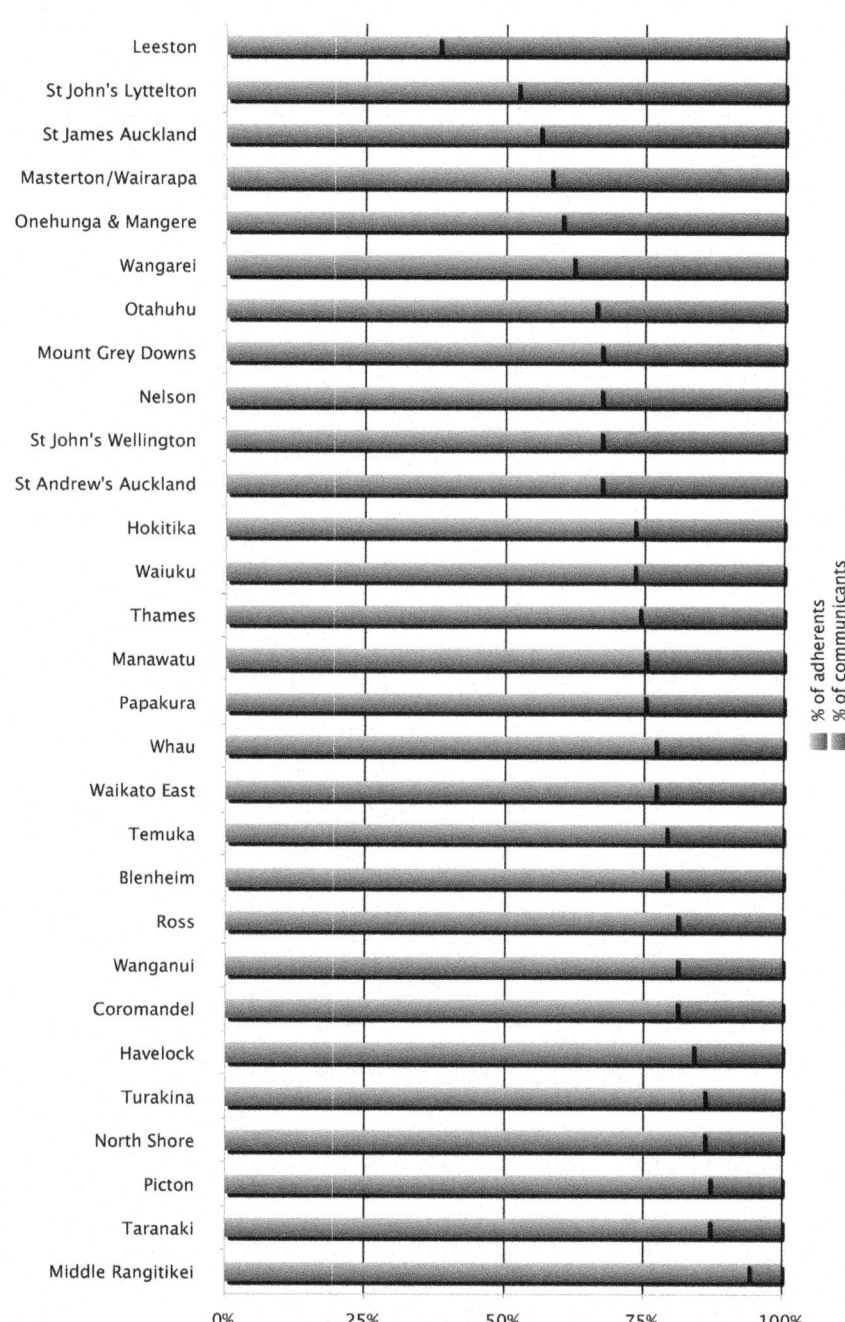

Figure 5: Church Membership 1874. *Proceedings of the General Assembly of the Presbyterian Church of New Zealand,* 1874.

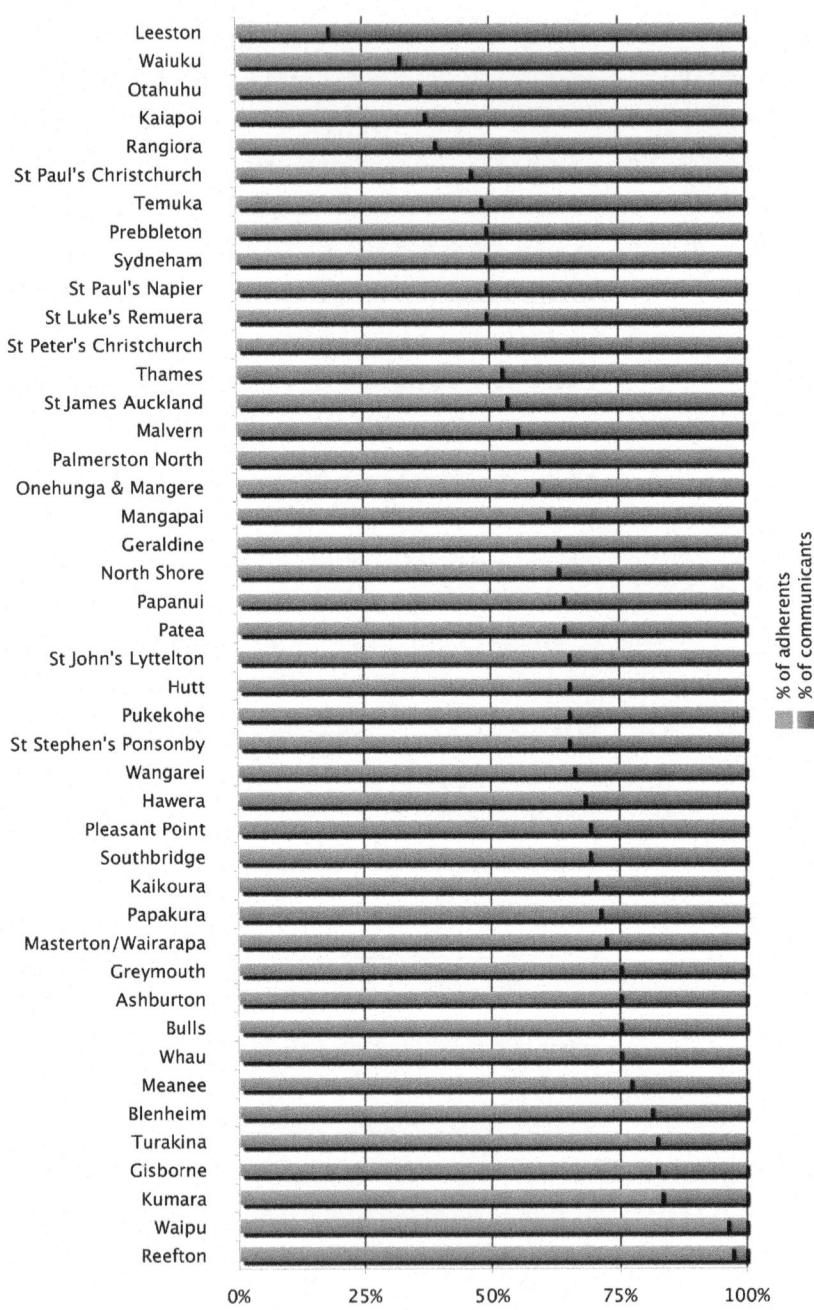

Figure 6: Church Membership 1883. *Proceedings of the General Assembly of the Presbyterian Church of New Zealand,* 1883.

11
'Mr Calvin and Mr Knox': The Calvinist Legacy in the Fiction and Poetry of New Zealand Scots

Kirstine Moffat

In 1972 New Zealand poet James K Baxter described the Calvinist influence on New Zealand literature and society as 'that austere, anti-aesthetic angel'.[1] This description emerged from a critical climate that diagnosed 'the awful disease of Puritanism' as the root of New Zealand's cultural ills.[2] Not only did social and literary commentators such as Gordon MacLauchlan and Bill Pearson castigate the secular Puritan inheritance, Pearson famously describing this tradition as 'a sour spit, a denial of life itself', they also regarded Puritanism as a force against which authors ought to react.[3] Robert Chapman highlighted the prevailing critical perception when he commented that 'the attitude which the New Zealand writer takes to his society . . . [is] based on . . . an attack on the distortion produced by an irrelevant puritanism of misplaced demands and guilts'.[4] Critics writing about this anti-Puritan New Zealand literary tradition herald 'the writers of [Frank] Sargeson's generation' (writing from the 1940s onwards) as the founding fathers of this literature of social critique and protest.[5]

I have previously challenged the two principles underlying this view of New Zealand's literary history—that New Zealand writers regard the Puritan inheritance as a solely negative force and that the

---

1. James K Baxter, *Aspects of Poetry in New Zealand* (Christchurch: Caxton, 1972), 22.
2. Jane Mander, *The Story of a New Zealand River* (Auckland: Vintage, 1999), 30.
3. Bill Pearson, 'Fretful Sleepers', in *Landfall*, 6 (1952): 225; Gordon McLaughlan, *The Passionless People* (Auckland: Cassell New Zealand, 1976).
4. Robert Chapman, 'Fiction and the Social Pattern', in *Essays on New Zealand Literature*, edited by Wystan Curnow (Auckland: Heineman, 1973), 98.
5. Lawrence Jones, 'Puritanism', in *The Oxford Companion to New Zealand Literature*, edited by Roger Robinson and Nelson Wattie (Melbourne, Auckland: Oxford University Press, 1998), 455.

creation of an anti-Puritan literary oeuvre begins with Sargeson—arguing that New Zealand authors engaged with Puritanism in complex ways and that murmurings of discontent about the Puritan legacy could be heard as early as the 1880s.[6] In this paper I would like to turn attention to a related issue, literary representations of Calvinism in literature written by New Zealand Scots. I contend that, as with the broader preoccupation with secular Puritanism, the New Zealand literary engagement with Calvinism has a long history that is decidedly more complex than Baxter's reference to the 'austere, anti-aesthetic angel' would seem to imply.

At this point it is necessary to briefly consider three key terms that tend to be used, sometimes interchangeably, in this context: Calvinism, Puritanism and Presbyterianism. They all come out of the Reformation and can seem to be synonymous. A careful, historical ordering provides some clarity. John Calvin's *Institutes of the Christian Religion* grew, by the late 1550s, to eighty chapters. In it he constructed a magisterial edifice for the Reformed faith, 'a system of tightly reasoned, logically formulated morals, policy, and dogma'.[7] It may be asserted with some certainty that strong reactions to Calvinism, particularly from the mid-twentieth century, have more to do with the manner in which morality was strictly enforced in Geneva by the Consistory than with a genuine understanding of Reformed theology. Peter Watson has referred to 'the dictatorship of terror in Geneva', what Daniel Boorstin calls the 'reign of biblical morality'.[8]

Calvin's ecclesiastical ordinances would provide a model for Reformed Churches in Europe and the New World. Watson claims that the regime in Geneva gave its name to the 'Puritan' movement.[9] Puritanism is particularly associated with the transplantation of the Reformed Church, and Calvinist morality, to the New World. In the popular imagination, now, the term has come to be almost exclusively associated with a particular cast of mind (the connotations of which are almost entirely negative).

---

6. Kirstine Moffat, 'Destruction, Transformation, Rebellion, Alienation: The Critique of Puritanism in Pre-1930 New Zealand Novels', in *Journal of New Zealand Literature*, 16 (1998): 86–96.
7. Peter Watson, *Ideas: A History of Thought and Invention, From Fire to Freud* (New York, London, Toronto, Sydney: Harper Perennial, 2005), 462.
8. *Ibid*, 463.
9. *Ibid*, 463.

Presbyterianism relates more to a form of church government and organization composed of ministers and elders and the congregation of churches within the jurisdiction of any such church court. The faith engine which, historically, provided the doctrine inside these churches is, of course, the Reformed faith. Presbyterianism is, and has been, the church visible in countless Scottish towns and villages and in Dunedin and the province of Otago, the area of New Zealand that all of the authors considered here either lived in or wrote about.

While the New Zealand authors of Scottish birth discussed in this paper do at times engage with Calvinist dogma, such as predestination and justification by faith, they react far more strongly to what some see as the tyranny of Calvinist Puritan morality and others regard as the template for a life of hard work, sound education, and egalitarian principles.

Specific references to either Calvinism or John Calvin are rare in New Zealand literature. Louisa Baker describes the villain of *The Perfect Union* (1908) as the 'son of a staunch Calvinist…who would not have averted perdition from the unelect if he could'.[10] In a novel otherwise unrelated to religion in New Zealand, Robert Carrick's *A Romance of Lake Wakatipu (A Legend of the Lakes): Being Episodes of Early Goldfields Life in New Zealand* (1892) does include a description of the 'sacramental Sabbath' in the Free Church settlement of Dunedin. 'Secular employment' is forbidden on this day, which is 'devoted to…sermons on Bell Hill or in the Valley, a little study of Calvin and a cold dinner'.[11] Likewise, in Wilhelmina Sherriff Elliot's *Service: A New Zealand Story* (1924), which will be considered in detail later in this paper, there is a passing reference to 'Mr Calvin and Mr Knox' in a passage questioning the orthodoxy of Presbyterian minister Cosmo Hallam.[12]

The coupling of Calvin and Knox and Calvin and Dunedin are significant because the authors considered here are all of Scottish birth and write predominantly about Southern New Zealand in their

---

10. Louisa Baker, *The Perfect Union* (London: Digby, Long, 1908), 40–1.
11. Robert Carrick, *A Romance of Lake Wakatipu (A Legend of the Lakes): Being Episodes of Early Goldfields Life in New Zealand with Itinerant, Statistical, Historical and Other Notes* (Wellington: George Disbury, 1892), 33.
12. Wilhelmina Sherriff Elliot, *Service: A New Zealand Story* (London: Stockwell, 1924), 15.

novels and poems. Dunedin and Otago have particularly close associations with Scotland. Established in 1848 under the auspices of the Lay Association of Members of the Free Church of Scotland, the Otago settlement was founded with the intent to 'build a moral and God-fearing community, enjoying Scottish forms of religious and educational provision'.[13] All of the authors discussed in this paper identify themselves as Scottish New Zealanders and write about Southern New Zealand, particularly Otago. Many of them write in a kind of Scots patois, seeking to evoke a Scottish cadence, vocabulary and accent through their poetry and prose.[14] Writing between 1861 and 1924, these seven authors, Reve Wardon, Constance Clyde, John Barr, Alexander Bathgate, Wilhelmina Sherriff Elliot, Dugald Ferguson and Bannerman Kaye, grew up in Presbyterian homes, many of them remaining within the church throughout their lives. These writers speak frequently of Presbyterianism, sometimes of the doctrines of sabbatarianism, predestination and original sin, and occasionally of Knox, but their references to Calvin and Calvinism are rare. Regardless of terminology, they all directly engage with the Calvinist inheritance, although in diverse ways, demonstrating that the New Zealand literary engagement with the Calvinist tradition is more complex than has been previously acknowledged.

The Scottish sensibilities of these authors are also visible in the literary models to which they turned for inspiration. In 'Otago and Scotland' Ferguson pays tribute to 'Scotia's minstrels': Burns, Ramsay, Campbell, Scott, Hogg and Tannahill.[15] Robert Burns was particularly beloved by New Zealand authors of Scottish birth. Elliot eulogises Burns' 'quenchless hate of wrong', while Barr hails Burns as the 'Minstrel Chief' and models his own poetry, such as the parodic 'On

---

13. RR McClean, 'Scottish Piety: The Free Church Settlement of Otago, 1848–1853', in *Building God's Own Country: Historical Essays on Religions in New Zealand*, edited by John Stenhouse and Jane Thomson (Dunedin: Otago University Press, 2004), 21.
14. All quotes in this paper are replicated as they appear in the published texts in order to keep the flavour and nuances of the original. Reading quotes aloud may help to clarify the meaning. Some passages will be translated in subsequent notes to assist readers.
15. Dugald Ferguson, 'Otago and Scotland', in Dugald Ferguson, *Castle Gay, and Other Poems* (Dunedin: Stone, Son and Co, 1912), 175.

a Rat', on that of his hero.[16] The other Scottish literary giant of particular influence on New Zealand writers of Scottish origin was Sir Walter Scott. Ferguson, whose historical epic about William Wallace was inspired by the fiction of his literary hero, lauded a Scott 'whose dazzling genius like a meteor burned' and whose 'brilliant mind… illumed the North'.[17]

Given that the authors considered here were steeped in Scottish literary traditions it is unsurprising that Calvinism is the central subject of so many of their poems and novels. Commentators writing about Scotland's literary history have pointed to the shaping power of the Calvinist inheritance. In 1840 Thomas Carlyle declared that,

> . . . Scottish literature and thought; Scottish industry; James Watt, David Hume, Walter Scott, Robert Burns; I find Knox and the Reformation acting in the heart's core of every one of these persona and phenomena; I find that without the Reformation they would not have been.[18]

As in New Zealand, twentieth-century critics have been insistent on the negative impact of Calvinism on Scottish culture. Edwin Muir perhaps best sums up this view when he writes that 'Calvinism . . . was a religion that outraged the imagination; and . . . helped to produce that captivity of imagination in Scotland . . . What Knox did was to rob Scotland of all the benefits of the Renaissance.'[19] Indeed, such was the antagonism towards Calvinism of some of the writers of the Scottish Renaissance of the 1920s and 1930s, such as Hugh MacDiarmid and Neil Gunn, that they 'tended to seek a revival of Scottish

---

16. Wilhelmina Sherriff Elliot, 'To Robert Burns', in Wilhelmina Sherriff Elliot, *From Zealandia: A Book of Verse* (London: JM Watkins, 1925), 147; John Barr, 'Awake My Muse', in John Barr, *Poems and Songs, Descriptive and Satirical* (Edinburgh: John Greig and Son, 1861), 240. Barr's 'On a Rat', in Barr, *Poems and Songs*, 14, is modelled on Robert Burns' 'To a Mouse'.
17. Dugald Ferguson, 'Sir Walter Scott', in Ferguson, *Castle Gay, and Other Poems*, 130. Ferguson also wrote a novel about William Wallace, *The King's Friend: A Tale of the Scottish Wars of Independence* (Paisley: Alexander Gardener, 1905).
18. Thomas Carlyle, 'The Hero as Priest', in Thomas Carlyle, *Thomas Carlyle's Collected Works, Volume XII: Heroes and Hero Worship* (London: Chapman and Hall, 1869), 171.
19. Edwin Muir, *John Knox: A Portrait of a Calvinist* (London: J Cape, 1930), 308–9.

community based on a Celtic or Jacobite past, rather than look back to Presbyterianism and Covenanting traditions'.[20]

These dualities are present within the Scottish literary tradition. John Galt's *Ringan Gilhaize* (1823), Sir Walter Scott's *Old Mortality* and George MacDonald's *Alec Forbes of Howglen* acknowledge that Calvinism bred in its adherents some redeeming features, such as moral toughness and a fierce, if sometimes misguided, dedication to a cause, and popular novels such as Annie S Swan's *The Forerunners* (1917) praise the Covenanters and Dissenters for their integrity and independence. However, from Burns' 'Holy Willie's Prayer' (1786), to James Hogg's *The Private Memoirs and Confessions of a Justified Sinner* (1824), to Robert Louis Stevenson's *Dr Jekyll and Mr Hyde* (1886), to George Douglas Brown's *The House of the Green Shutters* (1901), to Lewis Grassic Gibbon's *Sunset Song* (1935), Scottish writers castigate Calvinism as a repressive theological and social force responsible for warping the psyche of a nation and breeding fear and hypocrisy. Some New Zealand authors of Scottish birth were influenced by this tradition and clearly wish to contribute to the anti-Calvinist critique in a New Zealand context, while others wrote to praise and, indeed, proselytise, their Presbyterian faith.

The most damning of the early New Zealand literary critiques of Calvinism comes in Reve Wardon's 1892 novel *MacPherson's Gully*. I have been unable to discover any personal details about Wardon, but the names and background of his central characters and some of his language suggests a Scottish connection. The novel opens as a typical pioneer parable. Alick and Jeanie Spencer come to New Zealand in search of a better life. They work hard, read from 'the Guid Book' every night and attend their Presbyterian church regularly.[21] At first these virtues are rewarded. A combination of industry and economy enable the Spencers to buy a section and build a cottage, realising their dream of owning their own home.

Even in times of difficulty their faith remains strong. When Alick loses his job in a boot factory he remains undaunted and prays for

---

20. Professor Stuart Brown, quoted in George Rosie, *Curious Scotland: Tales from a Hidden History* (London: Granta, 2004), 36–7.
21. Reve Wardon, *Macpherson's Gully: A Tale of New Zealand Life: Containing Some Views of the Social Outlook from the Proletarian Standpoint* (Christchurch: Simpson and Williams, 1892), 6.

God's blessing on his new endeavour of searching for gold. After he hears of the death of his daughter his momentarily wavering faith is restored by his encounter with a mysterious old man who preaches a message of resignation to God's will, instructing Alick to rejoice in his poverty; for wealth 'promotes the growth of sordid selfishness' while poverty creates an awareness of 'the constant need of Divine Succour'.[22] The old man urges Alick not to grieve for his daughter who waits his coming 'in a purer atmosphere'.[23] Alick's confidence in a personal God of love and salvation is strengthened and at this point in the novel the reader is likely to be convinced that they are reading a Job-like morality tale of suffering and hardship that will eventually be rewarded.

However, Wardon sets up the morality convention only to undercut it. Having found some gold and about to realise his ambition to 'be the owner and occupier of a freehold farm', Alick dies in a flood on his way home.[24] His son dies of diphtheria and his wife goes mad and is committed to a mental institution. The reader perhaps expects to hear one last platitude at this stage, a reminder that the trials of this life are insignificant in the context of eternity. Wardon offers no such comfort. Shattering the expectations he so carefully constructed, he argues that Alick's death is an example of futility, that his industry is without purpose, that his faith in God is a delusion. Alick is a 'failure', whose 'brief appearance on the world's stage' will be followed by 'utter extinction'.[25]

Far from being a narrative of faith, Wardon's tragic parable is written not to instil belief in a Calvinist God but to illustrate the author's socialist beliefs, which are apparent in his subtitle: *A Tale of New Zealand Life: Containing Some Views of the Social Outlook from the Proletarian Standpoint*. An inset anti-capitalist speech from the Scottish socialist Mac locates Alick's fate within the historical dialectic of a proletariat who will never achieve wealth and stability however hard they work:

> ... the great bulk of the masses ... retain but the heritage of despair ... their lives a mere funeral procession to the

---

22. *Ibid*, 37–8.
23. *Ibid*.
24. *Ibid*, 26.
25. *Ibid*, 47.

> grave . . . I tell you that to-day the face of the poor man who strives to bring up his family honestly is held as securely to the grindstone as if he were chained thereto . . . [26]

Mac claims that the Church is the ally of the capitalists in the oppression of the people, with its message of 'the virtue of contentment . . . the duty of pious resignation'.[27] This helps to instil order and resignation into the working people, thus aiding the cause of the capitalists. At the same time the Church welcomes capitalists into the fold, allowing those who extort money and labour from the poor to cover their greed with 'the mantle of respectability' and 'the reputable robe of righteousness'.[28] Mac urges the people to throw off the shackles of the Church and establish a 'new Order . . . in which the selfish individualism now rampant in society will give place to a loyal regard for the common weal'.[29]

However, Wardon seems unconvinced of the ability to realise this better world. His atheism eventually trumps his socialism with a vision of nihilistic despair. Wardon ends with a savage attack on the Calvinist faith in which his hero has put his trust, declaring in a direct address to the reader that 'there is neither truth nor justice in the universe of God', and that the journey of each individual is 'hopelessly blank, utterly destitute of all permanent significance'.[30] For Wardon the 'whole sum of human existence' is a 'meaningless farce—a mere sardonic wrinkle on the passionless face of Time'.[31] He ends with an apocalyptic vision of the earth as 'an airless, waterless waste' circling aimlessly in space.[32]

Constance Clyde also plays genre and narrative games with her readers in her 1905 novel *A Pagan's Love*. Clyde is the penname of Constance McAdam, who was born near Glasgow in 1872 and arrived in Dunedin when she was seven. Her first short story appeared in the *Dunedin Star* and she moved to Sydney to work as a journalist

---

26. *Ibid*, 19.
27. *Ibid*, 19–20.
28. *Ibid*, 20.
29. *Ibid*, 21.
30. *Ibid*, 27.
31. *Ibid*, 47.
32. *Ibid*.

in 1898, sometimes writing under the pseudonym Clyde Wright.[33] As with *McPherson's Gully*, it initially appears as if Clyde intends to write a parable of Presbyterian salvation and redemption. Her protagonist Dorothea Wylding feels confined by the small Otago town of Waihoa in which she grows up. She leaves for the wider horizons of Sydney where she comes under the influence of a feminist activist and solo mother Ascot Wingfield and reconnects with her childhood sweetheart Edward Rallingshaw, now a committed atheist and socialist. Edward is already married and he tries to persuade Dorothea that marriage is an outmoded capitalist institution and that she should liberate herself from convention and enjoy a free love union with him. Tempted by both her love for Edward and by the example of the independent Ascot, Dorothea demands that God find her a new love in three months if he wants to prevent her union with Edward. Edward's death in a fire on the final day of the three-month bargain is interpreted by Dorothea as 'God's answer': 'Thus He had prevented her wickedness. Thus He had annulled on the very day of its commencement that impious alliance, and rebuked that blasphemous bargaining!'[34] Her 'puritanical mind' is restored and she returns to Waihoa and marries the Presbyterian minister John Archieson.[35] At this stage the narrative cycle of sin, repentance, salvation and restoration appears to be complete.

However, this is just the beginning of the real conversion at the heart of the novel. Dorothea's reintegration into the Presbyterian community is short-lived. She comes to believe that the pagan creed of Ascot and Edward, a combination of feminism, atheism and socialism, is the true creed and she leaves her husband to return to Sydney to work to improve working conditions for women. Jettisoning her Calvinist beliefs, which Clyde describes as 'this coarse, church-belled heathenism', Dorothea longs for a 'new religion . . . to bring new life to all, giving peace and harmony to these tired and aimless sojourners through this land of the Broken Cross'.[36]

---

33. AG Stephens Papers, Australasian Autobiographies, QMS–0095, Alexander Turnbull Library.
34. Constant Clyde, *A Pagan's Love* (London: Unwin, 1905), 272.
35. *Ibid*, 303.
36. *Ibid*, 217.

Dorothea's decision paves the way for the Reverend Archieson to undergo a similar awakening. At the beginning of the novel Archieson is a typically earnest Presbyterian minister 'sincerely anxious to do the will of God' and suspicious of anything unconventional.[37] His love for Dorothea and discovery of her history with Edward force him to 'lift the candle of experience to the face of truth and look'.[38] All his certainties are examined and challenged and the elders of his Waihoa church complain that he has become 'too heterodox'.[39] Archieson's final sermon succinctly captures the pagan moral vision Ascot and Edward embody and Dorothea and himself move towards. He questions whether 'there is such a thing as sin' and declares that 'it is not the higher but the broader life that we want; we need our minds enlarged rather than our souls purified'.[40] In a clarion call for individual choice and moral and intellectual freedom Archieson ends:

> . . . there comes a time to us all when we feel that we must break the bonds that bind us, however sacred they may seem; when we must go against the written word and forswear the signed pledge. There comes a time to many of us when we must forsake these quiet homes of ours, and breaking out into the world, let it do with us as it will, learning the Right at last only by having first known the Wrong. What was Christ, after all, but a Divine Adventurer wandering from the ordered courts of heaven down to this one lawless world, the Bohemia of the universe.[41]

Archieson's heterodoxy reunites him with Dorothea. The ex-Calvinist hero and heroine resolve to work together to free others from religious and moral bondage and promote 'a new morality and religion of love rather than law, of fulfillment rather than denial'.[42]

---

37. *Ibid*, 1.
38. *Ibid*, 306.
39. *Ibid*.
40. *Ibid*, 307.
41. *Ibid*, 309.
42. Lawrence Jones, 'The Novel', in *The Oxford History of New Zealand Literature*, edited by Terry Sturm (Auckland: Oxford University Press, 1991), 130.

The poetry of John Barr does not condemn Presbyterian belief in such a comprehensive way as Clyde. Born in Paisley in 1809, Barr immigrated to New Zealand in 1852. He bought a farm near Dunedin and became an important figure in the cultural life of the city, establishing the inaugural Burns Club, and becoming laureate of the Caledonian Society of Otago.[43] Many of Barr's poems are written in what Alan Riach terms a 'vernacular Scots'.[44] Barr writes of the virtues of prayer and faith and delights in the success of devout, honest men and women who work hard to achieve a better life for themselves and their children. His heroes are the 'jolly boys' who are not above the 'rough' work of 'ploughing', 'ditching' and 'splitting posts and nails' and the wives who transform 'humble cot[s]' into 'happy homes'.[45] Barr is critical of anything that threatens the wellbeing and success of these hard-working immigrants to New Zealand, in particular, class hierarchies, social pretensions and the abuse of alcohol.

While Barr favours the ballad and the humorous, satiric sketch, on occasion he adopts the role of moralist. This is particularly seen in his poems about the evils of drink. Barr adopts the voice of a lamenting wife in 'O Willie, Willie, My Gudeman' who weeps at the poverty her husband's 'weary drink' has brought her to: 'My claes are hangin' a' in rags, / My taes are through my shoon'.[46] For Willie's wife, alcohol is 'hemlock's juice' which is responsible for 'broken heart[s]' and even 'death'.[47] Likewise, in 'Drunken Davie Deil-Me-Care' the title character's drinking has brought poverty to himself and his family. Barr ends with a question and a plea:

> O Drunken Davie Deil-me-care
> Where now is a' your pride,
> When ye gaed decent to the kirk
> Wi' Nancy by your side?
> For heaven's sake hae done wi' drink,

---

43. Ronda Cooper, 'Barr, John 1809–1889', *Dictionary of New Zealand Biography*, updated 22 June 2007 http://www.dnzb.govt.nz/.
44. Alan Riach, 'Scotland', in *The Oxford Companion to New Zealand Literature*, edited by Roger Robinson and Nelson Wattie (Melbourne: Oxford University Press, 1998), 483.
45. 'Cheer Up, My Jolly Boys', in Barr, *Poems and Songs,* 68; 'There's Nae Place Like Our Ain Fireside', in *ibid*, 19.
46. Barr, *Poems and Songs*, 172.
47. *Ibid*, 174.

> For love o' wife and wean,
> And happy days may yet be yours,
> For a' that's come and gane.[48]

However, Barr's moralising relates only to the abuse of alcohol and not to the substance itself. He regards a drink as a natural reward at the end of a hard day's labour and is very critical of the Calvinist-Puritan suspicion of pleasure. In 'Noo Quat Your Fiddlin' and Your Fun' he rails against sanctimonious social reformers, who he describes as the 'unco guid', who attempt to banish 'gin and brandy', 'concerts, balls and races' and anything that involves alcohol, 'fiddles' or 'fun'.[49] In spite of the declared pious motivations of such reformers, Barr believes that their real agenda is a desire for 'carnal power . . . to rule the roast on every hand'.[50] The 'unco guid' also feature in Barr's poetry as hypocrites who 'drink on the sly' and 'tipple sherry cobblers', while condemning everyone else to a diet of 'beans and bran'.[51]

Barr is particularly derisive of Calvinist hypocrisy and self-righteous. The satirical 'Let Cannons Roar and Trumpets Blaw' punctures the posturings and pretensions of Jock the Precentor, whose sartorial splendour of a 'coat weel trimm'd wi' gold and lace' cannot conceal the effects of 'gin' on his 'vulgar, brazen face'.[52] Barr is incensed that it is the Jocks of the world who rise to positions of prominence and importance through their grandiose ideas of their own importance. The poem also contains a satirical deconstruction of the impact of Christianity on Maori, with Jock regaling a London audience on a trip back to Britain with a tale of

> . . . a' that the Kirk has dune
> For Maories that were waefu' blin',
> And hoo they ate the flesh and skin
> O' their ain mithers;
> But noo they're a' reclaimed frae sin,
> And live like brithers. [53]

---

48. *Ibid*, 7.
49. *Ibid*, 206.
50. *Ibid*, 207.
51. *Ibid*.
52. *Ibid*, 233.
53. Barr, 'Let Cannons Roar and Trumpets Blaw', in Barr, *Poems and Songs* 233.

Barr's 'The Hypocrite Gangs to the Kirk', clearly modelled on Burns 'Holy Willie's Prayer', is just as damning:

> With studied gait, or visage sour,
> He acts the saint, or Simon Pure,
> The better to beguile;
> He cares for no one but himself,
> His only aim is catching pelf,
> By every means that's vile.[54]

Barr is angered at the inability of the congregation and the community to see beneath the Hypocrite's pious exterior to the selfish greed that is his true nature. In spite of the way in which the Hypocrite 'cheats mankind by every quirk', he is 'often preferr'd / To men of worth who never swerv'd, / Or stained bright honour's name'.[55] However, the poet exacts his revenge on the Hypocrite, foretelling a 'future dark' in which he is 'laid in a dishonour'd grave, / A branded villain and a knave'. Barr clearly believed that a certain degree of Calvinist retribution and punishment was warranted.

The Hypocrite's crimes of duplicity and insincerity are compounded by his worship of wealth and his elevation of 'money' into 'his god'.[56] Throughout Barr's poetry there is a repeated refrain that 'the love of money is an evil root, / It changes men and makes them like the brute'.[57] Thus, while his poetry attacks the distortions of Calvinist theology by bigots and hypocrites rather than the church itself, he does warn that a belief in predestination can lead to a desire to be seen to be visibly favoured through temporal success and prosperity. This has the potential to foster greed and bolster what Barr regarded as the evils of capitalism. This is highlighted in 'O But Siller's Bonnie!' in which Barr castigates the way in which the avaricious 'Talk o' Christian duties, [that] they never feel' while trying to 'pluck' a neighbour 'every way [they] can'.[58] To those who 'worship a God that's

---

54. Barr, 'The Hypocrite Gangs to Kirk', in *ibid*, 247.
55. Barr, *Poems and Songs*, 248.
56. *Ibid*, 248.
57. Barr, 'The Love of Gold', in Barr, *Poems and Songs*, 95.
58. Barr, *Poems and Songs*, 193.

wrapped up in a purse' Barr has this advice: 'be wise, and think mair of your soul'.⁵⁹

Perhaps the most complicated engagement with Calvinist theology is to be found in Alexander Bathgate's 1913 novel, *Sodger Sandy's Bairn: Life in Otago Fifty Years Ago*. Born in 1845 in Peebles, Bathgate was educated at the University of Edinburgh. When his family came to New Zealand in 1863 he worked as a banker, barrister, newspaper director, novelist and poet. Apart from writing, Bathgate's main interest was conservation and civic improvement, organising the Dunedin Suburban Conservation Society and founding the Dunedin Art Gallery.⁶⁰ *Sodger Sandy's Bairn* opens with a scathing attack on Calvinist self-righteousness and hypocrisy. Listening to a fire and brimstone sermon on the text 'Flee from the Wrath to come' in his Scottish hometown Perblane, John Thompson

> . . . derives a grim pleasure from the denunciations being hurled from the pulpit at 'the wickit'. That somewhat vague epithet did not, if one might judge by the expression of his face, include John Thompson, though he could, without difficulty, have enumerated a goodly number of his fellow-hearers to whom, in his opinion, it might be justly applied, and the contemplation of their ultimate doom afforded him no little satisfaction.⁶¹

John is a severe, joyless miser who whips his son and sends him to bed without supper for daring to move in church and thus making him 'an object a' dereesion afore the hale congregation'. He refuses a friend an extension on a loan because financial difficulties are 'a judgment o' Providence on ye for yer sins'.⁶²

However, while the novel critiques aspects of the Calvinist character, the outworking of the narrative shows forces of retributive justice

---

59. Barr, 'Ye're Never Contented', in *ibid*, 46.
60. Geoffrey F Vine, 'Bathgate, Alexander 1845–1930', *Dictionary of New Zealand Biography*, updated 22 June 2007 http://www.dnzb.govt.nz/; Nelson Wattie, 'Bathgate, Alexander', in *The Oxford Companion to New Zealand Literature*, edited by Roger Robinson and Nelson Wattie (Auckland: Oxford, 1990), 41–2.
61. Alexander Bathgate, *Sodger Sandy's Bairn: Life in Otago Fifty Years Ago* (Sydney: New South Wales Bookstall, 1913), 7.
62. *Ibid*, 28.

at work. In Bathgate's world view the wages of sin are most definitely death. John excludes one son from his will, only to die in misery and want because Rob, the son he endows with his wealth, also inherits his own miserly, selfish disposition. After Rob's son John tries to rape his cousin Nancy he falls to a drunken death. Rob's determination to keep his money from his family is foiled when his holographic will is found to be illegal in New Zealand.

A Calvinist belief in the need for punishment and judgment is articulated by the title character, Sodger Sandy, really John Thompson's long lost rascal son who deserted his wife and fled to New Zealand. When Welsh evangelists try to 'save' him by preaching a message of 'Repent . . . if you would save your soul alive', Sandy replies that he has no forgiveness for himself:

> Why you dinna' ken what it is to repent. Man, Ah would gladly roast in the hell you speak o' to a' eternity if Ah could undae the past. Will ma repentance gi'e back her ruined life to the woman Ah lo'ed, or restore onybody Ah ha'e wranged to their former poseetion? Ah ha' ena' been an evil leevin' man [I have never been an evil living man], but still my selfish thochlessness [thoughtlessness] has been disastrous to others. For masel' Ah care nothing. Ah can trust God that made me, an' Wha'll maybe find mair excuse for me than Ah can find for masel'.[63]

The Welsh Methodists declare that Sandy is 'a blasphemer and a heathen', but Bathgate makes it clear that while he has contempt for Calvinist hypocrisy he concurs with Sandy's assessment that sin should be punished.[64] Indeed, while the novel challenges aspects of Calvinism, the novel ultimately regards Presbyterianism as the only worthwhile religion and the mark of a good Scot. The Welsh Methodists are not the only non-Presbyterian denomination to be found wanting. The funeral service in the Anglican prayer book is regarded as being a pallid send-off for Sandy, with a Scottish friend declaring that

---

63. *Ibid*, 133.
64. *Ibid*, 134.

'Sandy was a Presbyterian and…Ah'll pit up a bit of a prayer masel".[65] The Irish Catholics come in for even more abuse, attacked as being feckless, disrespectful of property rights on the gold fields and prone to violence as a means of getting their own way.

Like Bathgate, Wilhelmina Sherriff Elliot has a complex relationship with Calvinism. Born in Edinburgh in 1845, Elliot came to New Zealand with her parents, John and Elizabeth Bain, when she was thirteen. The family settled in Southland, with both a country estate and a town house in Invercargill. After the tragic death of her fiancé, Elliot worked as a teacher, and became a prominent member of the National Council of Women and a social activist who advocated pacifism, protective laws for workers, women on juries, prison reform, and proper provision for the dependants of propertied men.[66] Her 1924 novel, *Service: A New Zealand Story*, upholds a Presbyterian ethic of service and is dedicated to the Scottish Presbyterian minister and social activist Thomas Guthrie. However, the novel also highlights what Elliot regards as the limitations of the church.

The hero of the novel, Presbyterian minister Cosmo Hallam, works hard in his Queenstown parish and is beloved of his parishioners. Even the irreligious members of the community respect him, particularly when he heroically rescues a man trapped under a fallen tree, and he has significant success in stamping out swearing and drinking in his community. However, Hallam's theological views are distinctly nonconformist. Near the beginning of the novel, after listening to a sermon on the 'Oneness which flows through all life', a commercial traveller queries: 'Mr Calvin and Mr Knox / Is Mr Hallam orthodox?'[67] This unorthodoxy intensifies as the novel progresses. Hallam comes to regard 'creedal conventionality' as 'irksome', particularly petty denominational differences and debates, and feels that the church does not always do enough to address the 'vast needs of humanity', particularly those of the body such as hunger and homelessness.[68]

---

65. *Ibid*, 175.
66. Megan Hutching, 'Bain, Wilhelmina Sherriff 1848–1944', *Dictionary of New Zealand Biography*, updated 22 June 2007 http://www.dnzb.govt.nz/.
67. Elliot, *Service*, 15.
68. *Ibid*, 41–2.

Hallam's faith is severely tried when his children are killed and his wife Elvin temporarily blinded in a lightning strike. At first Hallam responds in orthodox fashion, preaching a sermon on the text 'Thy will be done'.[69] However, reflection ignites questions and discontent. Eventually Hallam finds it impossible to remain in 'doctrinal bounds'. He leaves New Zealand declaring: 'I must leave the Free Church of Scotland to be a free man in Scotland'.[70] He and his wife still believe wholeheartedly in Christian service, but of a practical rather than theological nature. In an inversion of the typical emigration pattern Cosmo and Elvin return to Edinburgh. New Zealand does not possess enough poverty and vice to provide an outlet for their mission, Edinburgh proving a more suitable hotbed of drunkenness and evil. Elvin pleads: 'Oh my Edinburgh! . . . Rouse thee! Purge thee of thy crimes! Not only is thy drunkenness a by-word; but the lust of thy dark plans are a stench unto humanity!'[71]

Elliot's message in *Service* reflects her own religious position, which is perhaps best described as a socialist, humanist, anti-denominational Christianity. In one of her poems, 'Anthem of the Universal' she expresses her faith in:

> One cosmic brotherhood,
> One universal good,
> One source, one sway!
> One law beholding us,
> One purpose moulding us,
> One God enfolding us
> In love always![72]

Dugald Ferguson is less conflicted about the merits of his own Presbyterian faith. Ferguson was born in the Western Highlands in 1833. Before settling in Otago in 1870, he spent time in Australia. In later years Ferguson moved to Waipu and then worked as a bookseller in Takapuna. He was best known for his collections of poetry and

---

69. *Ibid*, 54.
70. *Ibid*, 58.
71. *Ibid*, 46.
72. Elliot, 'Anthem of the Universal', *From Zealandia*, 174.

his novels, many of which ran to several editions.[73] Like himself, his heroes are all committed Presbyterians, their faith regarded by Ferguson as a proud marker of their Scottish heritage. Duncan Farquharson, the hero of *Bush Life in Australia and New Zealand* (1893), reads the Bible every day, keeps the Sabbath free of toil and prays for 'God's blessing upon his efforts'.[74] This faith in God, combined with a life of hard work, results in success for Ferguson's heroes, who emigrate to New Zealand in search of a better life, David Lochead, the hero of *Mates*, describing New Zealand as 'a splendid field for fortune-building'.[75] Avoiding 'low delights' and 'sensual pleasures vile', the 'high ideals' and 'stern control' of Duncan and David ensure that temporal blessings abound and that the heroes can look forward to the 'future happiness' of a heavenly 'crown'.[76]

In contrast, Ferguson's villains, such as the lawless bushranger Randal Marsden in *Bush Life*, come to a bad end. Marsden fashions a living from stealing cattle. In contrast to Duncan he is contemptuous of religion, declaring: 'The decorous man goes to church on Sunday, in superstitious fear of future damnation; the man of daring chooses to think for himself, and uses Sunday—like any other day—for his own pleasure, and scoffs at superstitious consequences'.[77] The 'conventional sobriety' of Duncan is ridiculed by Randal, who advocates a life of 'daring independence'.[78] However, it is the steady Duncan who succeeds, while Randal is captured for his crimes, refuses to repent and drowns while attempting to escape. Randal's pleasure-filled, irreverent life may hold a superficial appeal, but Ferguson the author models himself on his own Calvinist God, who he describes in a poem as a 'dread Judge' who condemns the ungodly to damnation.[79]

Such is Ferguson's devotion to Presbyterianism that all of the characters who come to a good end in his fiction are either born or convert

---

73. Nelson Wattie and Pauline Neale, 'Ferguson, Dugald', in *The Oxford Companion to New Zealand Literature*, (1990), 178.
74. Dugald Ferguson, *Bush Life in Australia and New Zealand* (London: Swan, Sonnenschein, 1893), 312.
75. Dugald Ferguson, *Mates* (London: Hodder and Stoughton, 1911), 15.
76. Dugald Ferguson, 'Evil Communications', in Dugald Ferguson, *Job and Other Sacred Poems* (Dunedin: James Horsburg, 1898), 157.
77. Ferguson, *Bush Life*, 150.
78. *Ibid*, 150.
79. Ferguson, 'Evil Communications', in *Job and Other Sacred Poems*, 157.

to what he regards as the true faith. In *Bush Life*, Duncan Farquarson rejoices when his friend Benjamin Lilly converts to Presbyterianism when he falls in love with the devout Teenie Sutherland. Ferguson's contempt for Catholicism, the archenemy of Presbyterianism, is apparent when he speaks of Lilly as ripe ground for conversion because he already possesses the necessary 'antagonism' to 'the leading Romish doctrines—such as the celibacy of the clergy, priestly absolution, papal infallibility'.[80] The lukewarm Catholic becomes a committed man of faith once he has been shown the light of the 'true' faith.

Ferguson's fiction and poetry also reveals a strict sabbatarianism. He frequently puts pen to paper to castigate those who work on Sundays, describing the Sabbath as 'the hallowed day of rest' and declaring that God will wreck a 'dreadful vengeance on their heads / Who trample on His Laws'.[81] In 'The Bible Appeal' he is equally troubled by the attempts of the New Zealand government to ban the Bible from schools and vows to 'fight those . . . / Who would yield the strong tow'r of the Protestant home / To the infidel's sneer or the sophists of Rome'. He regards himself as following in the heroic footsteps of the Covenanters, who he describes as: 'That stern race of iron, whose zeal for the Lord / Made them worship in fear with their hands on the sword'.[82]

Bannerman Kaye's 1900 novel *Haromi* is similarly complimentary to Calvinist-Presbyterian theology. Eliza Bannerman Maclaren was born in 1854 in Lossiemouth, the daughter of Presbyterian minister Peter Maclaren. The Presbyterian influence remained strong throughout her life. She married Albert Kaye in 1873 in Australia and the young couple moved to Christchurch where Kaye was instrumental in forming the Christchurch Young Women's Christian Association. Kaye led a Bible Class for many years and edited the Presbyterian Women's Missionary Union paper *Harvest Field*. Her tombstone in Karori cemetery reads: 'They rest from their labours and their works do follow them'.[83] The purpose of her novel, Kaye's only venture into

---

80. Ferguson, *Bush Life*, 356.
81. Ferguson, 'The Sabbath', in *Job and Other Sacred Poems*, 113.
82. Ferguson, 'The Bible Appeal', in *ibid*, 115.
83. Clare Simpson, 'Eliza Kaye', in *The Book of New Zealand Women: Ko kui ma te kaupapa*, edited by Charlotte Macdonald, Merimeri Penfold and Bridget Williams (Wellington: Bridget Williams Books, 1995), 342–3.

print, is to promote Protestant faith as the foundation of a better and more just world.

Kaye argues that Scottish Presbyterianism, with its emphasis that all are one in the sight of God, strips away the false hierarchies of class, gender and race. Actually, while *Haromi* does provide a fascinating critique of a class-bound patriarchal worldview, it does not do away with hierarchies altogether. Kaye inverts traditional hierarchies to produce a new hierarchy of Presbyterian faith in which belief separates the 'saved' from the 'damned'. Kaye's Presbyterian God is a God of love, forgiveness and inclusion, and through the course of the novel all of the central characters attain salvation through the example of God's representatives on earth, the shepherd Duncan Cameron and the Presbyterian ministers Mr MacArthur and Dugald MacLeod. The selfish and materialistic Millicent is transformed into the self-sacrificing 'angel lady' of the London slums; her violent half-brother James eventually devotes his life to converting North Island Maori; petty thief Jock McLennan becomes a Salvation Army preacher; and the hedonistic Robert Agnew resolves to paint pictures of Palestine as a means of sharing his new-found faith.[84]

It is through Robert that Kaye's feminist, Presbyterian, egalitarian message is particularly evident. At the beginning of the narrative the snobbish Robert expresses surprise at the esteem afforded to 'one of [Duncan's] class'. The minister's wife immediately reprimands him, declaring: 'Duncan Cameron is only a shepherd, it is true, but he is one of nature's gentlemen, which is a good deal more than can be said of many of those to whom the world cringes'.[85]

Robert's class snobbery is allied to racist and sexist attitudes. He is saved from these through the intervention of Duncan, who is the moral centre of the book and who epitomises Kaye's inclusive, feminist moral outlook. Robert has seduced the half-caste Haromi, who bears him a child. The first stage in Robert's redemption comes when Duncan convinces him that he must marry Haromi. Robert is reluctant, complaining that 'one can hardly imagine her in Society', and that 'a fellow likes to have a wife that will do him credit and can entertain ... and, you know ... when a girl has once made herself cheap—

---

84. Bannerman Kaye, *Haromi: A New Zealand Story* (London: Clarke, 1900), 431.
85. *Ibid*, 9.

well, anyhow it's not pleasant for a man to feel that his wife can't hold up her head as high as others'.[86] Duncan castigates Robert's hypocrisy:

> I'm thinkin' the verra de'ils in hell maun be lauchin' tae hear ye. Div ye think 'at there's twa Gods, ain for men an' ain for women, or 'at the Almighty hes twa laws, ain by whilk a man can 'tak his ain selfish wull ohn consequences, an' ain by whilk a wumman is dammed for yielding, moistly through loeing' ower muckle? I dinna haud the wumman free o' sin . . . but mostly the man is the greater sinner, an' moistly he tak's little tent o' the mischief he hes wrought. But, mon, there wull come a day when this sin wull burn intil yer hairt wi' a burnin'.[87]

True repentance comes to Robert with Haromi's death. She dies as Robert comes to make reparation. Her 'love-lit face and outstretched arms' as she drowns, suggestive of Christ on the cross, are imprinted on Robert's mind and he sees his actions and attitudes in a new way:

> Every thought and action with regard to Haromi seemed to start into prominence, and clearer and clearer the light upon them seemed to grow until, with a horror that was perfectly indescribable, he felt as if he stood before the Throne of God, and saw himself and his sin in the radiance that shone round about it. He shrieked aloud with terror . . . for Robert had awakened to a sense of his sin.[88]

Conversion transforms Robert's life. He revokes his old pursuit of pleasure, resolves to devote his art to God's service, and cares for his

---

86. *Ibid*, 381–2.
87. *Ibid*, 383. 'I'm thinking the very devils in hell must be laughing to hear you. Do you think that there are two Gods, one for men and one for women, or that the Almighty has two laws, one by which a man can take his own selfish will without consequences, and one by which a woman is damned for yielding, mostly through loving too much? I don't hold the woman free of sin…but mostly the man is the greater sinner, and mostly he takes little care of the mischief he has wrought. But, man, there will come a day when this sin will burn within your heart with a burning.' Translated by author.
88. *Ibid*, 408.

daughter. Most importantly, he recognises the hypocrisy, sexism, racism and bigotry of his former attitudes, finally acknowledging that all are one in the sight of God.

This paper, by way of exploring the works of seven authors who engage with Scottish Presbyterianism in their fiction, has attempted to challenge two of the assumptions which continue to dominate the world of New Zealand letters. Firstly, the fiction of Wardon and Clyde and the poetry of Barr highlight that a critique of a Calvinist-Puritan theological and secular inheritance was not the invention of Frank Sargeson and his heirs in the 1940s. Rather this tradition is as old as New Zealand literature itself and is clearly modelled on the work of eighteenth- and nineteenth-century authors such as Burns and Hogg. Secondly, and even more importantly, this paper has demonstrated that the engagement of New Zealand authors with Calvinism is not a succession of monochrome variations on the same theme. The nineteenth- and early twentieth-century authors considered in this paper respond to Calvinism in individual and complex ways. Yes, Wardon and Clyde reject Calvinist theology and Barr rails against Calvinist hypocrisy. But Bathgate and Elliot enter into a complex dialogue with Presbyterianism, highlighting both its enduring strengths and perceived limitations. And for Ferguson and Kaye the Calvinist-Presbyterian legacy in New Zealand is a positive one, capable of sweeping aside the barriers of race, class and gender and bringing about a better world.

12

Calvin in Australia and New Zealand

Ian Breward

Calvin's influence in our region has been refracted through confessions of the sixteenth and seventeenth centuries and the memories which migrant church members and ministers brought with them. There was little direct discussion of Calvin himself. What occurred happened at Assembly, in theological education, scholarly discussion, parish preaching and teaching and through the press.

Until the end of the nineteenth century, Calvinism retained considerable strength in the Presbyterian churches, both as a theological framework, but also as a social culture of self-improvement, which inspired politics, capitalism, education and ethics, as well as the patterns of church life. That was especially true of the Free Church of Scotland and its offshoots, in which Calvinism was given a new vitality after 1843. Missionary energy was important in building new societies overseas, though it could be self-righteous and light on social responsibility. It could also be opposed to inherited privilege and was strongly antiCatholic.

Theologians like Chalmers, Bannerman, Cunningham and Candlish made important contributions to this recovery of Calvinism. The doctrine of vocation energised the ways in which people saw their work as an offering to God and a blessing from God. Some Baptists, Congregationalists, Calvinistic Methodists and Churches of Christ also had a Calvinist heritage, but that was being subsumed into a more broadly based Evangelicalism, often suspicious of too much creedal definition.

The cultural patterns persisted, but Calvinist confessional identity was being eroded by the growing influence of scientific thinking, philosophical changes and wide-ranging attacks in the press on historic Calvinism and its alleged links with wowserism. Calvinism may not have been true Christianity, as some of its defenders claimed, but it certainly had a polarising influence because of the range of its claims to authority.

Within the major Presbyterian churches on both sides of the Tasman, the effect of changing attitudes to biblical authority, the influence of liberal theology and the paucity of ministers credibly able to deal critically with new paradigms of knowledge meant that Calvinism survived amongst a minority of conservative ministers, elders and laity, but even there was modified by Evangelical inputs, themselves under threat. The passing of the Declaratory Acts in the latter part of the nineteenth century were intended to ease consciences burdened by the by the detail of the Westminster Confession, but also weakened the integrity of classical Calvinism.

By the 1930s, there were signs of a reawakening of interest in Calvin, in part due to the growing influence of Barth and Brunner amongst English-speaking theologians and clergy. In congregations, however, use of the Shorter Catechism was in decline, for its teaching was no longer seen as suitable for Sunday Schools. The limitations of liberal theology were also becoming more obvious. The development of the ecumenical movement further challenged church leaders to re-assess their theological heritage. In our part of the world, reunion negotiations had a similar effect, by focussing attention on what was central to Christian identity.

By the end of the twentieth century, it was clear that a major cultural shift was taking place, which marginalised the churches as institutions, rejected the Christian assumptions of Australasian culture, changed the method and contents of education and lauded the benefits of multiculturalism. Australian Christians, in particular, found that Judaism, Islam, Buddhism and Hinduism were no longer the object of missionary work overseas, but challenged the place of Christianity at home in a different way from aggressive secularism and atheism which hoped for a future inspired by scientific rationality.[1]

Popular attacks on the allegedly narrow and unreasonable Calvinist morality, which had entered folklore in the seventeenth century, continued to be found in the press and other media. One of the most recent appeared in *Quadrant*, a significant Australian periodical, in

---

1. TR Frame, *Losing My Religion: Unbelief in Australia* (Sydney: University of NSW Press, 2009).

March 2007. Entitled 'The Puritan Anglicans of Sydney', its author, Peter Russell, argues that the diocese has been captured by Calvinist ideologues, who dominate Moore College and the Anglican Church League.

> The prime aim of this group is to preserve at all costs the Reformed Protestant character of the Sydney diocese and to vigilantly seek out and correct deviationism small or large . . . These developments have caused alarm to many, even on the old Evangelical/Low church side of Anglicanism, who believe that a blank and intolerant Calvinism dead to everything not in its direct purview has become the diocesan norm, and that the prayerful, reflective and tolerant strands of the broad Anglican inheritance are being ignored when they are not being actively disparaged.[2]

Most Calvinism is now of little public or political interest, replaced by other master narratives, though *Time* for 23 March 2009 suggested otherwise.[3] That has not always been the case. Dr Stuart Piggin has brought out its importance in his *Evangelical Christianity in Australia* (1996). There have been several studies of Calvinism in Australasia, but they do not adequately define what the term might mean, even in the theological sense, let alone in wider cultural terms.[4] Nor do they give adequate attention to the careful distinctions, which many leading historians, such as Basil Hall, make between Calvin and the developments introduced by some of his successors. These make a distinction between Calvin and Calvinism necessary, for they make too many assumptions about what Calvinism is and so overstate its influence.

---

2. Peter Russell, 'The Puritan Anglicans of Sydney', in *Quadrant*, (March 2007): 52.
3. David van Biema, '10 Ideas Changing the World Right Now: #3 The New Calvinism', *Time* 173/11 (23 March 2009): 50.
4. A Barkley, 'The Impact of Calvin in Australasia', in *John Calvin: His Influence in the Western World*, edited by WS Reid (Grand Rapids: Zondervan, 1982), 325-44; P Barnes, 'Australian Calvinism', in *Church Heritage*, 16/2 (2009): 118-26; CR Bale, 'Calvinism in Australia, 1788-2009', in *Engaging with Calvin*, edited by MD Thompson (Nottingham: Apollos, 2009), 274-97; RS Ward, 'Aspects of the Revival of Calvinism in Australia, 1938-78', in *Church Heritage*, 16/2 (2009): 94-117.

Calvinism includes emphasis on the supreme authority of Scripture; the sovereignty of God; justification by faith; salvation by grace alone, because of the universality of sin; imputed righteousness, stemming from the atonement; the necessity for Christians to grow in holiness; the importance of daily vocation; moderation in use of the created gifts of God; freedom in Christ; the importance of redeemed reason; accountability to God in final judgment and the importance of partnership in the God-given relationship of state and church. Such convictions were set out in confessional documents such as the Westminster standards and modifications like the Savoy *Declaration*. For Evangelicals who shared these convictions, confessional statements were unnecessary. Their foundation in the Bible and Christian experience was enough. They were more concerned about the separation of church and state as the basis for religious freedom, whereas Calvinists were in favour of embodying some of their social ethic in legislation, because they dared to hope for a more Christian society in the Australasian colonies.

Such convictions undoubtedly stem from Calvin, but there are important differences of emphasis in Calvin, notably in the intimate relation between listening to the Scriptures and reflecting theologically about the personal and cultural implications of God's revealed purposes. The systematic nature of the scholastic style theology of his successors has a different character from that of Calvin's *Institutes*. By the nineteenth century, it showed dangerous signs of ossification and inability to deal with the changing shape of knowledge, except by reiteration of what had been inherited. There was one important change—the translation of Calvin's writings, commentaries and letters into a set of published works in English between 1844 and 1855, which enabled people to read Calvin for themselves instead of through the eyes of his successors.

That can be seen in Professor Elder's *History of the Presbyterian Church of New Zealand*. He appreciated the importance of Calvin: 'He gave to western Europe a religion absolutely opposed to Roman Catholicism, based on the doctrines of Grace and Predestination and expressed with rigid logic and literary beauty'.[5] Elder recognised that Calvinism took different shapes in differing contexts. 'If Calvinism

---

5. J Elder, *History of the Presbyterian Church of New Zealand* (Christchurch: Presbyterian Bookroom, 1940), 4.

was somewhat hard, narrow and gloomy, it was virile and aggressive, and spread far more widely than Lutheranism . . . His doctrine became the fighting creed of militant Protestantism.'[6] Something of that was brought to New Zealand by the Scots and Irish.

> From Calvinism the Presbyterian Church in New Zealand inherited great and lasting traditions—a conviction of its responsibility to God and of its own mission as a Church, a strong ethical sense and a realisation of the necessity for instruction in the great tenets of the Faith. Calvinism, throughout its history, has shown, most of all, the value of a coherent and impressive system of faith which gives man a true sense of the presence of God, imbuing his life with the contagious thrill of a high purpose.[7]

In both nineteenth-century Australia and New Zealand, the direct influence of Calvin was limited, but the heritage of Scots-Irish Calvinism was an important part of Presbyterian identity, particularly through their influence in the wider culture.[8] Debates in the homeland on the Calvinist heritage were keenly followed in the colonies. Local disputes over the Sabbath, marriage law and the boundaries of grace amongst Presbyterians could still take place within a Calvinist theological framework up till the 1870s and 1880s. That could be seen in the debates over the 1843 Disruption, the attempts to reunite Presbyterians, disputes over state aid, and the contentions surrounding Dr JD Lang. In Melbourne, the Theological Hall had a Calvinist ethos, through Dr Adam Cairns, the first Principal, as well as through the later Professors, M MacDonald and JL Rentoul. The theological teaching in St Andrew's College, Sydney, had a similar character, though that began to change when Professor A Harper was appointed. In Dunedin, by contrast, the first Professor, William Salmond,

---

6. *Ibid*, 5.
7. *Ibid*, 10–11.
8. M Wood, *Presbyterians in Colonial Victoria* (Melbourne: Australian Scholarly Publishing, 2008); M Hutchinson, *Iron in Our Blood: A History of the Presbyterian Church in NSW, 1788–2001* (Sydney: Ferguson and CSAC, 2001); MD Prentis, *The Scots in Australia* (Sydney: University of NSW Press, 2008).

was from the outset a representative of those who were convinced that Calvinism needed to be rethought and restated.

In the Presbyterian Church of Otago and Southland, Dr James MacGregor showed that the intellectual depth of Calvinism was not exhausted. He had been one of Scotland's leading theologians, but migrated for family reasons and sought to restore some theological depth to the Presbyterians of the distant Scottish colony south of the Waitaki River. He was in regular published contact with North American Calvinists at Princeton, such as Charles Hodge, and before his death had completed an important study of apologetics. By the 1890s, however, the intellectual climate was changing and his approach no longer resonated widely.

In Melbourne, the preaching and writing of Dr Charles Strong, a migrant from the Church of Scotland, caused widespread concern amongst those of Free Church origins, for he was a disciple of Professor Caird of Glasgow University, seeking to adapt Christianity to modernity. Such views, influenced by Idealism, did not cause great concern in the Church of Scotland, where Calvinism was in serious decline, but they seemed threatening to the advocates of Calvinism in Victoria.[9] His ministerial certificate was withdrawn. After a brief return to Scotland, he returned to Melbourne and founded the 'Australian Church'.

Similar tensions emerged in Dunedin, where Professor Salmond, now Professor of Philosophy at Otago University, called Calvinist fundamentals into question in *The Reign of Grace* (1886). At First Church, Dunedin, the Rev. J Gibb was arousing conservative concerns for similar reasons, because of his critique of double predestination. In Wellington, the Rev. JG Smith's views on the atonement in *The Christ of the Cross* (1908) indicated that the recently united Presbyterian Church of New Zealand had significant ministers for whom the older Calvinism lacked authority and appeal. They wished to move much further to modify the Westminster Confession than the limited freedom permitted by the Declaratory Act.

Similar trends can be seen in the Congregational Churches on both sides of the Tasman. These reflected shifts taking place in England. Though they were never more than two percent of the population, they had some widely influential preachers and theologians in

---

9. Wood, *Presbyterians in Colonial Victoria*, 337ff.

Australia, such as Drs Bevan, Gosman, Kiek, Thatcher and Abba. In New Zealand, they lacked notable theological leaders.

Though the Calvinistic Methodists in Wales still had skilled defenders of historic Calvinism, Welsh migrants to Australia had to wrestle with issues of survival, rather than spending energy on theological debates. Some fifteen churches in Victoria in the nineteenth century were an inadequate base on which to build a Welsh-speaking denomination.[10] Only two congregations still survive. Their Calvinism has been replaced by Evangelicalism.

Baptists were a minority group, but were forming Unions to assist their work in New South Wales, Victoria and South Australia. The Strict and Particular Baptists had a strong Calvinist inheritance, leading them to adopt a sectarian stance to preserve their doctrinal distinctiveness. They had no theological leaders to help them effectively to adapt to a new cultural context. Within the wider Baptist community, Calvinist views were also in decline. CH Spurgeon was unashamedly a Calvinist, but his separation from the Baptist Union in England in 1887 won little support. Nevertheless, his sermons were widely read in Australasia, a number of graduates from his College migrated here and his son Thomas exercised an influential ministry in both Australia and New Zealand. Calvinism, however, was steadily being replaced by Evangelicalism, as the intellectual and emotional home of those who found the appeal of liberal theology unsatisfying. Few traces of Calvinism had survived by the beginning of the twenty-first century.[11]

The situation in the Church of England was more complex. Though *The Thirty-nine Articles* had significant Calvinist parallels and the *Irish Articles* even more, the initial ethos in Sydney was Evangelical. Some of the clergy were originally from the London Missionary Society, which selected some of its staff from the Calvinistic Methodists. Samuel Marsden had limited association with the Calvinist, the Rev. Charles Simeon, but is best understood as an Evangelical. With the

---

10. WN Gunson, 'The Contribution of the Calvinistic Methodist Movement to the Church History of Australia', in *Church Heritage*, 4/1 (1985): 28–59.
11. KR Manley, *From Woolloomooloo to 'Eternity': A History of Australian Baptists*, 2 volumes (Milton Keynes: Paternoster, 2006); D Parker, 'Jireh Particular Baptist Church, Brisbane', in *Baptist Quarterly*, 31/4 (1985): 159–78; M Chavura, 'A History of Calvinism in the Baptist Churches of New South Wales' (PhD Thesis, Macquarie University, 1994).

exception of the Evangelical Charles Perry of Melbourne, who had a somewhat tenuous link with Simeon at Cambridge, the first bishops all were High Church.

The appointment of Bishop Barker to Sydney marked a shift to Evangelicalism, which gradually put down roots and gave the diocese a distinctive character. That became decisive under Archbishop Mowll in the 1930s and was reinforced by the appointment of TC Hammond as Principal of Moore College from 1936 to 1953. While not a Calvinist, but a Cranmerian, he was well aware of the contribution made by Calvin and Calvinists to the Church of England and the Church of Ireland. He also realised that Evangelicalism needed a stronger theological foundation than the emphasis on personal experience, which was becoming influential.

Calvin, however, was almost unknown amongst the diocese's clergy. Marcus Loane, later to become a Principal of Moore College and the first Australian-born Archbishop of Sydney, gives a vivid description of how he came to read the *Institutes* in 1933–4, which were virtually unknown by other Sydney Anglicans, as an alternative to the teaching he was receiving at Moore College. He was captivated. 'I never knew another Moore College man or older Anglican clergyman who had read the *Institutes*. What directed my attention to Calvin was Reformation History. It seemed obvious that Calvin was to Protestants all that Thomas Aquinas was to Catholics.'[12]

During his term as Principal from 1953 to 1959, it was made compulsory in 1954 for all Moore students to read through the *Institutes*. That requirement is still in place, supported by Dr DB Knox, Principal from 1959 to 1985, making Moore almost unique in the Anglican Communion, as well as giving Calvin a place in the curriculum which is not matched by any of the Presbyterian theological colleges in Australia and New Zealand. No tutorials are given and there is no formal examination, but the requirement has created a diocesan climate which has a commitment to Reformed Christianity rarely found elsewhere in the Anglican Communion.

Australian Presbyterians had not altogether forgotten the historical Calvin. *The Messenger* (NSW) in 1909 published a series of articles on him in the issues of May 14, July 9, August 20 and September 3.

---

12. M Cameron, *An Enigmatic Life: David Broughton Knox: Father of Contemporary Sydney Anglicanism* (Sydney: Acorn Press, 2006), 135.

The first article pointed out that anyone familiar with the Shorter Catechism has been drinking in the theology of Calvin. His teaching had four features. They were the supremacy of God, the supremacy of the Bible, the supremacy of grace and the supremacy of Christ in his church. Calvin also insisted that, in the sacraments, believers 'take to themselves Christ Himself present in His divine-human character, and especially in all the loving self-abnegation of his atoning sacrifice'.[13] God's will was the ground of all events and His glory their end. Calvinism had no rest till it found the eternal in and behind the temporal.

That led to the question, How God was known? In an age when worship was overladen with ritual, and the government of the Church despotic, Calvin went back to the pure well-springs of the Bible, equipped for such study in ways equalled by few of his contemporaries. His stature as a commentator was still honoured. In practical terms, this commitment meant that when he dealt with worship 'his rule was to permit that only for which the Church could produce actual warrant'.[14] Yet he did not make the Bible a fetish. It was only the illuminating power of the Holy Spirit, which made it authoritative to conscience.

That same attachment to Scripture led him to his views on grace. The author of the article dealt frankly with the issues of election and reprobation, underlining that 'God's election does not prevent the Calvinist from preaching in its fullness to all the offer of salvation'.[15] Though there are difficulties in this opposition, we must hold contraries together, even though we cannot reconcile them here on earth.

Calvin gave new weight to the worth and dignity of man in the social institutions of states and churches. In that respect he was one of the founders of America. 'Calvin(ism) is distinguished by its spirit of nationality. It [sic] develops the individuality of peoples. It seeks its strength among the common people. It fosters in State and in church representative government. It opposes every despotism of pope or priest, or unlimited monarchy.'[16]

---

13. *The Messenger*, 14 May 1909, 313.
14. *Ibid.*
15. *Ibid.*
16. *Ibid*, 313–14.

Far from lulling Presbyterians into security, Calvinism is 'a trumpet call to holiness, a rousing command to action, to aggressive and missionary fervour'. And thus as Russell Lowell says, 'the doctrines of Calvin have produced some of the strongest and noblest characters the world has ever seen, the very fibre and substance of which Commonwealths are made'.[17]

In the issue of July 9, there were comments on Calvin's birth and humanity, the *Institutes*, Servetus and Calvin's contribution to Presbyterianism. Though its creedal principles have come from him, the editor argued that,

> . . . modern Presbyterianism does not bind itself to a hard and fast system of doctrine. It recognises, as Calvin did, the great mystery that besets the government of the universe, and enthrones God as Absolute Lord of All; but it sets up the love of God as well as His power, and declines to shut its eyes to the progress of Divine revelation. It see Christ as a Saviour for all mankind, and appeals to the freedom of man's will, believing that ultimate harmony between that freedom and the divine sovereignty will some day stand revealed.[18]

That was a reflection on current liberalising changes.

In addition to the editorial comments, the Rev. JC McDonald's fifteen minutes speech to the New South Wales Assembly was printed. He spoke on 'Calvin the Reformer', making some interesting comparisons with Luther, arguing that the limitations of his achievement necessitated a more radical reform. This was begun by Zwingli, 'but there is no doubt that the greatest exponent and the most powerful of that movement was John Calvin. He stamped the movement with his own spirit and temper through *The Institutes* and his leadership of the Reformed Church.'[19]

His challenge was to make a changed life the expression of a changed faith. 'The secret of the man is this, that his imagination, playing upon a primitive religious literature, helped him to see re-

---

17. *Ibid*, 314.
18. *Ibid*, 9 July 1909, 434.
19. *Ibid*, 441.

ligion as Jesus Himself saw it; and he set to work to make Christ's religion supreme in men's thoughts and lives. He sought to do this by two institutions, the holy Ministry and the Consistory.'[20] McDonald believed that his work was a heroic success, 'for nowhere was the will of God done so strongly and energetically as in Geneva'.[21] That was transmitted to Scotland through John Knox, who was proud to call Calvin his master.

Calvin was also the creator of Puritanism, whose influence in Scotland, England and America was massive and continuing. 'There are great conflicts to be waged, great wars to be fought, great victories to be won by this same spirit of Puritanism which we see raising itself and manifesting itself in our own fair land.'[22] For McDonald, Calvin's example calls us,

> . . . to gird up our loins and go forth to the same fight in which he spent his life, that we too, according to the measure of the power granted to us by God, may strive to make our community, our State, our Commonwealth, our Empire, part of the great Kingdom of our Lord and Saviour Jesus Christ.[23]

The final article was by the noted English Presbyterian, Dr O Dykes, who had spent some time in Victoria. He drew a contrast between the difficult times of the Reformation and the current missionary era. For Dykes, there was no sixteenth-century equal to Calvin in power of intellect, indeed no one since Augustine has been his peer. Even though the days of his intellectual ascendancy were over, the significance of his thought for philosophy and religion is unlikely ever to be exhausted. 'If this be at all a just estimate, it is obvious that Calvin is a large enough figure to allow different people to walk around and survey him from quite different sides, each taking note of the aspect which appeals most to themselves.'[24]

Reformer, churchman, divine, exegete, Calvin can afford to lose a few chips from his greatness as time goes by, and as the world's

---

20. *Ibid.*
21. *Ibid.*
22. *Ibid*, 441–2.
23. *Ibid*, 442.
24. *Ibid*, 3 September 1909, 556.

standards of measurement change, but remain memorable to the last. Dykes was surprised that the sources of Calvin's greatest impact in his time 'are the things which have proved most temporary, which as living forces are now almost everywhere decayed'.[25] It was his advocacy of Augustinian theology which has been his lasting legacy. That was explained by his clear-cut French intellect 'which proved with remorseless logic the cohesion of all the dogmas in the Augustinian system, worked it out to its furthest deductions, and expounded it with admirable French lucidity of statement'.[26] Scholars now would lay less emphasis on Calvin's logic and more on his gift for holding paradoxes together in a biblical manner.

The move of Lutherans away from positions, which had originally been occupied by all the first generation of Reformers, left Calvin's heirs to dominate the field in many parts of Europe. Their churches' confessions constitute his major significance as a divine, for they were largely drawn from the *Institutes*. They provided persecuted Christians with indispensable spiritual resources in the sixteenth and seventeenth centuries. Calvinism gave them a sense of unity and brotherhood. They suffered for the same sacred cause, bore each other up, sharing each other's disasters and successes, offered one another asylum and gave mutual aid. The stern teaching sustained them in struggle and endurance, 'for it was a masculine creed for strong men',[27] in the struggle against Catholicism. They were convinced that they were God's chosen fighters against His enemies, with tenacity in defeat and confidence against the deadliest odds.

> We in our piping times of peace and goodwill, with a weak-kneed faith and universal toleration for all sorts of and no creeds, can afford to think well and hope well of all men. But our forefathers fought as men chosen to be saints in the eternal purpose of God, ordained to be His witnesses and combatants for the truth against the ancient lie of Antichrist; His foe. To them the line of cleavage between elect and non-elect ran clear and

---

25. *Ibid.*
26. *Ibid.*
27. *Ibid.*

broad. And it followed that with God on their side they were predestined for victory in the end.[28]

'Moreover—and this was the best lesson of all—they learnt to count all temporal loss, even of life itself, a price cheerfully to be paid and reckoned small in comparison with the prize they were sure to win. They fought for the glory of God and for the kingdom of heaven. That cause deserved every sacrifice.'[29] Such was the faith that was called for in such arduous times. 'It was a stern hard faith, but it was one to live and die for. It poured its iron into the blood of these strong men.'[30] When that use had been served, the immediate work of Calvin was done, when the battle for Protestant freedom against Papal tyranny was won.

Every period has its own distinctive task for the Kingdom:

> We do not repudiate or deny the awful dogmas of election and predestination on which their souls fed; they have their place in the teaching of the New Testament and in the Body of our Christian faith. But other aspects of truth have in our day come to the front, and it is on larger, wider, more gracious truths we now need to nurture our souls for the very different work given to us to do. We are the sons of a missionary era. It is the world-wide mercy of the Gospel—the expansive compassion and all-embracing redemption of Christ—that we have to carry abroad through the whole race of our fellow men. . . . But let us honour the brave men who fought and suffered in the great days of old. And let us not forget the wise deep thinker, whose lessons made them what they were.[31]

In the 1920s and 1930s, major doctrinal disputes centred round Professor Samuel Angus, who taught at St Andrew's College in Sydney. He argued that his major departures from classical Christianity were

---

28. *Ibid.*
29. *Ibid.*
30. *Ibid.*
31. *Ibid*, 566.

justified by the Declaratory Act, and defended his conclusions as in accord with the message of the Scriptures in a succession of lively and widely read books. Attempts to try him for heresy after 1933 were unsuccessful and ended with his death in 1943. Though some of his critics dealt with his views in terms of the Westminster Confession, there was no significant reference to Calvin in their writings and speeches. Interest in him had not disappeared, but was found mainly amongst minority Presbyterian groups in an attenuated form.

A coalition, however, appeared in 1939. It was the Calvinistic Society of Australia. Formed in Melbourne on 15 June of that year, it was an initiative of the Rev. Arthur Allen of the Reformed Presbyterian Church of Geelong. Its committee included prominent members of the Presbyterian Church of Victoria, such as Professor J Gillies, the Reverends Aeneas Macdonald of Murrumbeena, JC Jamieson, leader of the Youth Department and WH Leembruggen, a Methodist. Maxwell Bradshaw, a young lawyer from Swanton's Hawthorn parish, was also on the Committee, later to become a key opponent of church union. Allen had been a student at the Free Church College, Edinburgh, where Professor MacLean had been one of the founders of the *Evangelical Quarterly* in 1929 and given Allen a vision of a scholarly journal of similar character. That began in 1942, edited by Allen and R Swanton, then a young minister at Hawthorn in Victoria, who remained an editor till 1988, along with able deputy editors.

The significance of the *Reformed Theological Review* grew with inclusion of Sydney Anglicans and Lutherans amongst its regular authors. It became an invaluable forum for the discussion of theological issues from both a Reformed and Evangelical perspective and was respected internationally. Though the Calvinistic Society ran occasional conferences, its influence had declined by the 1950s and the beginnings of reunion negotiations between Congregationalists, Methodists and Presbyterians from the 1960s. A Westminster Society was founded in New South Wales in 1948, later opposing reunion and providing a forum for some younger ministers with conflictual personalities, such as the Reverends G Kerr and R Donaldson, who found their selective brand of Calvinism a satisfying foundation for resistance to majority opinion in the Presbyterian Church of Australia. They also built relations with their New Zealand counterparts in the Westminster Fellowship. In the aftermath of the trial of Principal

L Geering for heresy in 1966, Kerr left the Presbyterian Church of Australia in 1967, which had made no pronouncement on the Geering case, and formed the Presbyterian Reformed Church, which eventually revoked his ministerial status in 1982. He took his own life in 1988.

The most important twentieth-century addition to Calvinist ranks came with considerable postwar Dutch migration. Some of them happily joined the Presbyterian Church of Australia and New Zealand, but many from the *Gereformeerde Kerk* found them too liberal for their comfort and they formed the Reformed Churches of Australia in May 1952, with the support of the Presbyterian Church of Eastern Australia and Free Presbyterian Church.[32] They were too small to provide a home and insistence on singing only unaccompanied psalms was off-putting to the Dutch. Nevertheless, they co-operated in forming the Reformed Theological College in Geelong in 1955, which had close relations with the Free University in Amsterdam, though local hopes for a similar Calvinist university were never realised. The academic stature of the college was enhanced by the arrival of Professor K Runia who taught from 1957 to 1971 and published widely. Other Dutch scholars, such as J Schep reinforced its academic reputation and brought the scholarship of Kuyper and Bavinck to provide a far wider and deeper Calvinist scholarship and professional education to the Reformed and Australian Presbyterian Churches, which provided its constituency. The Reformed Churches also established schools, some of which were named after Calvin.

In New Zealand, the Reverends PB Fraser and T Miller upheld nineteenth-century Calvinism. Fraser's magazine, *The Biblical Recorder* also had an evangelistic and eschatological interest, which owed more to American Dispensationalism than to orthodox Calvinism. Such views were opposed by JTV Steele, a passionate admirer of Calvin, who wrote an article attacking the Assembly evangelist, entitled 'Calvinism or Pietism' for *The Outlook*, 30 December 1931. There was also interest in Calvin in *Foursquare*, the magazine of the Young Men's Bible Class Union. Articles pointing out his continuing importance were written by influential younger ministers, such as AC Watson (later Moderator General of the Presbyterian Church of

---

32. *A Church En Route: 40 Years Reformed Churches of Australia*, edited by JW Deenick (Melbourne: Reformed Churches. 1991).

Australia), JTV Steele and HJ Ryburn in 1933. That year the Life and Work Committee, convened by RS Watson, was asked by the General Assembly to prepare material to celebrate the publication of the *Institutes* in 1936.

An order of service, modelled on Calvin's liturgy, was produced for use in August, extracts from the *Institutes* were combined in a booklet called *The Life of a Christian Man* and a series of articles appeared in *The Outlook*. They covered Calvin's teaching, his churchmanship, his worship, his contribution to Christian ethics, his role as man of God and minister, his role as reformer and the humanity he displayed in his correspondence. They were clearly linked with current theological concerns, which made Calvin relevant once again. Unfortunately the majority of the articles are anonymous, but we can confidently say that this celebration of Calvin owed a great deal to JM Bates.

Bates had done doctoral studies in Zurich under Professor E Brunner on Calvin's doctrine of the church. It was a very competent thesis, drawing on sources in Latin, French and German, dealing with the chronological development of the doctrine in Calvin's writing. While recognising the limitations of Calvin's doctrine of Scripture, Bates recognised that it had modern possibilities, which were not open in the sixteenth century. Faith and order were fruitfully combined, because Calvin had such penetrating insight into spiritual and historical reality. Unfortunately, Bates did not have the money to return to Zurich for the oral and so the degree was never awarded, despite being fully up to doctoral standard.

Bates shared his enthusiasm and respect for Calvin with others, especially JTV Steele, with whom he set up *The New Zealand Journal of Theology* in 1931. Unfortunately, it was not financially viable and closed in 1935. It opened up not only the importance of Calvin for a new generation, but also dealt with the new theologies emerging in Europe, which stressed the importance of wrestling with the original writings of the Reformers, instead of being content with the thought of their successors. Bates' *Manual of Doctrine* (1950) showed how that foundation could be relevant for laity, combined with attention to contemporary theology.

Not all agreed with either Bates' method or conclusions. Many Dutch migrants found New Zealand Presbyterians too liberal and became part of the Reformed Churches set up in Australia, wondering out loud if Presbyterianism could survive.[33] In 1950, the Westminster Fellowship was founded, in which two of Thomas Miller's sons, Rob and Graham, played an active part. Graham had been an influential missionary in Vanuatu and had a powerful ministry in Papakura after his return to New Zealand. He had an important influence on a number of young men, such as Graham Hughes, who were considering the ministry. I was influenced by him, during my compulsory military training in Papakura. He introduced me to Calvin, by giving me a copy of the *Institutes* and making me aware of Banner of Truth publications that began to appear in 1955.

By 1957 the *Evangelical Presbyterian* had a circulation of some 1200. It aimed to be more popular than its Australian counterpart. When both the Millers accepted calls to Australia in 1966, the editorship was taken over by the Rev. A Gunn of Manurewa. He had a keen mind, had studied and ministered in Scotland and gave the magazine a sharper polemical edge, with occasional reference to Calvin, in the theological turmoil of the 1960s. The visits of Billy Graham gave Evangelicalism a new lease of life and brought greatly increased numbers of students to the Theological Hall, Dunedin. Calvin was made more accessible by the writings of Mitchell Hunter, Wendel and the Torrances, even though there was not a specific course on Calvin. Dr John Roxborogh came closest to that in the new century with his course on 'Reformed History, theology and practice'. Reunion negotiations also led to Calvin being given attention, especially in relation to church and ministry. The same was true as dialogue with Roman Catholics began, for they were interested to understand what role the Reformation played in contemporary Presbyterianism and how it might illuminate theological differences.

Another important re-entry point for Calvin was the Scottish Church Service Society, which drew attention to the importance of Calvin's liturgical publications and the biblical principles on which they were based. The Society had offshoots in both Australia and New Zealand. The Church of Scotland's *The Book of Common Order* was widely used and Calvin's views were also important in the composition of the Uniting Church's *Uniting in Worship*. In New Zealand, a magazine for ministers was established in 1954, entitled *Forum*. From

---

33. JW Deenick, *Will Presbyterianism survive in New Zealand?* (Auckland: Reformed Publications, 1961).

time to time it published articles on Calvin and on the Reformed heritage, though there was no commemoration of Calvin's death on its tercentenary in 1964.

In Australia, interest in Calvin was awakened in an unexpected quarter during the 1950s and 1960s. Some Tasmanian Baptists rediscovered him as part of their struggles over identity, even though their reading was selective. The Evangelical Presbyterian Church was formed in late 1961 and then the Southern Presbyterian Church and the Australian Free Church emerged out of splits over interpreting both the Bible and Calvin. The Evangelical Free Church, for example, rejected common grace.

More importantly, the appointment of Professor George Yule to the Chair of Church History in the Theological Hall, Ormond College, Melbourne, led many Presbyterian, Congregational and Methodist students to a new appreciation of the importance of Luther and Calvin. Yule also was very influential in the reunion negotiations, along with Davis McCaughey, the Master of Ormond College, in the 1960s and 1970s, which led to the formation of the Uniting Church in 1977.

Its *Basis of Union* recognised the importance of the Apostles' and Nicene Creeds, along with the Scots Confession, the Heidelberg Catechism, the Westminster Confession, the Savoy Declaration and John Wesley's sermons as indispensable parts of its Catholic and Reformed identity. How that identity was defined was uncertain, given the variety of theological views which had appeared by the first decade of the twenty-first century.

Ministers were also committed by their ordination vows to teach these historic documents, as well as being influenced by modern scholarship in their proclamation of the Gospel. Study of the Reformation was compulsory for ministerial students in all Uniting Church theological colleges. Study of Calvin and the Reformation was also important in the theological colleges of the continuing Presbyterian Church. Harold Whitney was the first Principal in Brisbane and the author of *The Teaching of Calvin for Today* (1959). Robert Miller taught church history in Melbourne and was followed by Stewart Gill. Allan Harman and Douglas Kelly were also committed to upholding the importance of Calvin. Many Presbyterian students attended Moore College before the New South Wales college was set up in Burwood. In 1992, Dr Peter Cameron, of St Andrew's College was convicted of heresy over his view of Scripture and the ordination of women, which had been ended in 1991.[34] Professor Nigel Lee in Brisbane was another strong Calvinist, influenced both by North American and South African colleagues of similar convictions.

Moore College continues to insist that its students read the *Institutes*. Recently retired Archbishop Peter Jensen has set out the importance of this in an article published in 2009, 'Calvin among the Students: Shaping Theological Education'.[35] He himself had done research on Calvin under Professor P Collinson, then at Sydney University, before going to Oxford for doctoral studies. He found many negative attitudes to Calvinism there, with a consensus among critics that it was intellectually barren and morally flawed. Jensen, however, was surprised to discover how seriously Calvin was taken by Roman Catholics, because of his theological depth. 'The nub of the matter is this: John Calvin expounded the Bible in such a clear way that virtually no one else has matched him in showing us what God is like and therefore what we are like . . . He is the apostle of the majesty of God.'[36] Hostility to Calvin, Jensen suggests, often springs from hostility to the God of the Bible. Interestingly, Jensen describes himself as a Cranmerian and rejects the criticism that Moore is a narrowly Calvinist seminary. His views need to be given careful attention.

He points out that Dr Broughton Knox insisted students should read Calvin, because he wanted them to have read one great work of theology during their course. In his own lectures he did not hesitate to disagree with Calvin and taught his students how to critically test him and other theologians. Jensen is convinced that study of Calvin can still be profitable for students and ministers. During the 1960s, he provided resources against secularisation, the temptation to be anti-intellectual, or to make personal experience the basis of Christianity. Tragically both Australian culture and churches have suffered amnesia on the content of Christianity and its public implications. Churches, with once proud theological traditions, are now unable to meet the challenge of secularisation, or the overall challenge to Christianity.

---

34. P Cameron, *Trial for Heresy* (Sydney: Doubleday, 1993).
35. Thompson, *Engaging with Calvin*, 255.
36. *Ibid*, 19.

Assimilating Calvin is a major theological task, forcing readers to grapple with great Christian ideas and to see that our culture does not have the last word. Calvin shows that Christianity involves a series of intellectual commitments that cohere intimately. Parts cannot be bartered without consequences. Furthermore, Calvin integrates the theological disciplines and is consistently biblical in a way that it is vital for preachers and pastors, who cannot be specialists, when they seek to bring the Word of God to bear on the lives of their congregation. They must have a thorough education, which means far more than pietistic meanderings, or reliance on the atomistic versions of Christianity provided by specialists. Calvin and his contemporaries confronted perennial issues and transcend their century, speaking powerfully to us precisely because they are not of our times. 'But to become Calvinist, in the sense of taking his theology without critical appreciation is a mistake which condemns the student to living in the wrong place at the wrong time.'[37]

True theological education, for Jensen, means knowing God ever more deeply, where He has chosen to be found. That leads to knowing ourselves in a new way. Such views have no place in the contemporary writings, based on scientific atheism. Calvin is an indispensable reminder that true wisdom is not found in human reason, because of our depravity. That portrait is very unattractive and it is not surprising that it is rejected by many Christians, seduced by our culture into believing that human freedom rests on our essential goodness and the wisdom of our choices. That brings God down to our level, whereas Calvin insists that our depravity leaves no place for saving agencies other than the majesty and grace of God. Those who fear that they will lose their freedom by totally turning to God need to hear Calvin's insistence that we only become free, when God is the centre of our lives. True piety, according to Calvin, rests on obedience to the revealed Word of God, giving us assurance that the God who rules all things is also the Father who cares for us. That gave Calvin boldness to obey God, no matter what the situation.

For Archbishop Jensen, 'This theology is the best explanation of the Gospel of Jesus Christ and of the world in which we live.'[38] Such a theology provides the foundation for a seminary, which is not only

---

37. *Ibid*, 262.
38. *Ibid*, 272.

an educational institution, but a proving ground for those who would be preachers and pastors. Jensen's eloquent justification for the study of Calvin may not win wide assent, but is a reminder of the value of studying and living Calvin's theology in the twenty-first century.

The year 2009 saw the holding of Calvin conferences in Dunedin at the University of Otago, at United Theological College, Presbyterian Theological College and Moore College in Sydney and in Melbourne's United Faculty of Theology. Local scholars combined with eminent overseas authorities to underline the importance of Calvin for contemporary theological disciplines and for theological education and ministry. Three collections of articles will ensure that the issues raised are not quickly forgotten.

Even though these gatherings will not ensure that Calvin will have new life in congregations of the denominations concerned, they are a reminder that he is not forgotten by them, as seemed likely at the beginning of the twentieth century. The small Calvinist churches remain marginal, but committed. If the larger denominations of Anglicans, Presbyterians and the Uniting Church continue, through their younger scholars and ministers, to encourage the study of Calvin, that may provide a theological leaven in both Australia and New Zealand, which contributes to significant renewal.

Contributors

Ian Breward is Emeritus Professor of Church History, United Faculty of Theology, and Senior Fellow in the History Department, University of Melbourne. From 1966-82 he was Professor of Church History at Knox Theological Hall, Dunedin, New Zealand, and held the same position at Ormond College, Melbourne from 1982-99. In 1975 he was Moderator of the General Assembly of the Presbyterian Church of New Zealand. His many publications include *A History of the Churches in Australasia* (Oxford University Press, 2001) and *A History of the Australian Churches* (Allen and Unwin, 1993)

Ali Clarke works as a freelance historian and as an archivist at the Hocken Collections, University of Otago. She is particularly interested in the social and religious history of nineteenth-century New Zealand. Her publications include *Holiday Seasons: Christmas, New Year and Easter in Nineteenth-Century New Zealand* (2007), *A Living Tradition: A Centennial History of Knox College, Dunedin* (2009), and *Born to a Changing World: Childbirth in Nineteenth-Century New Zealand* (2012). She is currently researching and writing a history of the University of Otago.

Jason Goroncy is Lecturer and Dean of Studies at the Knox Centre for Ministry and Leadership in Dunedin. He is the author of *Hallowed Be Thy Name: The Sanctification of All in the Soteriology of Peter Taylor Forsyth* (T&T Clark, 2013) and editor of *Descending on Humanity and Intervening in History: Notes from the Pulpit Ministry of P. T. Forsyth* (Wipf and Stock, 2013). He also serves as a member of the Theology Network for the General Council of the World Communion of Reformed Churches.

Brett Knowles is a retired Senior Lecturer in Church History. He has held academic positions at the University of Otago, at the Sydney College of Divinity in Australia and at Sekolah Tinggi Teologi Tawangmangu (Tawangmangu Theological College), Tawangmangu, Central Java, Indonesia. He has published a history of the New Life Churches of New Zealand as well as a number of articles on New Zealand Pentecostalism. He has also edited and co-edited publications for the Department of Theology & Religion and the Department of History at the University of Otago.

Peter Matheson taught Church History in Edinburgh and Otago Universities and was Principal of the theological seminary the Uniting Church of Australia in Melbourne; his research is in Renaissance and Reformation and in New Zealand church history; recent books are *The Imaginative World of the Reformation* (Fortress Press, 2001) and *Argula von Grumbach: Schriften* (Verein für Reformationsgeschichte, 2010). He is a retired Presbyterian minister, and President of the St Martin Island Community in Otago, an offshoot of the Iona Community.

Elsie McKee is the Archibald Alexander Professor of Reformation Studies and the History of Worship at Princeton Theological Seminary. Her research has focused on John Calvin's theology and ministerial practice, and on the lay reformer Katharina Schuetz Zell. McKee has been a guest professor in Europe (Göttingen) and Africa (Kananga, Democratic Republic of Congo where she was born and reared), and has lectured on Calvin around the world. Recent publications include *John Calvin: Institutes of the Christian Religion* (Wm. B. Eerdmans Publishing Company, 2009) *Katharina Schuetz Zell, Church Mother: The Writings of a Protestant Reformer in Sixteenth-Century Germany* (University of Chicago, 2006) *John Calvin: Writings on Pastoral Piety* (Paulist, 2001) *Katharina Schuetz Zell: The Life and Thought of a Sixteenth-Century Reformer* (Brill, 1999)

Kirstine Moffat was born in Scotland and came to New Zealand at the age of seven. She is now a Senior Lecturer in English at the University of Waikato where her research and publications focus primarily on nineteenth and early twentieth century New Zealand settlement writing, with publications in the *Journal of New Zealand Literature, Im-*

migrants & Minorities, New Literatures Review, History Compass, and *the Journal of Commonwealth Literature*. She is the editor of a recent edition of Jean Devanny's *Lenore Divine* (Otago Colonial Texts Series, 2012). As well as books, music is one of Kirstine's abiding passions. She started to learn the piano when she was five and is the author of *Piano Forte: Stories and Soundscapes from Colonial New Zealand* (Otago University Press, 2011).

Murray Rae is Professor of Theology at the University of Otago and Head of the Department of Theology & Religion where he teaches courses in Systematic Theology and Ethics. His research interests include the work of Søren Kierkegaard, theological hermeneutics Maori engagements with Christianity and theology and the built environment. He is editor of the *Journal of Theological Interpretation* monograph series and his publications include *Mana Maori and Christianity*, (Wellington: Huia, 2012), *Kierkegaard and* Theology (London: Continuum, 2010), History *and Hermeneutics* (London: T&T Clark, 2005) and *Kierkegaard's Vision of the Incarnation* (Oxford: Clarendon, 1997)

Graham Redding is Principal of the Knox Centre for Ministry and Leadership in Dunedin, New Zealand and is a former Moderator of the Presbyterian Church of Aotearoa New Zealand. He has written extensively on the subject of prayer and worship in the Reformed tradition, with particular reference to John Calvin. His book *Prayer and the Priesthood of Christ in the Reformed Tradition* was published by T&T Clark in 2003.

John Roxborogh is a mission historian and retired theological educator living in Dunedin, New Zealand. He studied Thomas Chalmers and the mission of the church at the University of Aberdeen, served in parish ministry in Wellington, and taught in Seminary Theology Malaysia, Laidlaw College, and the Knox Centre for Ministry and Leadership. He has also taught Presbyterianism through the University of Otago and the Ecumenical Institute for Distance Theological Studies. He is interested in governance and theology and involved in projects on Christianity in Southeast Asia, syncretism and identity, and the implications of digitization and social media for mission studies.

John Stenhouse is Associate Professor in the Department of History at the University of Otago. He teaches courses in the history of science, religious history and intellectual history. He is currently writing a book on missionary science in the modern world and researching the history of eugenics in New Zealand. Recent publications include 'Religion and Society' in *The New Oxford History of New Zealand* and 'Selwyn through settler eyes,' in *A Controversial Churchman: Essays on George Selwyn, Bishop of New Zealand and Litchfield, and Sarah Selwyn*.

Randall Zachman is Professor of Reformation Studies at the University of Notre Dame. His research interests lie in the history of Christian thought from the Reformation period to the present. Zachman is the author of *Reconsidering John Calvin* (Cambridge University Press, 2012), *Image and Word in the Theology of John Calvin* (University of Notre Dame Press, 2007), *John Calvin as Teacher, Pastor, and Theologian: The Shape of his Writing and Thought* (Baker Academic, 2006), and *The Assurance of Faith: Conscience in the Theology of Martin Luther and John Calvin* (Westminster John Knox Press, 2005)

Index

A
Abba, R, 241
Adam, P, 15
alcohol, 126, 167, 195-6, 223-4
Alexander of Hales, 115
allegorical reading, 90
Alleine, J, 134
Allen, A, 248
Ambrose, 115
Angus, S, 247
Anthropomorphites, 92
antiCalvinism, 145, 151
antiCatholicism, 137, 235
Antiochus IV Epiphanes, 118
antipuritanism, 145, 149, 151, 169
Aquinas, T, 242
Aristotle, 112, 113, 114
Arminianism, 129, 178
Arnold, M, 150-1, 181
astronomy, 112-14
atonement, 8, 102, 131, 138, 184, 238, 240
Augustine, 24, 37, 115, 124, 116, 245
Awad, NG, 21
Axelsen, AE, 183

B
Bach, JS, 39
Badius, C, 31
Bain, E, 228
Bain, J, 228
Baird, J, 186, 189-91
Bannerman, J, 235
baptism, 8, 37-8, 189-212
Barber, L, 159
Barker, Bishop, 242
Barkley, A, 237
Barnes, P, 237
Barnett, T, 199
Barr, J, 216-7, 223-6, 234
Barrie, JM, 181
Barth, K, 24, 30, 79, 96, 185, 186, 187, 236
Basil the Great, 115
Bates, J, 168
Bates, JM, 174, 180, 186-7, 250
Bathgate, A, 216, 226-8, 234
Bavinck, H, 249
Baxter, JK, 143, 145, 149, 172, 213-4
Baxter, R, 134, 175
Bebbington, D, 172-3
Beecher, HW, 175
Belich, J, 155, 160, 166
Benedict, P, 127
Bennett, M, 192
Benoit, J-D, 16, 34
Bevan, LD, 241
Beza, T, 18
Bible, (See also 'Scripture') 14, 16, 18, 19, 22, 24, 25, 31, 39, 62, 63, 65, 76, 90, 115, 117, 139, 146, 163, 164, 168, 179, 186, 231, 238, 243, 252, 253
Biblical infallibility, 177
Binney, J, 154
Blackie, D, 202
Blaikie, A, 198
Bonhoeffer, D, 187

Boorstin, D, 214
Boston, T, 134
Boswell, J, 133
Bourgoing, F, 17
Boyd, KM, 198
Bucer, M, 68, 75
Bullinger, H, 13, 27, 75
Burnet, G, 208
Bradshaw, M, 248
Breen, Q, 33
Breward, I, 145, 174, 176, 192
Brookes, B, 154
Brown, G, 202
Brown, GD, 218
Brown, J, 200
Brown, S, 123, 130, 133, 138
Brown, W, 133
Brunner, E, 185, 236, 250
Buchanan, C, 133
Buckle, HT, 166
Bulloch, J, 131
Bultmann, R, 187
Bunting, J, 135
Burns, R, 129, 133, 143, 150, 168, 171-2, 216-8, 225, 234
Burns, T, 152, 156, 202

C

Caird, J, 240
Cairns, A, 239
Calvinism, 8, 123-42, 143-70, 171-88, 189-212, 214-8, 228, 235-41, 243, 244, 246, 248, 249, 253
Calvinistic Society of Australia, 248
Cameron, M, 242
Cameron, P, 253
Campbell, A, 216
Campbell, G, 134
Campbell, JMcL, 125, 129-32, 140-2, 179
Candlish, RS, 235
capitalism, 14, 124, 225, 235
Capito, W, 75
Cargill, W, 156
Carlstadt, A, 98

Carlyle, T, 150, 217
catechesis 18, 77,
catechism, 15, 17, 63, 105
   Genevan, 16, 36
   Heidelberg, 252
   Longer, 128
   Shorter, 128, 184, 236, 243
Cattle, W, 151
Cecil, R, 133, 136
Chalmers, T, 123-42
Chapman, RM, 145-9, 152, 213
Charters, S, 135
Chauvet, R, 17
Chavura, M, 241
Cheyne, AC, 132, 141, 180
Chicand, G, 70, 74
Chisholm, James, 175, 181, 201
Chisholm, John, 180
Christ, 4-12, 19, 20, 21, 22, 27, 28, 34, 36-8, 40, 46, 47, 56-7 76, 80, 81, 86-9, 91, 93, 95, 100, 101, 105, 107, 115, 119, 138, 165, 168, 208, 222, 233, 238, 243, 244, 245, 247, 254
   coming of, 106, 108, 109
   death of, 5, 6, 8, 102, 108, 109, 179
   divinity of, 193
   faith in, 42, 56
   humanity of, 5, 45, 116
   resurrection of, 6, 100, 108
   school of, 97
   union with, 6, 10, 37
Christian life, 10-12, 140, 164
Christian Socialism, 169, 186
Christie, J, 207-8
Chrysostom, 21, 115, 116
Church, 4, 10, 11, 13, 14, 16, 19, 23-9, 33-4, 36, 38, 39, 66, 68, 77, 80-1, 83-7, 91, 95, 97, 104, 109, 110, 126, 128, 129, 131, 155, 202, 209, 215, 220, 228, 238, 243
   marks of, 13, 38
Church, I, 194
Church of Scotland, 7, 123-4, 126, 128, 130-2, 156, 181, 229, 235, 240, 251

Church Service Society, 186, 251
Cicero, 47, 112
Clarke, A, 209
Clarkson, T, 133
Clauburger, J, 72
Clyde, C, 216, 220-1, 223, 234
Coleridge, ST, 181
Colladon, N, 21
Collinson, P, 150, 253
communion (see Lord's supper)
Company of Pastors, 17, 19, 61-3, 68, 73-5
confession, 3, 7, 10, 55
conscience, 22, 50, 54-6, 132, 243
Consistory, 17, 19, 62, 69-71, 73, 74, 194, 214, 245
Cooper, A, 161
Cooper, R, 223
Cooper, T, 176
Cop, M, 17
Cop, N, 75
Copland, J, 158-9, 199
Cottret, B, 15, 30
Council of Trent, 174
Covenanters, 124, 128-9, 181-2, 231, 218
Cranach, L, 27
Cromwell, O, 144, 150
Cunningham, W, 131, 137, 176, 235

D

Daley, C, 161
Dante, 31
Darwin, C, 124, 151, 157, 179
d'Aubigne, M, 124
Davidson, AK, 152, 153
Davin, D, 147, 149
de Boer, E, 18, 73
de Boiville, M, 70-1
de Greef, W, 15
death, 6, 9, 10, 36, 46, 47, 72, 89, 100, 103, 227
Declaratory Acts, 123, 124, 141, 142, 236, 240, 248
Deenick, JW, 251
depravity, 3, 6, 41, 43, 49, 137, 138, 143, 154, 254
Des Chesnais, LeM, 177
Des Gallars, N, 17, 66
DeVries, D, 30
Dick, ER, 165
Dickie, J, 176, 185, 187
Dickson, J, 177
Dickson, N, 182
discipline, 11, 15, 19-20, 51, 61, 69, 77, 124, 128, 130, 158, 184, 194, 195, 197-202, 209, 210
dispensationalism, 249
Disruption, 124, 146, 156, 176, 181-2, 239
Dissenters, 151, 156, 218
divine economy, 93-5
doctrine, 9, 14, 18, 20, 25, 34, 43, 58, 81, 82, 86, 93, 95, 98-9 105, 114, 116, 117, 133, 139-40, 143, 171, 178, 184, 194, 215, 216, 231, 238, 239, 244, 250
Doddridge, P, 134
Donaldson, R, 248
Dougherty, I, 153
Drummond, AL, 131
Duff, O, 153
Dunlop, J, 176
Dykes, O, 245-6

E

Earle, A, 151
Edwards, J, 133, 135
Elder, J, 238
Eliot, TS, 39
Elliot, W, 200
Elliot, WS, 215-7, 228-9, 234
Emerson, RW, 181
Engammare, M, 28
Enlightenment, 150, 151, 157, 172, 173
Erasmus, 65
Erskine, T, 131, 139, 140
eternal life, 5, 47

Evangelicalism, 119, 127, 129-32, 134, 136, 140, 146-7, 151-2, 154, 156, 160-1, 167, 172-3, 175, 183, 184, 186, 188, 235-7, 241-2, 248, 251-2
excommunication, 3, 4, 10, 18, 69

F

Fabri, J, 73-4
faith, 5, 11, 18, 23, 25, 33, 36, 38, 56-8, 72, 83, 85-7, 127, 130, 137-8, 191, 208, 219, 223, 244, 246, 247
fall, 41, 45, 47-50, 52, 99, 165
Farel, W, 5, 18, 62, 75
feminism, 149, 154, 160, 163-7, 221, 232
Ferguson, D, 217, 229-31, 234
Findlay, Dr, 171
Fish, HS, 165
Fletcher, J, 135
forgiveness, 7, 10, 56, 68, 227, 232
Frame, TR, 236
Fraser, IW, 186
Fraser, PB, 185, 249
Free Church, 123-7, 131, 132, 140, 146, 147, 152, 156, 176, 181, 182, 195, 200, 215, 216, 229, 235, 240, 248
freedom, 71, 108, 183, 222, 238, 240, 244, 247, 252, 254
French Confession, 15
Froude, JA, 184
Fulton, C, 165
Fundamentalism, 184-5

G

Galt, J, 218
Geering, L, 155, 188, 249
Genevan Academy 17, 18, 19
Gerrish, B, 27-8, 37, 38
Gibb, J, 159, 166, 179, 183, 186-7, 240
Gibbon, LG, 218

Gill, S, 252
Gillies, J, 248
Gillies, Rev., 176
Glover, D, 149
God, 8-11, 14, 21-6, 27-9, 30-7, 40, 43-8, 51-2, 54-8, 77, 82-7, 89-93, 95-7, 98-9, 102, 104-10, 113, 130, 184, 219, 225, 230, 232, 233, 235, 238-9, 243-5, 247, 253-4
  children of, 56, 59
  freedom of, 24,
  image of, 45-7, 49-51, 54, 56
  knowledge of, 41-2, 48, 98, 115, 157
  power of, 114
  sovereignty of, 179, 183, 184, 238, 244
  union with, 46-7
Godly Commonwealth, 126, 142, 156, 168
Gordon, B, 14, 18, 31
Gorman, J, 172
Gosman, A, 241
grace, 7, 9, 26, 38, 46, 55, 67, 76, 87, 106, 107, 175, 178, 183, 192, 208-9, 238, 243, 252, 254
Graham, B, 251
gratitude, 42-5, 48, 108
Gray, A, 202
Greene-McCreight, K, 88-9
Gregory the Great, 104
Grosse, C, 62, 70
Gunn, A, 251
Gunson, WN, 241
Guthrie, T, 228

H

Hageman, H, 5
Hall, B, 237
Hamilton. I, 123, 132
Hamilton, W, 157
Hammond, TC, 242
Hanna, W, 139
Harman, A, 252
Harper, A, 239
Hart, TA, 37

Harvey, G, 182
Helm, P, 22
Helvetic Confession, 13, 27
Henry, M, 134
heresy, 139, 155, 159, 243, 179, 249, 253
Hewitson, W, 174, 176
Hill, DO, 182
Hill, G, 123-4, 132, 134
Hindemith, P, 39
Hinton, A, 165
historical criticism, 82
Hodge, C, 177, 185, 240
Hogg, J, 129, 216, 218, 234
Holland, S, 152
Holy Spirit, 5, 9, 25, 31, 37-8, 51, 52, 82, 84, 92, 95, 98, 110, 113, 138, 208, 243
Homer, 112, 115
Hooker, R, 174
Horace, 103, 112
Horton, RF, 180
Hughes, G, 251
humility, 23, 41-60, 85
Hunnius, 116
Hunter, M, 251
Hutching, M, 228
Hutchinson, M, 239
Hyde, R, 149

I
Idealism, 238
Irenaeus, 105
Irving, E, 130
Irwin, CH, 181

J
Jamieson, JC, 248
Jensen, P, 253-5
Jesuits, 177
Jews, 88, 101, 100, 102, 105-8, 113-4, 116
Johnston, AD, 190
Johnstone, W, 194
Jones, JW, 173
Jones, L, 149, 213, 222

Jones, TS, 135
justification, 9, 215, 238

K
Kant, I, 157
Kaye, A, 231
Kaye, B, 216, 231-4
Keddie, J, 174
Kelly, C, 192
Kelly, D, 252
Kendall, T, 153
Kenyon, J, 166
Kerr, G, 248
Kiek, ES, 241
King, G, 185
Kingdon, RM, 61, 69, 70, 71
Kingsley, C, 150
Kipling, R, 171
Kirk, J, 128
Knight, F, 191
knowledge, 33, 37, 41-59, 76, 92, 93, 114, 180, 236, 238
Knox, B, 253
Knox, DB, 242
Knox, J, 97, 124, 128, 129, 149, 172, 177, 181, 186, 215-7, 228, 245
Knox College, 159, 176
Kuyper, A, 249

L
Lang, JD, 239
Law, R, 161
Lean, F, 202
Lecointe, G, 70
Lee, JA, 164
Lee, M, 164
Lee, N, 253
Leembruggen, WH, 248
Leishman, W, 198
Leneman, L, 192, 198
Leo XIII, Pope, 168
Levesque, A, 154
Lewis, A, 23
Lewis, JJ, 201
Liberalism, 142, 173, 180, 185-6
Lister, Jane, 162-64

Lister, Joseph, 157
Lister, S, 161, 163-5, 168
Lister, W, 162
literal sense, 90-2
liturgy, 15, 31, 36, 64, 67, 68, 250
  communion, 3-12
Loane, M, 242
Lochore, R, 200
Lombard, P, 115
Lord's Supper, 3-12, 18, 36, 62, 66, 70, 76, 204-9
love, 11, 47, 49, 51, 52, 57-9, 106, 107, 130, 147, 168, 206, 232, 244
  of self, 42, 52-3, 55-7
Lowell, R, 244
Luther, M, 24-5, 27, 34, 46, 98, 109, 183, 244, 252
Lutheran, 66, 67, 120, 239, 247, 248

M

Macdonald, A, 248
MacDonald, G, 218
MacDonald, M, 239
MacGregor, A, 207
MacGregor, D, 157-9
MacGregor, J, 174, 176-9, 190-2, 207, 240
Mack, B, 126
Mackie, A, 193
Mackie, G, 193
Maclaren, P, 231
MacLauchlan, G, 213
Maclean, D, 248
Maclean, S, 189
Mander, J, 213
Manley, KR, 241
Manningham, T, 150
Maori, 151, 152, 154, 190, 224, 232
Marcion, 106-7
marriage, 18, 64, 71, 75, 198-200, 209, 221, 239
Marsden, S, 241
Marx, K, 124

Massam, Professor, 178
Matheson, P, 179, 182
Matthews, E, 189-92
Matthews, H, 189-92
McCaughey, D, 252
McClean, RR, 216
McDonald, JC, 244-5
McGill, P, 200
McIlvanney, L, 150
McKee, EA, 49, 62, 64, 68, 70, 72, 76
McKinlay, Mrs J, 182
McLeod, L, 123
McLintock, AH, 153, 156
McNeill, JT, 20
M'Crie, CG, 128,
M'Crie, T, 134
Melchizedek, 99-100
Melville, A, 124, 129
Miller, G, 251
Miller, H, 182
Miller, J, 162
Miller, R, 251-2
Miller, T, 249, 251
miraculous exchange, 6, 8
Mitchison, R, 192, 198
modernity, 38, 151, 240
Moehn, WHTh, 35
Moffat, K, 149, 214
Moir, J, 202
Moody and Sankey, 184
Moore College, 172, 237, 242, 252-3, 255
More, H, 133, 146
Morley, J, 184
Morrison, H, 165
Mowll, Archbishop, 242
Münster, S, 65
Murray, DM, 208

N

Naphy, W, 69
Neale, P, 230
Nettleton, J, 150
Neville, Bishop, 168, 171
Newton, J, 133

Nichols, J, 15
Nicol, H, 165
Noll, M, 125, 126
Norton, J, 166, 168

O

Oberman, H, 31
O'Connell, K, 162, 168
O'Connor, PS, 153
Oecolampadius, J, 75
Oliver, WH, 148, 172
Olssen, E, 154, 161, 162
Origen, 90, 107
Ott, H, 16
Ovid, 102, 112
Owen, J, 134
Oxford Movement, 124

P

Page, D, 164, 167
Pak, GS, 116
Parker, D, 241
Parker, THL, 20-1, 22, 25, 26, 28, 32, 34, 89, 90
Pascal, B, 133
pastoral care, 11, 17, 20, 24, 67, 75, 76, 77, 126, 187
Pearson, C, 174, 180, 186, 187
Pearson, WH, 149, 213
Perry, C, 242
Peterson, J, 200
Pettegree, A, 127
Philip, A, 140
Pietism, 172
Piggin, S, 237
plain sense, 90-3, 95-6
Plato, 47, 112
Pliny, 112, 113, 114
Porter, F, 191
Poullain, V, 72-3
Poupin, A, 63, 67-9, 71-4,
prayer, 3, 7, 9, 58, 66, 67, 68, 69, 77, 156, 223
preaching, 5, 13-40, 62-5, 73-4, 76-7, 81, 111, 126-7, 184
predestination, 123-4, 127, 131-3, 139, 141, 171, 179, 180, 190, 216, 225, 238, 247
Prentis, MD, 239
Pringle, W, 15, 87, 124
prohibition, 159-60, 162-3, 167
Puritanism, 8, 128, 176, 144-9, 172, 213-4, 245

R

Rae, M, 11
Rainy, R, 177
Raitt, MA, 200
Ramsay, A, 216
Ramsay, MS, 206
reason, 50, 86, 131, 238, 254
reconciliation, 10, 29, 56
Redding, G, 8
Reed, AH, 153
Reformation, 15, 17, 84, 129, 131, 172, 217, 245, 251, 252
Rentoul, JL, 239
resurrection, 9, 72, 101
Revivalism, 146, 160, 184-5, 187
Reynolds, R, 164-6
Reynolds, W, 164
Riach, A, 223
Ritschl, A, 181
Ritschl, D, 27
Robinson, M, 14, 19, 24
Roman Church, 104, 109, 110
Rosie, G, 218
Roussel, B, 72
Roxborogh, WJ, 130, 185, 251
Rule of faith, 93, 94
Runia, K, 249
Russell, P, 237
Rutherford, S, 134, 181
Ryburn, H, 250

S

Sabbatarianism, 167, 171, 216, 231
sacrament, 4, 10, 13, 18, 27, 28, 36-8, 62, 69, 76-7, 87, 115, 185, 189-212, 243
Salmond, JD, 186

Salmond, W, 159, 176, 178-9, 190, 239-40
salvation, 5, 6, 11, 30, 33, 35, 76, 107, 126, 130, 190, 191, 209, 219, 221, 232, 238, 243
Sargeson, F, 149, 213-4, 234
Savoy Declaration, 238, 252
Schep, J, 249
Schleiermacher, FDE, 181
Schmidt, LE, 208
Schwöbel, C, 26, 34
science, 52, 113, 127, 129, 139, 151, 159
Scot's Confession, 128
Scott, AJ, 130, 131, 139
Scott, W, 129, 133, 216, 217
Scripture, (see also 'Bible') 18, 20, 22, 25, 26, 29, 30-2, 35, 56, 63, 65, 79-96, 97-120, 130, 136, 150, 157, 165, 168, 173, 180, 184, 207, 238, 243, 248, 250, 253
  inspiration of, 82, 83, 92, 95, 139, 178, 184
  unity of, 94-5
secularism, 144, 147, 152, 155, 159, 160-1, 163, 166, 236, 253
Servetus, 61, 88, 177, 187, 244
sex, 147, 154, 195-8, 200, 202, 209
Simeon, C, 136, 241-2
Simpson, C, 231
sin, 3, 7-11, 37, 41-2, 44-5, 47, 49-52, 55-7, 68, 86, 98, 102, 103, 137, 138, 166, 193, 194, 198-99, 200, 201, 2 08, 221, 222, 224, 226, 227, 233, 238
  original, 45, 148, 189, 216
Sinclair, K, 152-3
Singer, M, 99
Small, JD, 14, 38
Smellie, A, 182
Smith, A, 181
Smith, D, 125
Smith JG, 240
Smith, RM, 198
Smith, WR, 178
Smout, C, 198
Sola Scriptura, 109-10

Somerville, J, 152
Somerville, R, 179
soul, 5, 9-10, 28, 29, 36, 46-7, 76, 143, 206, 222, 247
Spencer, H, 157
Spierling, K, 194
Spurgeon, CH, 241
Spurgeon, T, 241
Stanley, Dean, 171
Steele, JTV, 186-7, 249-50
Steinfel, P, 14
Stenhouse, J, 147, 158, 162
Stephens, AG, 221
Stevenson, RL, 218
Stout, R, 158-9, 164
Strong, C, 240
Stuart, DM, 158, 203-4
Sumpter, DJ, 201
Swan, AS, 218
Swanton, R, 248
Synod of Otago and Southland, 123, 157-9, 180, 193, 201, 203, 206

T

Tannahill, R, 216
Tennyson, AL, 181
Thatcher, GW, 241
Thirty Nine Articles, 183, 241
Thomlinson, K, 161
Thompson, B, 3, 10, 36
Thompson, MD, 253-4
Thomson, A, 140
Thomson, E, 203
Thomson, G, 203-4
Thomson, GM, 159
Thomson, JH, 182
Thomson, W, 203-4
Tillich, P, 187
Todd, C, 200
Todd, M, 128
Torrance, JB, 130, 131, 251
Torrance, TF, 140, 251
Treadwell, J, 179
Trinity, 116, 187
Turretin, F, 176

U

University of Otago, 143, 157-8, 164, 179, 240, 255
Updike, J, 29

V

Van Biema, D, 237
Vanhoozer, K, 31
Vine, GF, 226
Viret, 19, 34, 62
Virgil, 112, 115

W

Waddell, R, 163-4, 179
Waddington, E, 189
Walchenbach, JR, 21
Wallace, P, 165
Wallace, W 217
Ward, RS, 237
Wardon, R, 216, 218-20, 234
Warfield, B, 185
waterfront strike, 152, 168
Watson, AC, 249
Watson, P, 214
Watson, RS, 250
Wattie, N, 226, 230
Watts, DW, 80, 81
Webster, J, 34
Wendel, F, 251
Wesley, J, 252
Westminster Confession, 123-5, 127, 130-3, 138-9, 141, 159, 174, 176-80, 184, 236, 240, 248, 252
Westminster Fellowship, 248, 250
Westminster Society, 248

Westphal, J, 66-7, 73
Whitney, H, 252
Whyte, A, 177, 183
Wilberforce, W, 133, 146
Wilcox, PJ, 19
Wilkie, Y, 177, 205
William of Orange, 128
Wilson, A, 194, 201
Witte, J, 70, 71
Wohlers, J, 192
Womens' Christian Temperance Union, 164-5, 167
Wood, M, 239, 240
Word (of God), 4, 11, 13-40, 71, 76-7, 83-8, 91, 93-5, 108, 186, 254
Wordsworth, W, 133, 181
worship, 4, 11, 18, 25, 31, 38, 39, 62, 64, 68, 101, 104, 126, 128, 186, 225, 231, 243
Wright DF, 22, 140
Wright, I, 200
Wyber, I, 200

X

Xenophon, 113

Y

Yule, G, 252

Z

Zachman, R, 20, 27, 98
Zell, M, 72, 75
Zwingli, H, 5, 13, 34, 75, 185, 244,

Lightning Source UK Ltd.
Milton Keynes UK
UKOW01f0443070218

317473UK00002B/172/P